P9-CKW-905

Evaluating Sexual Harassment

Evaluating Sexual Harassment

PSYCHOLOGICAL, SOCIAL, *and* LEGAL CONSIDERATIONS *in* FORENSIC EXAMINATIONS

William E. Foote
Jane Goodman-Delahunty

AMERICAN PSYCHOLOGICAL ASSOCIATION
WASHINGTON, DC

Published by
American Psychological Association
750 First Street, NE
Washington, DC 20002
www.apa.org

To order
APA Order Department
P.O. Box 92984
Washington, DC 20090-2984
Tel: (800) 374-2721
Direct: (202) 336-5510
Fax: (202) 336-5502
TDD/TTY: (202) 336-6123
Online: www.apa.org/books/
E-mail: order@apa.org

In the U.K., Europe, Africa, and the Middle East, copies may be ordered from
American Psychological Association
3 Henrietta Street
Covent Garden, London
WC2E 8LU England

Typeset in Goudy by World Composition Services, Inc., Sterling, VA

Printer: Book-mart Press, Inc., North Bergen, NJ
Cover Designer: Berg Design, Albany, NY
Technical/Production Editor: Rosemary Moulton

Library of Congress Cataloging-in-Publication Data

Foote, William E.
Evaluating sexual harassment : psychological, social, and legal considerations in forensic examinations / William E. Foote, Jane Goodman-Delahunty.
p. cm.
Includes bibliographical references and index.
ISBN 1-59147-101-X (hardcover : alk. paper)
1. Forensic psychology. 2. Sexual harassment. I. Goodman-Delahunty, Jane. II. Title.

RA1148.F54 2004
363.25'953—dc22 2004000027

British Library Cataloguing-in-Publication Data
A CIP record is available from the British Library.

Printed in the United States of America
First Edition

CONTENTS

Acknowledgments .... *vii*

Introduction 3

Chapter 1. Sexual Harassment: An Evolving Social–Psychological Phenomenon 13

Chapter 2. Harassers, Harassment Contexts, Same-Sex Harassment, Workplace Romance, and Harassment Theories 27

Chapter 3. The Legal Framework in Sexual Harassment Cases 47

Chapter 4. The Forensic Evaluation: Practical, Legal, and Ethical Contours 73

Chapter 5. Assessing Liability Issues 101

Chapter 6. Evaluation of Damages 121

Chapter 7. Alternate Dispute Resolution in Sexual Harassment Claims: Neutral Fact-Finding, Mediation, and Arbitration 151

Appendix A. Complex Case Involving Male on Female Sexual Harassment Allegations 161

Appendix B. Allegations of Male on Male Sexual Harassment and Retaliation 181

References 197
Table of Authorities 231
Index 233
About the Authors 241

ACKNOWLEDGMENTS

This book was a long time in the writing and required many helping hands to reach completion. We had excellent secretarial help beginning with Polly Stipke through the capable hands of Krisan Smith, and as the manuscript took its close-to-final form, the thoughtful and diligent care of Rhea Clothier. Their generation and cross-checking of references was invaluable. Kerri Repa, who passed away suddenly last year, spent many hours in the library tracking down references. We are also indebted to a number of friends and colleagues who commented on drafts of chapters along the way, particularly Dan Shuman and Stu Greenberg. Reviewers Beth Clark and Nancy Baker provided detailed comments that enhanced the manuscript. Bill Foote thanks his children, Jenny and Jeremy, for their constant support. His wife, Cheryl Rowe Foote, was his rock and encouragement. Without her to pick up the dropped balls and clean up the broken plates, this book would have never been completed.

Evaluating Sexual Harassment

INTRODUCTION

The workplace is an arena of human interaction in which both the best and the worst of behavior occur. Because work addresses a broad range of human needs, the stakes of interactions are often higher in the workplace than they are in similar contacts occurring in voluntary, social settings (Warr, 1982). Work provides, at a minimum, temporal structure for the day. Social contact in the workplace is primary for some workers, and for others it provides a basis for substantial social interaction outside of work. Work is also a means of self-definition: What one does can serve as shorthand for one's social identity. Most fundamentally, employment provides income. For most people, this aspect of work makes it a mandatory, rather than an optional, activity.

Power plays a pivotal role in the workplace (Bargh & Raymond, 1995; Kidder, Lafleur, & Wells, 1995; Leeser & O'Donohue, 1997). Most employees are subject to the power of employers and supervisors who have the authority to hire or fire, to promote or demote, to assign duties and hours, to set working conditions, and to specify coworkers. How people in authority exercise their control often determines whether an employee has positive experiences or endures work to support self and family. The disparity in power between the employer and employee distinguishes these relationships from purely social ones and from those that occur between coworkers or others of equal status.

By working, people contribute to the success of the national economy and constitute a resource to the nation. Preservation of this national resource is an important political goal. Factors that deter people's capacity to function in the workplace, to produce goods, and to provide services are of concern to business and government. Losses to the U.S. government in productivity, turnover, and sick leave caused by sexual harassment over a 2-year period were estimated at $270 billion (U.S. Merit Systems Protection Board, 1988). Legislation such as the Civil Rights Act of 1964 and the Americans With Disabilities Act of 1990 and numerous court decisions acknowledge the importance of protecting individuals from hindrances to their functionality in the workplace (*Meritor Savings Bank, FSB v. Vinson*, 1986). One of those hindrances now commonly acknowledged is sexual harassment. Both state and federal laws have clearly established the right to work in an environment free from sexual harassment.

Forensic assessment and consultation are relatively new and evolving areas of psychological practice. Nonetheless, mental health experts have provided testimony on an array of issues in sexual harassment cases. For example, social psychologists have provided critical evidence at trial by pointing out features of the workplace that promoted sexualized conduct and an atmosphere conducive to harassment (*Jensen v. Eveleth Taconite Co.*, 1997). Mental health professionals typically provide evidence concerning the nature and scope of emotional damages caused to the plaintiff by workplace sexual harassment (Cooke, 1996; Hellkamp & Lewis, 1995). In some cases, psychological and psychiatric expertise is sought on liability issues, such as the extent to which the defendant was legally responsible for causing the alleged sexual harassment (Feldman-Schorrig, 1995). In cases in which this testimony is admitted, the psychologist must address psychological issues beyond those relevant to an evaluation of emotional injury alone.

Beyond the trial, psychologists have at times participated in sexual harassment litigation when a decision in a case is reviewed on appeal. For example, the American Psychological Association submitted an amicus brief when the issue of psychological injury as a necessary element of sexual harassment was appealed to the U.S. Supreme Court (*Harris v. Forklift Systems, Inc.*, 1993; Goodman-Delahunty, 1999), and mental health and trauma professionals submitted an amicus brief when the issue of same-sex harassment was appealed to the U.S. Supreme Court (*Oncale v. Sundowner Offshore Services, Inc.*, 1998; National Organization on Male Sexual Victimization, 1998). Less well documented and evaluated are contributions a psychologist may make in proceedings before trial or prior to the commencement of litigation through efforts at investigation, mediation, and arbitration.

This book provides psychologists with essential information to conduct an evidence-based forensic practice involving sexual harassment cases. The book acquaints readers with clinical and social–scientific literature on sexual harassment and applies those findings to issues that psychologists must consider in preparing ethically sound and well-substantiated forensic reports and testimony.

INTENDED AUDIENCE

This book is intended to be a resource for all those working in sexual harassment cases, including psychologists, psychiatrists, lawyers, judges, and human resource professionals. For clinical psychologists and psychiatrists who have some forensic experience but have not worked in sexual harassment cases, the book is designed to provide a solid base for initiating practice in this area. The research review, extensive discussion of the determination of damages, and detailed discussion of the case sequence encourage the psychologist or psychiatrist new to this area to seek supervision from an experienced forensic practitioner and to enter into this work with greater confidence.

For the experienced forensic psychologist or psychiatrist, this book provides a ready summary of the relevant research, even in areas that are not usually on the "need-to-know" list. For example, the review of issues related to liability may allow the experienced forensic practitioner to examine these issues in the course of already familiar forensic examination procedures. The chapter on alternative dispute resolution introduces an aspect of practice that takes the forensic practitioner out of the expert witness role and into the realm of prevention, intervention, and active problem solving. For many, this is a new arena of practice that should, as is ethically necessary, be undertaken with consultation and supervision (American Psychological Association, 2002).

For human resource professionals, this book offers a basis for understanding how people's interactions in the workplace may result in claims of sexual harassment. Understanding harassers and their patterns of behavior is an important part of this mix, as is understanding how different people perceive and react to potentially harassing events in the workplace. A grasp of the impact of sexual harassment on harassment targets can lead to more effective risk management and care of employees and to the development of preventive measures that can reduce employee turnover and use of sick leave.

For lawyers, this book provides insight into the large body of research comprising the scientific and factual bases for forensic evaluation of plaintiffs in sexual harassment cases. Revised Federal Rule of Evidence 702 (Federal Rules of Evidence, 2000) requires that experts testifying about scientifically based subject matter base their opinions on research of acceptable validity and reliability. Two U.S. Supreme Court cases outlined standards for admitting expert testimony (*Daubert v. Merrell Dow Pharmaceuticals, Inc.*, 1993; *Kumho Tire Co. v. Carmichael*, 1999), arguably increasing the degree to which psychologists must rely on psychological research as a basis for their testimony (Goodman-Delahunty & Foote, 1995). This book goes beyond a discussion of the extant research in sexual harassment by applying the research findings to issues likely to arise in civil rights or tort litigation. Lawyers may use this material to aid their clients in making strategic decisions about litigation or in preparing more sophisticated and comprehensive examinations of mental health experts.

For judges, magistrates, industrial relations tribunals, and other fact-finding bodies, this book provides significant background in the body of knowledge on sexual harassment. As a foundation for understanding the sometimes complex dynamics of sexual harassment of plaintiffs by defendants, this book can help fact finders evaluate scientific bases of expert testimony of mental health experts. In addition, portions of the book that address assessment procedures and ethics inform the court on issues to consider in deciding whether to admit expert evidence.

A SHORT HISTORY OF THE TERM *SEXUAL HARASSMENT*

Despite extensive interest in and media publicity about sexual harassment, there is little consensus about its definition, and the meaning of the term remains confusing to many. Claims of sexual harassment are often met with intense skepticism, and conclusions that they must be bogus are commonplace. Some of the controversy stems from a gender gap in perceptions of sexual harassment, discussed in depth in chapter 5. Other confusion may be attributable to the fact that situations to which the term applies have evolved over time as social science and law on the topic have developed. Practitioners who are familiar with these developments are better equipped to deal with clients and courts whose understandings may reflect a limited grasp of the concepts, perhaps because of their age, cultural background, or naive notions about sexual harassment.

For example, elderly jurors and judges may view claims differently from men and women who came of age late in the twentieth century and who are often unfamiliar with civil rights history and expect sexual equity in the workplace. Cross-cultural differences may underlie different views about acceptable sexual conduct in the workplace. Certain clients do not use the term *sexual harassment*, for example, if they are focused on what they perceive as a racist motive underlying the conduct at issue or if they are unaware that the legal definition encompasses phenomena other than conduct that implies ordinary sexual attraction, such as certain forms of workplace intimidation or bullying.

Legislation prohibiting sexual harassment had its origins in the Civil Rights Act of 1964 (Title VII). However, that act was implemented mainly to address racial discrimination in the workplace, and ironically, the inclusion of *sex* as a protected category on the basis of which discrimination was outlawed was a political strategy designed to prevent the act's passage. The language of the act does not even include the term *sexual harassment* (Civil Rights Act of 1964).

The term *sexual harassment* is attributed to Catherine A. MacKinnon, a professor at the University of Michigan Law School, who coined it in the mid 1970s and has since applied it to a range of gender-based workplace interactions (MacKinnon, 1979). In 1974, the term was used by a group of women at Cornell University who spoke out against the harassment of female colleagues who quit their jobs because of unwanted advances from their supervisors (Brownmiller & Alexander, 1992). After the women's movement and the ideology of feminism flowered in the 1970s, the bare bones legislation outlawing discrimination "because of . . . sex," which initially applied only to unequal treatment of males and females in the workplace in terms of tangible workplace benefits such as salaries and promotional opportunities, was extended to detrimental workplace conduct occurring *because of sex*, thus taking on flesh in the form of sexual harassment. The first case in which the U.S. Supreme Court incorporated her theories of sexual harassment under Title VII was *Meritor v. Vinson* (*Meritor Savings Bank, FSB v. Vinson*, 1986).

The year 1991 was a watershed of sorts for sexual harassment. In the summer, the *Tailhook* scandal erupted following accusations that naval aviators sexually assaulted women who were required to run a gauntlet of males at an annual meeting in Las Vegas. Revelations from this episode provided clear examples of the most blatant forms of sexual harassment, sexual touching and coercion, painting an ugly picture of gender relations in the military. Several months later, President George H. W. Bush nominated U.S. Court of Appeals Judge Clarence Thomas to the U.S. Supreme Court. During his confirmation hearings, televised in daily nationwide broadcasts, a number of events ensued, which took discussions of sexual harassment into almost every household. At the outset, most Americans viewed Thomas as a conservative African American who had served as chairman of the U.S. Equal Employment Opportunity Commission (EEOC) from 1982 to 1990, a controversial period for civil rights under the administrations of presidents Ronald Reagan and George Bush.

When a former commission employee, now a respected law professor, Anita Hill, came forward with allegations that Thomas had sexually harassed her on a number of occasions while he headed the agency charged with enforcing laws prohibiting sexual harassment (Hill & Jordan, 1995), the country was riveted. Political rhetoric, depending on the source, painted Hill as a lying, manipulative, disgruntled ex-subordinate (Brock, 1993) or as a long-suffering victim of a superior who had the capacity to destroy her career (Mayer & Abramson, 1995). The Hill–Thomas controversy brought to the American public descriptions of sexual harassment incidents not unlike those endured or observed by many workingwomen, such as workplace conversations about pubic hairs on soda cans and descriptions of the sexual organs of pornographic video actors. Many women had little difficulty believing the allegations; many men who discredited Hill's allegations had fundamental difficulty understanding the offensiveness of this sort of verbal or physical sexual conduct on the job (Hill & Jordan, 1995).

The issues, starkly backlit by the U.S. Senate hearings and subsequent media debate, prompted an explosion of sexual harassment litigation and research in the 1990s. In that decade, prominent researchers at the University of Illinois (Fitzgerald, Gelfand, & Drasgow, 1995), Illinois State University (Pryor, Giedd, & Williams, 1995), the University of Arizona (Gutek & O'Connor, 1995), and St. Louis University (Wiener, Watts, Goldkamp, & Gasper, 1995), as well as many others, expanded our understanding of sexual harassment.

Even before his election to the presidency in 1992, Bill Clinton was plagued by sex-related scandals. One of these emerged in the civil rights claim (based on sections 1983 and 1985 of chapter 42 of the U.S. Code) filed by Paula Jones against the president. This case served as the legal basis for the perjured deposition testimony that resulted in attempts to impeach Bill Clinton (*Plaintiff Jones's Appeal to the 8th Circuit Court, Jones v. Clinton*, 1996). The underlying lawsuit alleged that Clinton, while governor of Arkansas, attempted to coerce Ms. Jones, an employee of the Arkansas Industrial Development Commission, to engage in sexual acts with him. In the subsequent furor surrounding President Clinton's sexual activities with White House intern Monica Lewinsky, the 1999 out-of-court settlement was eclipsed. To many, the Jones case was pure political theater designed to undermine the Clinton presidency, a venue to force him to respond under oath to questions about his sexual peccadilloes. To others, this case signaled that sexual harassment could occur at the highest levels of employment. Still others viewed it as an indication that even he who fills the role of the most powerful figure in the world is answerable to the law for his actions.

Since 1980, when the EEOC processed one charge of sexual harassment, the number of claims has increased steadily to approximately 15,000 annually. In 1998, the U.S. Supreme Court upheld a decision that men may be sexually harassed by other men (*Oncale v. Sundowner Offshore Services, Inc.*, 1998). This case added impetus to investigations of same-sex harassment that had already commenced (Foote & Goodman-Delahunty, 1999; Stockdale, Visio, & Batra, 1999; Waldo, Berdahl, & Fitzgerald, 1998). In the same year, the U.S. Supreme Court issued decisions elaborating on the responsibilities of employees and employers in dealing with workplace sexual harassment (*Burlington Industries, Inc. v. Ellerth*, 1998; *Faragher v.*

TABLE 1
Equal Employment Opportunity Commission and State Fair Employment Agency Charge Data, 1992–2001

Year	Total charges filed	% charges filed by men	Monetary awards (millions)[a] ($)
1992	10,532	9.1	12.7
1993	11,908	9.1	25.1
1994	14,420	9.9	22.5
1995	15,549	9.9	24.3
1996	15,342	10.0	27.8
1997	15,889	11.6	49.5
1998	15,618	12.9	34.3
1999	15,222	12.1	50.3
2000	15,836	13.6	54.6
2001	15,475	13.7	53.0

[a] Does not include monetary awards obtained through litigation.

City of Boca Raton, 1998). These cases increased the emphasis on education programs and internal systems for reporting and resolving sexual harassment complaints. Women continue to file the greater number of charges, but claims by men have increased and since 2000 comprise 13% to 14% of the charges (see Table 1).

In early litigation, the relief available under Title VII to compensate plaintiffs in sexual harassment cases was limited, and unless the plaintiff was fired and could claim monetary damages derived from lost wages, no compensation was available. Since the act was amended in 1991, allowing for the recovery of monetary compensation for psychological or psychiatric injury, claims specifying those injuries have increased (McDonald & Kulick, 2001). The demand for qualified forensic psychologists to provide helpful evaluative information to assist courts in resolving these claims has increased commensurately.

PURPOSE OF THE BOOK

In many civil cases, the major controversies center on causation of harm and credibility of the witnesses. Workplace sexual harassment cases are no different in this regard and may, in fact, present greater challenges than many other types of cases because of the classic credibility contests that devolve into *he said/she said* disputes in which there are no witnesses to the core events in issue. The body of research on different aspects of sexual harassment that bears on questions of causation and credibility continues to proliferate. However, its implications for practitioners, and precisely how a forensic consultant should apply this almost overwhelming body of information within the constantly evolving legal framework is considerably less apparent. This book provides a road map of sorts for forensic evaluators, outlining and elaborating considerations drawn from the research and law and applying them to the task of a workplace forensic assessment. As such, it provides a useful benchmark regarding legal and ethical standards for competent forensic evaluations in workplace sexual harassment cases. We appreciate that not all experts approach this material and the task in the same manner, and many may emphasize different aspects of the literature from those that we have chosen to highlight.

The material in this book is organized in three major sections. In the first section, chapters 1 through 3, we acquaint readers with fundamental background information intended to provide perspective regarding the prevalence of sexual harassment, the causes of sexual harassment, and legal theories. Chapters 4 through 6 constitute the second major section. These chapters lead the reader through a practical sequence of steps to perform a competent and thorough evaluation in a sexual harassment case. The progression moves from initial consultation through in-court testimony, focusing first on information gathering, second on uses of the data regarding causation or liability, and third on the consequences or harms and damages. In the final section, chapter 7 reviews the expanding roles for forensic psychologists in applying this information prior to trial to investigate harassment complaints and to resolve them prior to formal litigation. This sequence first enables readers to familiarize themselves with existing research, theories, and legal cases and then to apply this information in a practical way to develop forensic skills and increase their competence in conducting ethical and comprehensive evaluations in workplace sexual harassment cases. We have included two appendixes in this volume. Both are disguised case reports adapted from real sexual harassment cases and are included to provide examples of the issues encountered in these cases and how one psychologist chose to examine those issues. The first reflects allegations of severe sexual harassment in a situation involving a plaintiff with multiple trauma in her history. The second involved allegations of same-sex harassment filed by a male plaintiff who claims he was a target of retaliation.

Chapter 1 provides an overview of the prevalence and incidence of different types of workplace sexual harassment. An understanding of this topic permits evaluators to assess whether the type of claim they are addressing fits within the commonly experienced forms of sexual harassment or whether it is atypical. The implications of that information may influence conclusions that can be drawn about the types of harms claimed, the credibility of the claimant, and the extent to which the general literature can be extended and generalized to the specific case presented. The less typical a claim, the less likely it is that the evaluator can rely on the general research literature. In chapter 2, the contexts that promote or inhibit harassing conduct are examined in light of current theories of sexual harassment.

Insight into this body of research permits the evaluator to better assess the credibility of the parties and the likelihood that harassment was a causal factor in producing the claimed symptoms or consequences. Chapter 3 outlines the legal framework that applies in sexual harassment cases and acquaints the reader with landmark cases that reflect the evolution of the legal theories that can lead to liability on the part of an employer. An understanding of the legal framework on sexual harassment is integral to effective consultation and testimony. Because not all sexual misconduct amounts to sexual harassment, it is critical to understand how the law distinguishes between those cases of incivility and misconduct that are trivial and those that can result in an employer's liability.

With this background, readers are better equipped to move to the chapters addressing the consultation process. Chapter 4 takes readers through the stages and processes of consultation in a sexual harassment case from the time of referral through trial with particular emphasis on ethical issues, including the "Ethical Principles of Psychologists and Code of Conduct" (American Psychological Association, 2002) and the role of the Federal Rules of Evidence (2000) in shaping the contours of evaluation and testimony. Chapter 5 focuses on issues pertaining to whether sexual harassment occurred. Chapter 6 presents a model for evaluating the psychological consequences of sexual harassment, including consideration of alternative sources of the emotional reactions commonly reported by sexual harassment plaintiffs. Finally, in acknowledgment of the expanding opportunities for psychologists to serve as consultants to employers and claimants outside of the trial process itself, chapter 7 discusses the roles psychologists may play in resolving sexual harassment cases though investigation, fact-finding, and mediation.

The authors wanted this book to provide both mental health providers and members of legal professions with a tool for dealing more knowledgeably with sexual harassment cases. It is hoped that we have done this in a balanced and helpful way so that plaintiffs, defendants, and the public will receive improved services.

1

SEXUAL HARASSMENT: AN EVOLVING SOCIAL–PSYCHOLOGICAL PHENOMENON

This chapter provides the reader with an overview of who is sexually harassed, who does the harassing, and where and how the harassment is likely to occur. The forensic evaluator needs to be familiar with aspects of sexual coercion and other forms of harassment that can constitute a hostile work environment. Familiarity with sexual harassment research findings enables a forensic psychologist to place a specific case within the larger context of the phenomenon of sexual harassment. The chapter begins by reviewing large-scale empirical-studies research of sexual harassment in civilian, federal, and military contexts conducted in the past 25 years. Next, factors related to the targets of sexual harassment are examined, including the age, race, and vulnerability of the target.

Social scientists have quantified many aspects of sexual harassment using different research methods and somewhat different definitions of sexual harassment, depending on the research objectives, making it difficult to aggregate and generalize the results. The term *harassment* has a different meaning and significance in everyday conversation from the technical, legal meaning. Many laypersons are insensitive to the differences. For example, a common misconception is that legally actionable harassment entails only unwanted physical touching or groping. Thus, researchers who inquire whether participants were ever sexually harassed may receive responses that underestimate legally significant conduct. Better questioning techniques avoid conclusory, ambiguous terms such as *sexual harassment* and, instead, ask about types of conduct experienced. Investigators interested in assessing the full spectrum of social sexual conduct, from mild verbal compliments at one extreme to forcible sexual assault at the other, have been criticized by lawyers for confounding innocuous social conduct and criminally culpable conduct with some forms of actionable sexual harassment. Even when the focus of the research is actionable sexual harassment, many studies do not take legal definitions into account, limiting conclusions regarding the application of the findings to legal cases.

LARGE GROUP SURVEYS

To appreciate who is sexually harassed and how people evaluate workplace behaviors in the light of their harassing qualities, one may find it helpful to understand the prevalence of sexual harassment in terms of base rates, indicating how often something happens in the real world (Otto, 1994). For example, when a forensic psychologist evaluates a workplace incident, if the plaintiff alleges that the defendant committed acts that the research indicates occur very rarely, this may prompt the examiner to probe more closely the plaintiff's credibility. The studies summarized in the sections that follow reflect employees' self-reported experiences in a diverse range of work settings.

The 1976 *Redbook* Survey

A survey soliciting information on sexual harassment was published in the January 1976 issue of the women's magazine, *Redbook* (Safran, 1976). The results of this groundbreaking study appeared in the May 1976 issue of the same publication. About 9,000 women responded, and many included letters describing their experiences in detail. The majority of the respondents were married women in their 20s and early 30s. However, the sample also included never-married and divorced women and women drawn from several generations of Americans. Of the respondents, 88% reported the experience of unwanted sexual activity on the job.

Although the sampling method was susceptible to response bias because women who were not harassed may not have been motivated to complete the survey and the magazine readership may have included more readers in restricted age ranges and socioeconomic groups, the study highlighted the pervasiveness and negative personal impact of sexual harassment. The popular forum of the study exposed the phenomenon of sexual harassment to a broad cross section of American women and helped them voice their experiences and validate their reactions to those experiences. One caveat to bear in mind is that these data may not reflect the incidence of actionable sexual harassment, as the query about unwanted sexual activity included more conduct than is prohibited by law.

The 1985 Los Angeles Survey

One early, well-controlled, and broadly based study of sexual harassment was conducted in Los Angeles County, California (Gutek, 1985). As part of a telephone survey, the researchers spoke with a randomly selected sample of adults, 827 women and 405 men, who were working a minimum of 20 hours a week. The participants were drawn from a mix of occupational classifications. Women had fewer managerial, skilled, semiskilled and unskilled positions than men, but more clerical jobs. More than two thirds of the men (72%) came from workplaces in which men predominated, and more than half of the women (59%) came from workplaces in which women outnumbered men. Workplaces were generally segregated along gender lines: Women worked with women; men worked with men.

Respondents reported whether they had a series of experiences on the job. Separately, they indicated whether they labeled the same conduct as sexual harassment. Table 1.1 summarizes their responses. To a small degree,

TABLE 1.1
Experiences of On-the-Job Sexual Behavior

	Experienced on any job		Labeled as harassment	
Type of behavior	Women (%)	Men (%)	Women (%)	Men (%)
Complimentary comments	68.1	60.7	18.9	10.4
Insulting comments	23.3	19.3	19.9	12.1
Complimentary looks and gestures	66.6	56.3	16.2	8.1
Insulting looks and gestures	20.3	19.3	15.4	9.6
Nonsexual touching	74.4	78	3.6	3.5
Sexual touching	33.1	33.3	24.2	12.3
Expected socializing[a]	12	8.4	10.9	7.4
Expected sexual activity	7.7	3.5	7.6	3.2
Experienced sexual harassment			53.1	37.3

Note. From *Sex and the Workplace* (p. 46), by B. A. Gutek, 1985, San Francisco: Jossey-Bass. Copyright 1985 by Jossey-Bass. Adapted with permission.
[a]As a job requirement.

women consistently experienced more sexually related experiences than did men. Larger gender differences emerged in the labeling of behavior as harassment. In general, women were more likely to define a behavior as harassing than were men. Over half of the women surveyed said they had been sexually harassed, although no legal definition was provided. A little over a third of the men concluded that their experiences constituted harassment.

U.S. Merit Systems Protection Board Surveys

In part stimulated by earlier small-scale research, the U.S. Merit Systems Protection Board (USMSPB) conducted a series of three studies that assessed the nature and extent of sexual harassment among federal employees (U.S. Merit Systems Protection Board, 1981, 1988, 1994). Although some researchers viewed women as the sole targets of sexual harassment (Crull, 1982; Koss et al., 1994), the USMSPB made no such assumptions and polled all employees concerning their experiences of sexually offensive behavior in the workplace. The scale of these surveys was large: The 1981 study polled 20,314 men and women; the 1987 and the 1994 studies analyzed replies of over 8,000 federal workers. The 1981 study yielded a response rate of 85%; response rates for the 1988 and 1994 studies were 66% and 61%, respectively. All three studies yielded approximately equal numbers of returns from men and women, even though in 1994 the federal workforce consisted of 57% men and 43% women. In all of these studies, the interval assessed was the previous 2 years of the worker's life. Thus, these are measures of incidence as opposed to lifetime prevalence.

The methodology used and the samples assessed in the three studies were similar, providing a rare opportunity to examine trends in sexual harassment incidence over a 13-year period. Although the federal workplace may differ in some significant respects from private work settings, these data provide a general picture of the incidence and nature of sexually harassing behaviors in a range of work environments. Table 1.2 shows the percentage of women and men in the sample who experienced seven types of sexual harassment in the 2-year period preceding the survey.

Table 1.2 indicates that across the years sampled, the incidence of sexual harassment was remarkably stable. A closer look reveals that for women, the incidence of verbal harassment increased over the 13 years spanned by the studies. The only category to show a decline was that of "pressure for dates." For more serious forms of harassment, the levels either increased (as in the case of "deliberate touching") or stayed about the same. The most severe category, "actual or attempted rape or assault," showed a fourfold increase over the course of the surveys.

TABLE 1.2
U.S. Merit Systems Protection Board 2-Year Incidence Data for Seven Kinds of Sexual Harassment for Women and Men Across a Series of Three Studies

	Study					
	1982		1987		1994	
Type of behavior	Women (%)	Men (%)	Women (%)	Men (%)	Women (%)	Men (%)
Sexual remarks	33	10	35	12	37	14
Suggestive looks	28	8	28	9	29	9
Pressure for dates	26	7	15	4	13	4
Deliberate touching	15	3	26	8	24	8
Pressure for sexual favors	9	2	9	3	7	2
Letters and calls	9	3	12	4	10	4
Actual or attempted rape or assault	1	0.3	0.8	0.3	4	2

Note. From *Sexual Harassment in the Federal Workplace: Trends, Progress, Continuing Challenges* (p. 58), by U.S. Merit Systems Protection Board, 1995, Washington, DC: U.S. Government Printing Office. In the public domain.

As shown in Table 1.2, the most striking comparison between the men's and women's data is the overall lower incidence of sexual harassment experiences for men. In general, men experienced about one third to one fifth the number of sexually offensive experiences that women experienced over the years spanned by the study. The gender difference was especially marked in reports of experiences of more serious acts, including deliberate touching and actual or attempted rape or assault. This rather shocking disparity may accurately reflect women's greater susceptibility to harassment. In the alternative, it may demonstrate the reluctance on the part of male participants to report these events. These data are also striking in that the incidence of sexually harassing acts among men traced the same trends as were observed among women over the study interval. This increase may be related to a number of factors. Although men report far fewer sexually harassing experiences than do women, the incidence and nature of the harassment are significant and constitute a basis for concern for researchers, policymakers, and forensic consultants.

The Department of Defense Surveys

The USMSPB studies, which included military personnel, prompted concern about the incidence of sexual harassment for women and men serving in the armed forces of the United States (Niebuhr, 1997). These studies indicated that the rates of sexual harassment experiences among military women were higher, in a range of 44% to 47% in the 1987 study, compared with an average of 42% among nonmilitary female personnel. The levels of sexual harassment among military men varied from 11% to 16% in 1987 compared with rates of 14% among civilian men. In 1988, the Department of Defense organized the Task Force on Women in the Military to review the status of women in the armed forces. The group was to offer recommendations about a range of issues including whether women should be placed in combat roles and to explore the barriers to women's participation in the military, including the presence of sexual harassment. The task force recommended that the secretary of defense conduct a survey to determine the incidence of sexual harassment in the military and the effectiveness of existing programs for reducing sexual harassment. The secretary of defense mandated the 1988 Department of Defense Survey, followed in 1995 by a survey to replicate and extend the first survey (Bastian, Lancaster, & Reyst, 1996; Martindale, 1990).

The format of the first survey (Martindale, 1990) was similar to that used in the earlier USMSPB studies. The 1995 study, conducted by the Defense Manpower Data Center, included a research team from the University of Illinois (Lancaster, 1999) and used both the old (Form A) and new (Form B) instruments, allowing for continuity and comparisons across times. The use of Form B facilitated comparisons with data from civilian samples (Fitzgerald et al., 1988). The 1988 and 1995 Form A inquired about the incidence of sexual harassment in the 12 months before the survey.

Because women make up a significantly smaller proportion of military personnel than men, women were oversampled in both studies to allow better statistical control over the data. The 1988 study surveyed 10,752 men and 9,497 women, and 13,599 personnel completed the 1995 study. Overall, the incidence of unwanted sexual attention among men was approximately one fourth the incidence among women. Both women and men reported fewer incidents of unwanted sexual attention in 1994 than they reported in the 1988 research: The incidence of unwanted sexual attention dropped from 64% to 55% among women and from 17% to 14% among men.

Table 1.3 shows the incidence of unwanted sexual attention for women across the two sampling intervals. "Attempts" refers to "attempts to get your participation in any other sexual activities" (Bastian et al., 1996, p. 9). Less severe types of unwanted sexual attention (sexual teasing, suggestive looks) in the workplace are frequent experiences for military women, as are instances of sexual touching, whistles, and calls. More serious behaviors, such as pressure for sexual favors, attempts to involve the target in sexual activities, rape, and sexual assault, occur significantly less frequently in this military sample.

A similar reduction in the frequency of harassing behaviors over the 7 years spanned by the study was observed among men. Table 1.3 shows

TABLE 1.3
The Department of Defense Studies: Incidence of Unwanted Sexual Attention by Type of Behavior for Women and Men

	Study			
	1988		1995	
Type of behavior	Women (%)	Men (%)	Women (%)	Men (%)
Sexual remarks	52	13	44	10
Suggestive looks	44	10	37	7
Pressure for dates	26	3	22	2
Deliberate touching	38	9	29	6
Pressure for sexual favors	15	2	11	1
Letters and calls	14	3	12	2
Actual or attempted rape or assault	5	<0.5	4	<0.5

Note. From *Department of Defense 1995 Sexual Harassment Survey* (p. 9), by L. D. Bastian, A. R. Lancaster, and H. E. Reyst, 1996, December, Washington, DC: U.S. Government Printing Office. In the public domain.

that among men as well as women, sexual teasing, jokes, and remarks were the most common experiences, followed closely by sexual looks and gestures.

The University of Illinois researchers had some reservations about the usefulness of these data and adapted the Sexual Experiences Questionnaire (SEQ) to produce the Sexual Experiences Questionnaire–Department of Defense version (SEQ-DoD), which included questions specifically designed to assess the sexual harassment experiences of men as well as women (Hay & Elig, 1999). The SEQ-DoD inquired about unwanted sex-related experiences in the military during the previous 12 months. The items listed behaviors without defining them as sexual harassment. For example, one item read "Made unwanted attempts to establish a romantic sexual relationship with you despite your efforts to discourage it" (Fitzgerald, Magley, Drasgow, & Waldo, 1999, p. 248).

The researchers clustered sex-related experiences into four categories or types of sexual harassment: sexist hostility, sexual hostility, unwanted sexual attention, and sexual assault. Sexist hostility included activities of gender-based harassment such as being treated differently because of one's gender, the presence of sexually offensive materials, or being the recipient of sexist remarks. Sexual hostility included offensive sexual stories or jokes, offensive remarks about the respondent's appearance or body, or the harassers' exposing themselves physically (e.g., "mooning"). Unwanted sexual attention included requests for dates, touching that made the respondent uncomfortable, or having sex with the respondent without consent or against the person's will. In some analyses (Bastian et al., 1996), sexual assault was examined separately from unwanted sexual attention in acknowledgment

TABLE 1.4
Department of Defense Form B Data:
Reports of Unwanted Sex as a Function of Gender

Unwanted experience	Women (%)	Men (%)
Sexual coercion	13	2
Sexual attention	42	8
Sexist hostility	63	15
Sexual hostility	70	35
Any type of sex experience	78	38

Note. From "Measuring Sexual Harassment in the Military: The Sexual Experiences Questionnaire (SEQ-DoD)," by L. F. Fitzgerald, V. J. Magley, F. Drasgow, and C. R. Waldo, 1999, *Military Psychology, 11,* pp. 252–253. Copyright 1999 by Lawrence Erlbaum Associates, Inc. Adapted with permission.

of the fact that this is a distinct and more serious class of behavior that may be the subject of a criminal prosecution. Sexual coercion included bribing the target to engage in sexual behavior, treating the respondent badly for refusing sex, or implying better treatment if the respondent was sexually cooperative. Table 1.4 shows the incidence of these behaviors as a function of gender (Fitzgerald, Magley, et al., 1999). Sexual hostility was the most common experience between both genders, followed by sexist hostility. Unwanted sexual attention occurred at a lower, yet substantial, rate, especially for women.

The 1995 data were further analyzed to assess whether individuals experienced more than one type of unwanted sexual conduct. Table 1.5

TABLE 1.5
Department of Defense Form B Data:
Reports of Single and Multiple Forms of Sexual Harassment

Unwanted experience	Women (%)	Men (%)
None	24	64
Sexist hostility	8	2
Sexual hostility	8	18
Unwanted sexual attention	1	—
Sexist hostility and sexual hostility	24	9
Sexist hostility and unwanted sexual attention	1	—
Sexual hostility and unwanted sexual attention	4	3
Sexist hostility, sexual hostility, and unwanted sexual attention	21	3
Sexist hostility, sexual hostility, unwanted sexual attention, and sexual coercion	9	1

Note. Dashes indicate that data were not reported. From "Measuring Sexual Harassment in the Military: The Sexual Experiences Questionnaire (SEQ-DoD)," by L. F. Fitzgerald, V. J. Magley, F. Drasgow, and C. R. Waldo, 1999, *Military Psychology, 11,* pp. 255–256. Copyright 1999 by Lawrence Erlbaum Associates, Inc. Adapted with permission.

displays the extent to which female and male personnel experienced single and multiple forms of harassment. More than twice as many men as women experienced no sexual harassment during the relevant period. Among women, unwanted sexual attention rarely occurred in isolation from other harassment experiences and most often occurred in combination with sexist and sexual hostility and sexual coercion. Likewise, sexual coercion occurred rarely in the absence of sexist hostility, sexual hostility, and unwanted sexual attention. Among men, sexual hostility was the most frequent experience, followed by sexist and sexual hostility. For men, unwanted sexual attention rarely occurred in the absence of sexual hostility and sexist hostility.

Lessons From the Incidence Studies

Although in the large-scale studies conducted in the civilian workplace, in government civil service, and in the military, researchers used broad and varying definitions of unwanted sexual attention, several observations concerning the incidence of sexual harassment in the United States over the past 25 years can be made. First, women are more often targets of sexual harassment than are men. Depending on the setting and the questions asked, women report harassment experiences at a rate two to seven times the incidence among men. Questionnaires that included inquiries about abusive verbal behavior allowed men to report more harassing experiences. The types of harassment experienced by men versus women differ in that men experience more gender-based hostility and verbal harassment than do women.

Second, studies of similar populations over time indicate few consistent trends. In some settings, harassing behaviors appeared to decline. For example, most types of harassing experiences decreased in the years between the two DoD studies. Conversely, the incidence of sexual comments and sexual touching increased in the years examined in the USMSPB studies.

For the forensic practitioner, studies of the base rates of sexual harassment in the general population suggest that sexual remarks and suggestive looks are common workplace experiences. Even deliberate, unwanted touching is a relatively common experience, affecting about 25% of women and about 8% of men. In contrast, the incidence of sexual harassment complaints is much lower (Fitzgerald, Swan, & Fischer, 1995). For example, the 1995 DoD Survey (Bastian et al., 1996) showed that only 14% of participants who were harassed reported the incident to a supervisor. The data reflect a substantial gap between the incidence of unpleasant workplace experiences and the number of complaints made by employees in those settings. Reasons for this gap are discussed in chapter 6.

VARIABLES AFFECTING THE INCIDENCE OF SEXUAL HARASSMENT EXPERIENCES

As previously noted, gender is one critical variable that determines the experience of sexual harassment in the workplace. One reason that gender influences perceptions of harassing episodes is that gender role stereotypes influence the reasons provided for attributing responsibility to targets of harassment. Women are traditionally expected to be more passive and vulnerable, whereas men are expected to be more aggressive and powerful and less vulnerable. Vulnerability is also influenced by the extent to which a target is seen to violate social morality norms. For instance, a married woman who is unfaithful to her spouse and is then a target of sexual assault or harassment is seen as more responsible for the victimization than is a woman who is not unfaithful or promiscuous (Viki & Abrams, 2002). Thus, attributions as to whether harassment occurred and who is to blame for sexual harassment may be influenced by the target's gender, perceived vulnerability, and conformity with gender role stereotypes and social morality stereotypes. Coworkers and employers of a female target who works in a nontraditional occupation (e.g., firefighter, law enforcement officer, plumber), and thus appears less passive and vulnerable than a target employed in a traditional occupation consistent with stereotypical norms (e.g., teacher, nurse, secretary, waitress), may be less likely to perceive harassment than would coworkers and employers of the more traditional female target. Similarly, when a target is a man, expectations that men are less vulnerable may also decrease the perception that he was harassed. Violations of gender role expectations are somewhat more acceptable among women than men, perhaps because the gender role of men is more strictly defined than is that of women (Kite & Whitely, 1998). Thus, gender can play an important role in how and how frequently different harassing episodes are perceived (Baker, Terpstra, & Cutler, 1990; Sheffey & Tindale, 1992). Other demographic variables, such as age and race, also are relevant.

Age

Gutek (1995) noted that among the women in her sample, 57% of those who reported sexual harassment were under the age of 35 years. The 1981 USMSPB survey showed that the incidence of sexual harassment decreased as a function of age. Figure 1.1 displays reported harassment by target age and gender (adapted from U.S. Merit Systems Protection Board, 1981, p. 43).

The 1994 USMSPB study did not report parallel data by age and gender of the harassment targets but compared the ages of individuals who

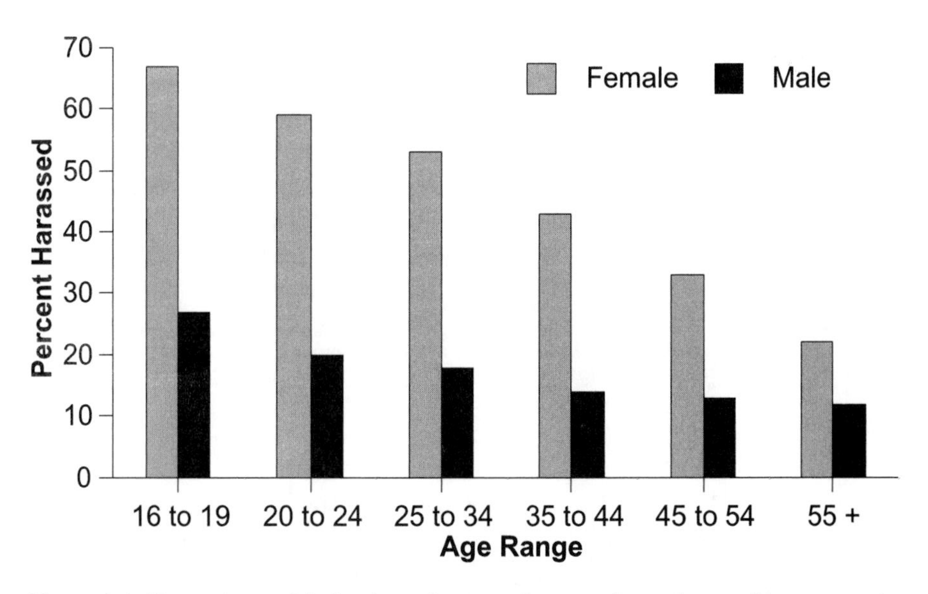

Figure 1.1. Percentage of federal employees who experienced sexual harassment by age and gender. From *Sexual Harassment in the Federal Workplace: Is It a Problem?* (p. 43), by U.S. Merit Systems Protection Board, 1981, Washington, DC: U.S. Government Printing Office. In the public domain.

were harassed with those who were not harassed. Table 1.6 displays these results.

The 1995 DoD study did not report incidence data by age of participants. However, a subsequent study reworked those data to examine the characteristics of the target compared with the characteristics of the harasser (DuBois, Knapp, Faley, & Kustis, 1998). Table 1.7 displays the gender and relative age of harassers and targets.

TABLE 1.6
Percentage of Respondents Who Did and Did Not Experience Sexual Harassment as a Function of Age of Target

	Men		Women	
Target's age	Targets	Nontargets	Targets	Nontargets
34 and younger	19	16	29	19
35 to 44	82	84	71	81
45 and older	41	54	32	49

Note. From *Sexual Harassment in the Federal Workplace: Trends, Progress, Continuing Challenges* (p. 60), by U.S. Merit Systems Protection Board, 1994–1995, Washington, DC: U.S. Government Printing Office. In the public domain.

TABLE 1.7
Percentage of Respondents Who Experienced Sexual Harassment as a Function of the Relative Age of the Harasser

Relative age of harasser	Women		Men	
	Opposite gender	Same gender	Opposite gender	Same gender
Older	76	60	32	59
Same age	13	21	21	21
Younger	11	19	47	20

Note. From "An Empirical Examination of Same- and Other-Gender Sexual Harassment in the Workplace," by C. L. Z. DuBois, D. E. Knapp, R. H. Faley, and G. A. Kustis, 1998, *Sex Roles, 39,* p. 739. Copyright 1998 by Cathy DuBois, PhD, and Kluwer Academic/Plenum. Adapted with permission.

These data show a pattern of harassment that varies as a function of both the gender of the target and the gender of the harasser. Among female targets, the pattern is uniform for same-sex and other-sex harassment: The harasser is more likely to be older. Among men, the pattern differs. Women who harass men tend to be younger than the male targets. Men who harass other men are more likely to be older than the male targets.

Race

The 1981 USMSPB study was the first to examine the issue of the target's race. This study showed few differences among female targets: White, Hispanic, and African American women experienced approximately equal rates of sexual harassment. However, among male targets, minority status (African American and Native American) was correlated with higher levels of harassment. Subsequent USMSPB studies did not report data by race.

Other researchers directly addressed the issue of sexual harassment and race. In 1993, Wyatt and Riederle (1995) conducted a telephone survey of more than 100 African American and 100 White women between the ages of 18 and 36 years. The participants were matched for age, education, number of children, and marital status. Of this group, 44% reported "unwanted requests, comments, or actions of a sexual nature that respondents did not welcome" (Wyatt & Riederle, 1995, p. 313). Among the African American women, 34% reported at least one incident of sexual harassment at work compared with similar reports by 53% of the White women. Wyatt and Riederle suggested that this difference might reflect underreporting by African American women.

The 1995 DoD study (Fitzgerald, Magley, et al., 1999) gathered race data from participants. One surprising result was that Native American men and women experienced a higher rate of all sorts of sexually harassing experiences than did those of other racial groups. Hispanic women reported somewhat fewer incidents, and White, African American, and Asian American women also reported fewer incidents of harassment. The gap across the racial groups was approximately 14%. Among men, Native Americans again reported the highest rates of harassment, at about the 50% level. African American, Hispanic, White, and Asian American participants showed lower rates, with the Asian American group reporting only a 36% incidence. Fitzgerald, Magley, et al. offered no rationale for the racial differences noted in the study.

Other researchers mined the DoD data for differences related to race (Bergman & Drasgow, 2003). This research repeated the finding that Native American women experienced the highest levels of harassment. Blacks and Hispanics were harassed less, and Asian and White targets reported lower overall harassment and better outcomes. Increases in harassment yielded increases in negative outcomes.

Research has revealed that the perceived seriousness of sexual harassment or assault is also influenced by racial stereotypes. For example, African American rape victims are generally perceived as more responsible for the attack and as less traumatized than are White victims (Hall, 1998; Willis, 1992). The perceived seriousness of a rape or sexual harassment of an African American woman is also reduced because of racial stereotypes of African American women as promiscuous (McNair & Neville, 1996). Regardless of the race of the target, victims of interracial rape are seen as more responsible for the assault than are victims of intraracial rape (George & Martinez, 2002).

Overall, results of studies related to race are inconsistent. Proportionally, African American women are targets of sexual harassment less often than are members of other racial and ethnic groups. In many different settings, Native American women and men appear to be singled out for harassment more than members of other racial and ethnic groups.

SUMMARY

Unwanted sexual experiences in the workplace are common. Inappropriate verbal behavior was reported by 33% to 66% of women and 10% to 15% of men. Incidents involving unwanted touching or other similar activities were reported by 15% to 38% of women and 1% to 12% of men. Incidents involving demands for sexual activity were reported by 8% to 16% of women and up to 2% of men.

The incidence data also indicate that younger workers are more likely to be recipients of a range of unwanted sexual experiences on the job. Perhaps this is because youth is an important component of sexual attractiveness in our society (Sprecher, Sullivan, & Hatfield, 1994). Both the absolute age and the relative youth of the target of sexual harassment compared with the age of the harasser may make the targets more vulnerable to sexual behavior in the workplace.

Because many women and some men experience sexual harassment as a relatively common event in the workplace, a potential plaintiff is likely to have been exposed to a number of situations involving a hostile work environment or adverse sexual experiences on the job. Exploration of prior experiences in the forensic evaluation of a sexual harassment plaintiff may provide insight about stress tolerance or individual reactions to particular stressors. For example, one worker may have been the recipient of substantial harassment over a long period of time in a previous job. However, in the job where the current harassment allegedly occurred, the same worker may have tolerated similar harassment for a short time and then complained to supervisors or resigned from the position. Inquiry into the differences between the jobs, the particular kind of harassment, other stressors in the person's life, and other variables may elucidate that worker's differential reactions. We explore those differences in later chapters of this book.

2

HARASSERS, HARASSMENT CONTEXTS, SAME-SEX HARASSMENT, WORKPLACE ROMANCE, AND HARASSMENT THEORIES

The goal of this chapter is to familiarize the psychologist with current theoretical perspectives on sexual harassment. Research on four topics is central to many theoretical discussions concerning sexual harassment: sexual harassers, work context, same-sex harassment, and workplace romances. This chapter reviews research on these topics and evaluates theoretical approaches applied to the phenomenon of sexual harassment.

THE HARASSER

In the last chapter, we delineated characteristics of workers likely to be targets of sexual harassment. This section focuses on the other side of the harassment dyad as well as the harasser and reviews the characteristics, both demographic and behavioral, of those who harass others in the workplace. This discussion aims to deepen the forensic psychologist's understanding of the complexity of sexual harassment. An understanding of the harasser provides the forensic consultant with insight into the relationships that harassers have with their targets and the kinds of thinking or conduct that predicate harassing activities. In evaluating *he said/she said* conflicts, the psychologist may use information about the alleged harasser to make judgments about credibility.

Status Relative to Target

The USMSPB researchers asked harassment targets who harassed them (USMSPB, 1981, 1988, 1994). As Table 2.1 indicates, both men and women are most likely to be harassed by a coworker or other employee of equivalent status. When coworker harassment occurs, men are somewhat more likely than women to be targets. In situations in which the harasser is a supervisor, women are the predominant targets.

These data provide some evidence of *contrapower* sexual harassment that arises when a subordinate harasses a supervisor (Rospenda, Richman, & Nawyn, 1998). The evidence from these studies indicates that subordinates rarely harass women but that harassment by a subordinate is more common among men. The 1995 DoD survey examined the relationship between harasser and target (Bastian et al., 1996). Military personnel work with both civilians and other members of the military, thus harassers could belong to either group. Although the power dynamic between civilians and military personnel is sometimes ill defined, for members of the military, every harasser has a designated rank relative to the target. The incidence of harassment of military personnel by civilians was very low among both men and women: Only 6% of women and 7% of men reported that civilians bothered them.

In contrast, the incidence of harassment by a military person was significantly higher. Table 2.2 displays data based on a single harassing event by the military status of the harasser and may reflect an incident involving multiple harassers. Thus, the percentages do not add up to 100%. Consistent with the USMSPB data, women in the military are more likely than men

TABLE 2.1
Status of Harasser Relative to Target

	1980		1987		1994	
Harasser	Women (%)	Men (%)	Women (%)	Men (%)	Women (%)	Men (%)
Coworker or other employee	65	76	69	77	77	79
Immediate or higher supervisor	37	14	29	19	28	14
Subordinate	4	16	2	10	3	11
Other or Unknown	6	5	10	10	7	6

Note. From *Sexual Harassment in the Federal Workplace: Trends, Progress, Continuing Challenges* (p. 19), by U.S. Merit Systems Protection Board, 1995, Washington, DC: U.S. Government Printing Office. In the public domain.

TABLE 2.2
Data for a Single Harassing Event by Military Status of Harasser

Status of harasser	Women (%)	Men (%)
Unit commander	4	2
Immediate military supervisor	18	11
Other military personnel of higher rank or grade	43	21
Military coworker	44	52
Military subordinate	10	15
Military training instructor	2	1
Other military person	24	22

Note. From *Department of Defense 1995 Sexual Harassment* Survey (DMDC Report No. 96-014, p. 39), by L. D. Bastian, A. R. Lancaster, and H. E. Reyst, 1996, December, Washington, DC: U.S. Government Printing Office. In the public domain.

to be harassed by a person of superior rank; military men are more likely to be harassed by coworkers.

In summary, two large-scale studies differ in their results. In civilian settings, the harasser is most likely to be a coworker. The probability of being harassed by someone of superior rank is much higher for women in military jobs than is the probability of being harassed by someone of equal or lower rank. For men, the civilian and military contexts are similar: Men are more probable targets of someone of equal rank or of a subordinate than of a superior.

Personality Characteristics of Harassers

Social scientists have expended considerable research effort to define the characteristics of men who harass women and the contexts in which harassment occurs (Begany & Milburn, 2002; Pryor, 1987; Pryor et al., 1995; Pryor & Stoller, 1994; Pryor & Whalen, 1997; Rudman & Borgida, 1995). A series of studies used the Likelihood to Sexually Harass (LSH) scale (Pryor, 1987) to identify characteristics of men who harass women. The LSH scale is derived from research on attitudinal components toward rape (Malmuth, 1981). The scale uses 10 scenarios in which a man in a power relationship with a woman has the potential to use that power to obtain sexual favors from the woman. In the initial validation study (Pryor, 1987), the LSH scale correlated with existing measures of sex role stereotyping, likelihood to rape, and impaired perspective taking. The latter scale asks the person to *step into the shoes* of another individual. The foregoing research is important to the forensic practitioner as it indicates that not every employee is equally likely to sexually harass others. This research illuminated three kinds of harassing men: men who are naive about heterosexual relationships, men who are exploitative in their relationships with women, and men who dislike or despise women. No parallel research has been conducted on women who harass men.

Misperceiving Harassers

Not all men who sexually harass women are would-be rapists, women haters, or men who enjoy exploiting women. Many men are positively oriented toward women and, in fact, seek a social or sexual relationship with them. However, in some cases, men misconstrue or misperceive the dress or behavior of women as sexually provocative. In nonwork settings, misperceptions of this sort are relatively common (Abbey, 1987). The extent to which a woman sits, stands close to, or touches a man often causes both male and female observers to conclude that the woman is interested in a romantic relationship (Abbey & Melby, 1986). However, compared with female observers, men are more likely to interpret these behaviors as cues that the woman's intentions are sexual. This misperception phenomenon is congruent with an extensive literature (e.g., Blumenthal, 1998; Gutek, 1995; J. D. Johnson, Benson, Teasdale, Simmons, & Reed, 1997; Katz, Hannon, & Whitten, 1996), which indicates that compared with women, men generally interpret ambiguous circumstances as less sexually harassing (Stockdale, 1993).

The misperceiving harasser mistakes the workplace for a location in which sexual relationships are appropriate. These harassers often repeatedly ask women at work for dates or engage in discussions concerning sexual matters. The harasser's misperceptions may be based on beliefs that relationships with women are adversarial and aggressive and that women who are friendly are expressing sexual desires (Stockdale, 1993). In short, the same cognitive patterns that characterize men who are high in LSH are evident in men who merely misperceive ordinary workplace interactions. Whether this is a continuum of cognitive distortion is still open to research investigation. Misperception may play a different role among harassers who engage in quid pro quo harassment, although they may be similar to exploitative men high in LSH in that they are more likely to see sexual favors as a commodity that can be traded for a salary increase or improved working conditions. "The seduction/imposition harasser is, on the other hand, one who attempts to use the organizational setting to obtain sexual gratification" (Stockdale, 1993, p. 93).

Exploitative Harassers

The research has demonstrated that "men who are high in LSH tend to (a) hold adversarial sexual beliefs, (b) find it difficult to assume others' perspectives, (c) endorse traditional male sex role stereotypes, (d) are high in authoritarianism, and (e) report a higher likelihood of rape" (Pryor & Stoller, 1994, p. 164). They concluded that the LSH scale measures the "readiness to use social power for sexually exploitive purposes" (Pryor & Stoller, 1994, p. 164). In addition, men who scored high on LSH cognitively connected sexuality to social dominance (Pryor & Stoller, 1994). In other words, men who are more likely to sexually harass women tend to view sexual relationships as involving a power differential in which the man is more powerful. Other research (Bargh & Raymond, 1995; Bargh, Raymond, Pryor, & Strack, 1995) suggests that the link between power and sexual interest may be a much more fundamental element of how men appraise women across a broad range of situations. These studies indicate that whenever a man is in a more powerful role relative to a woman, he is likely to see her as more sexually attractive.

Men who score high in LSH are more likely to engage in behavior consistent with those beliefs. In one study (Rudman & Borgida, 1995), men high in LSH were placed in a simulated interview with a female job applicant. Compared with men low in LSH, men high in LSH asked more sexist questions during the interview, sat closer to the woman, and engaged in more sexualized behavior toward her. These men rated the woman's friendliness and attractiveness higher than did the men who were less likely to harass. Men with higher LSH scores are more likely to harbor pro-rape and authoritarian attitudes (Begany & Milburn, 2002). Pro-rape attitudes are reflected by positive responses to statements like "women who dress in sexy clothes are asking to be raped," or "most women would enjoy being raped." Additional research examined the constructs of benign and hostile sexism as they related to LSH. The data indicate that high LSH men are more likely to show evidence of hostile sexism but not of the benign variety.

Men who are more likely to sexually harass women are more likely to express stereotyped attitudes toward women and male–female relationships. They are more likely to believe that women "accept and even enjoy male domination, even when it means physical coercion" (Pryor & Stoller, 1994, p. 167). High LSH men process social interactions differently from men males whose cognitive processes are not distorted in this manner. This differential processing is likely to emerge when these men are placed in a position of power over a woman in a work context. In these contexts, the exploitative men high in LSH are more likely to engage in sexist behavior.

Misogynistic Harassers

In some harassment situations, the harasser is not so much expressing a desire to have sex with someone in the workplace but is expressing hostile or negative feelings toward members of that gender (Pryor & Whalen, 1997). Although some women harbor generic hatred of men, because hostility to the opposite gender has historically been encountered more often among men, women-hating or misogyny is better recognized. Hostile work environment cases often involve elements of misogyny. The presence of pornography in the workplace, the use of negative sexually based terms for women, the derision of women's abilities, and frank taunts designed to offend women are examples of this sort of harassment. The misogynistic harasser is more likely to emerge as part of a group in a situation in which the person singled out for harassment is in some way different from the other workers. A salient example is a woman who is attempting to work in a formerly all-male occupation, for instance as a police officer, firefighter or soldier. Misogynistic harassers are more likely to divide the social world into male and female categories and to express traditional sexist attitudes.

From a forensic perspective, understanding the harasser is important for consultation, training, and testimony in sexual harassment cases. Appreciation that sexual harassment is often based on enduring beliefs on the part of the harasser suggests that individuals who are accused of consistent, egregious workplace sexual harassment display cognitive distortions in their perception of women, themselves, and how people signal sexual or romantic intentions. The misperceiving harasser tends to evaluate the friendly, cooperative, and collegial behavior of a coworker, supervisor, or subordinate as an indication that the person desires a sexual relationship. The exploitative harasser is likely to hold adversarial beliefs about women and to share many cognitive distortions with men who rape. The misogynist, on the other hand, simply dislikes women in the workplace and is likely to divide the world into gender-based groups, punishing those who attempt to break the traditional gender norms and rules. Harassers do not exist in a vacuum but in a social and work context in which their tendency to exploit, demean, or misperceive may or may not be fostered.

HARASSMENT CONTEXTS

Although sexual harassment has been the experience of a majority of women and a substantial portion of men, sexual harassment experiences are comparatively rare in some settings, and differences in the incidence rates of sexual harassment among organizations are large (Gruber, 1997). Various factors contribute to the situational or contextual workplace climate, which may promote or inhibit the incidence and prevalence of sexual harassment.

Work Group Composition and Type of Workplace Setting

One obvious factor that captured the attention of early researchers of sexual harassment was the relative proportion of men and women in a given organization or department and how that affected the incidence of harassment. As more women entered formerly exclusive male preserves, researchers examined the influence on small-group behavior of the gender distribution (Kanter, 1977). The sexes remained segregated in many workplaces. For example, in the Los Angeles study described earlier, 62% of men worked in jobs in which fewer than 20% of the workers were women, but only 40% of women worked in jobs in which fewer than 20% of the workers were men (Gutek, 1985). Even women employed by organizations that had a more equal overall gender mix were often assigned to work groups that were gender skewed. Women in traditionally male-dominated jobs experienced significantly more sexual harassment than women in jobs that included a larger proportion of women and women in jobs in which men's and women's work was integrated so that sex roles were less salient (Gutek, 1985). Subsequent research on traditionally male-dominated occupations, such as the military and police departments, indicates that the rates of sexual harassment of all types in these organizations are significantly higher than those of harassment in more gender-neutral job contexts (Gruber, 1997). Other studies have shown that in some groups in which women constitute a majority, sexual harassment is more probable (Fain & Anderton, 1987).

Organizational Responses to Harassment

The workplace in which sexual harassment occurs is not a neutral environment, and public or private employers respond in different ways to the problem of sexual harassment. At one end of the continuum is the organization that deals proactively with the problem by using educational interventions with supervisory and line staff, developing clear policies concerning harassment, developing and publicizing mechanisms for targets to report harassment, and establishing a system for dealing with those complaints in a way that protects the target and sanctions the harasser. Other organizations may ignore the problem and assume that harassment targets can fend for themselves. Some may even overtly or covertly encourage harassers. The extent of harassment in an organization is influenced by these factors (Gruber, 1998). Factors that potentially predict the incidence of harassment in a work group of staff in a university were examined by O'Hare and O'Donohue (1998). A number of policies that fall under the control of managers are positively correlated with the incidence of harassment.

These include (a) a lack of knowledge about grievance procedures, (b) a generally unprofessional atmosphere, and (c) the existence of sexist attitudes in the workplace. In job situations in which impersonal forms of sexual harassment (sexually explicit pictures in the workplace, sexual graffiti, sexual material on the office computers, or sexual entertainment at office parties) are present, women experience higher rates of unwanted sexual attention (Dekker & Barling, 1998).

Research has revealed that the policy of the employer is expressed in *local norms* of the organization (Pryor et al., 1995; Pryor, LaVite, & Stoller, 1993). The reactions of work group leaders or management are significant in encouraging or inhibiting the incidence of harassment. "Potential harassers may perceive that they are free to harass if management tolerates or condones such behavior" (Pryor et al., 1995, p. 70). For example, a reanalysis of the 1988 DoD study data revealed that in units in which men perceived the commanding officer as neutral or indifferent to sexual harassment, women experienced more harassment than they did in less tolerant settings (Pryor et al., 1995). A similar review of the USMSPB data from the 1981 and 1988 samples showed that in settings in which management was seen to discourage complaints about sexual harassment, more women were harassed (Pryor et al., 1995).

In an analysis of the 1995 DoD data, researchers examined the impact of three factors reflecting organizational climate: (a) the implementation of practices related to policies and procedures, (b) the provision of resources for targets, and (c) the provision of training (J. H. Williams, Fitzgerald, & Drasgow, 1999). All factors were considered a priori to have a high potential to affect the incidence of harassment in military organizations. However, only the implementation variable attained statistical significance, and this variable exceeded the impact of any other in this rich and extensive study. The extent to which the organization enforced the rules was inversely related to the dissatisfaction of workers in their jobs and in their supervisors.

In summary, how an organization addresses harassment issues is a very important determinant of whether employees are harassed at work. The presence of a policy prohibiting harassment and a complaint procedure are critical, but only if they are applied in practice do they inhibit the occurrence of sexual harassment in that organization. In short, if harassers know they can get away with sexual harassment, they do it.

SAME-SEX HARASSMENT

Although researchers have gathered data from both men and women, most of the focus of sexual harassment research has been on female targets of sexual harassment. One reason for this disparity is obvious: Women are the predominant targets of sexual harassment. Failure to study male targets of sexual harassment may also be based in part on paradigmatic assumptions concerning who harasses and who is the victim of that harassment (Vaux, 1993). Some researchers have begun to investigate the sexual harassment of men (Berdahl, Magley, & Waldo, 1996; DuBois et al., 1998; Magley, Waldo, Drasgow, & Fitzgerald, 1999; Waldo et al., 1998).

For men, the experience of sexual harassment is more likely to be same-sex harassment. The 1988 DoD study data were analyzed to determine the incidence and patterns of same-sex harassment (DuBois et al., 1998). This research revealed that almost all women (99%) were harassed by men. Although men were more likely (65%) to be harassed by women, a substantial proportion (35%) were harassed by men. Of those participants harassed by members of the same sex, about 90% were men. These results were generally replicated in an analysis of the 1995 DoD data (Magley et al., 1999) and in two samples drawn from civilian workplaces (Waldo et al., 1998).

Research reflects a different form of workplace harassment for men than for women. When men are harassed by women, some 45% are likely to experience sexually charged verbal abuse (sexual hostility); about 33% report incidents of verbal abuse directed to the male gender (sexist hostility); and slightly fewer, 32.8%, report unwanted sexual attention. A small proportion (about 4%) report sexual coercion (Magley et al., 1999). Men who are harassed by other men report the largest proportion of harassment in the form of sexual hostility (84%) with significantly less sexist hostility (16%), unwanted sexual attention (7%), and incidents of sexual coercion (1.7%). Thus, men who are harassed by men are predominantly targets of vulgar jokes, teasing, put-downs, or sexual hazing (DuBois et al., 1998). This type of sexual harassment enforces the heterosexual male gender role or hypermasculine norms (Waldo et al., 1998). Hypermasculinity is a rigid male sex role stereotyped identity comprising callous attitudes toward women, a conception of violence as manly, and a view of danger as exciting (Mosher & Sirkin, 1984).

Although lesbian or bisexual women report harassment based on sexual orientation (Day & Schoenrade, 2000; Evans & Broido, 2002; Schneider, 1991), large-scale studies indicate that women being harassed by other women on the basis of sexual orientation appears not to be a major problem. Rather, lesbian or bisexual women tend to be harassed by men who use the women's sexual orientation as a basis for gender hostility (Brogan, Frank, Elon, Sivanesan, & O'Hanlan, 1999). To our knowledge, no systematic research on the topic of same-sex harassment of women has been published.

Although no research has directly addressed the question, it appears that sexual harassers of men are rarely gay men (Magley et al., 1999), although men who are perceived as gay are frequently targets of gender-based harassment (Herek, 1989). The high incidence of male-on-male harassment makes it likely that many targets of same-sex harassment are heterosexual or men who do not conform to traditional stereotypes of hypermasculinity, such as transsexuals, bisexuals, and homosexuals. Much same-sex harassment experienced by men expresses homophobia, heterosexual biases, and antigay bias: Men call other men *queer* or *faggot*. This type of harassment solidifies traditional hypermasculine sex role stereotypes and reinforces *homo-anathema*, "the reaction to homosexuals as a hated and feared outgroup" (Pryor & Whalen, 1997, p. 140).

Current research may underestimate the incidence and prevalence of sexual harassment of men. Men may be less likely to report harassment because of embarrassment or shame about being the target of such acts. Men are about half as likely to report a sexually harassing experience as women in the same organization. This disparity increases as the severity of the sexual harassment increases with men reporting only one fifth the number of experiences of unwanted sexual attention and one sixteenth the rate of sexually coercive experiences (Fitzgerald, Drasgow et al., 1999).

Researchers have been slow to recognize that men may suffer ill effects from sexually harassing experiences. Some researchers suggest that men may experience unwanted verbal behavior or sexual attention but do not regard this as unpleasant or as harassment (Berdahl et al., 1996; Waldo et al., 1998). However, other research indicates that sexual harassment hurts men just as much as it does women, and "the data suggest no basis for assuming that harassment affects men any differently from women, given equal frequency, intensity and offensiveness" (Magley et al., 1999, p. 297). There are some indications that "the impact of the harassment on the professional and personal lives of male targets of same-gender harassment is far more devastating than that reported by male targets of other gender sexual harassment" (DuBois et al., 1998, p. 744).

WORKPLACE ROMANCES

As women entered the workplace in increasing numbers, opportunities for romantic relationships between employees increased (Gutek, 1985; Pierce, 1998). Approximately 33% of all romantic relationships begin or occur in the workplace (Bureau of National Affairs, 1988). These relationships are part of ordinary human interaction and, from the perspective of many, improve the morale and work performance of both the participants in the romance and their coworkers. Participation in a workplace romance has been shown to correlate with an employee's own level of intrinsic work motivation, job involvement, and satisfaction with work (Karl & Sutton, 2000; Pierce, 1998).

However, workplace romances are rife with pitfalls for the involved workers, their coworkers, and their employers (Gutek, 1985; Hoffman, Clinebell, & Kilpatrick, 1997). In some cases, the romance has a direct effect on coworkers by disrupting lines of communication and work alliances or by creating the impression that the romantic parties will favor each other more than deserving coworkers (Hoffman et al., 1997). Many times, workers are concerned that relationships in the office will disrupt productivity (Powell, 2000; Pryor, 1995).

In general, both workers and supervisors agree that whether they take place in the workplace or in nonwork settings, workers' personal relationships are private, and the employer has a limited right to intervene (T. J. Brown & Allgeier, 1995; Karl & Sutton, 2000). However, certain aspects of workplace romances stimulate more concern by observers. For example, if the two workers are of unequal status, one serving as a supervisor and the other as a subordinate, the relationship is more likely to be viewed as inappropriate, especially by female observers (T. J. Brown & Allgeier, 1995; G. E. Jones, 1999; Karl & Sutton, 2000; Powell, 2000). If one of the romantic couple is married, this effect is compounded (G. E. Jones, 1999). However, the gender of the participants has an impact on this perception: If a woman is married, she is seen more negatively than a man who is involved in an adulterous workplace relationship.

Gender has an impact on whether coworkers approve of workplace romances. Generally, women have less positive attitudes about workplace romances than do men (Karl & Sutton, 2000; Pierce, 1998). Ironically, however, women are more likely to have been involved in such relationships (Pierce, 1998). Likewise, gender has an impact upon the motives attributed to the players. A repeated finding is that men are assumed to enter into workplace relationships primarily for selfish motives, such as stroking their egos, and only secondarily for genuine love and very rarely to achieve some goal, such as promotion in their job (Anderson & Fisher, 1991; G. E. Jones, 1999). On the other hand, women are seen to be primarily motivated by love, much less motivated by ego, yet substantially motivated by job goals. G. E. Jones found similar rankings for people who themselves were participants in workplace romances. Some 13% of women who were in workplace romances rated job goals as their primary reason, but none of the men admitted to such motivations.

The most problematical workplace romances are those that go sour, a fertile breeding ground for sexual harassment lawsuits (Hoffman et al., 1997). For example, in a survey of human relations professionals by the Society for Human Resources Management (1998), 24% of respondents said that workplace romances resulted in complaints of sexual harassment. In the workplace, ex-lovers who are coworkers must often continue to interact on a daily basis with someone with whom they may have significant conflict.

An additional complication arises when only one of the participants may not want to continue the relationship, resulting in a situation in which the attempts for dates and reconciliation are experienced by the rejecting party as unwanted.

Alleged harassing behavior after a romantic relationship has been the topic of some research (Powell, 1986; T. Reilly, Carpenter, Dull, & Bartlett, 1982; Summers & Myklebust, 1992). In general, these studies indicate that when the alleged harasser and the target have had a romantic relationship, both male and female observers are less likely to view subsequent behavior as harassing. In other words, the context of a prior romantic relationship may prime observers to assess subsequent on-the-job sexually related behavior as invited by the target. Similarly, if the target engages in overtly sexual activities (deliberately brushing up against the alleged harasser or suggesting a willingness to exchange sex for some advantage under the alleged harasser's control), sexual harassment determinations are less likely.

Workplace romances are more likely to be seen as harassment when one of the parties is a supervisor and the other is a subordinate (Pierce, Aguinis, & Adams, 2000; Summers & Myklebust, 1992). As suggested by the data concerning attribution of motives for romances, those who attribute love motives to the accused harasser and job-related motivations to the complainant are less likely to label the behaviors as harassment. The opposite situation is also true: Those who view the motives of the accused as based on job goals and those of the complainant as based on love are also more likely to view the scenario as one of harassment.

For the forensic psychologist, a history of a workplace romance in the context of a sexual harassment complaint must be carefully assessed. Because valid sexual harassment complaints may arise from romance contexts, the mere history of such relationships does not quench inquiry into other aspects of the relationship history. Particularly, the use of work-related incentives or retaliation by the alleged harasser in relation to the alleged target may signal harassment developing from a romantic relationship. In balance, it is appropriate for the psychologist to conduct a review of the relationship to determine if the sexual harassment complaint arose from an attempt on the part of a partner to retaliate against the scorning other. Close review of collateral source data is critical to this inquiry. The review of depositions, interviews with coworkers (if possible), and the creation of time lines can facilitate decision making.

CURRENT THEORETICAL FORMULATIONS

Most theories related to sexual harassment focus on *why* sexual harassment occurs. Two recent articles review the origins of sexual harassment

(Stockdale et al., 1999; Tangri & Hayes, 1997) and a third, by a legal scholar, reviews theoretical underpinnings of legal decision making in sexual harassment litigation (Franke, 1997). These reviews acquaint psychologists with the four major perspectives on the origins of sexual harassment in the workplace. The first derives from biological models of human behavior. The second focuses on power as the fundamental dynamic underlying sexual harassment. The third emphasizes how organizations are structured and how that structure facilitates sexual harassment. The fourth is more individually focused and centers on the relationship between the characteristics of individuals and work contexts. Sexual harassment research is still in its infancy (Pryor et al., 1995), and much of the theoretical work has been piecemeal and focused on specific issues. Some recent formulations ambitiously attempt to synthesize elements of the existing theories to predict when and how sexual harassment will occur.

Biological Theories

Theorists have attempted to explain sexual harassment in terms of fundamental biological processes that cause people to harass each other in the workplace (Tangri & Hayes, 1997). One argument is based on hormonal drives. Men are presumably driven by hormones to dominate and control women in all situations, one of which is the workplace. The tendency of men to objectify women in these contexts is seen as an expression of men's higher order conceptualizing faculties.

A variant on the biological model highlights patterns of human behavior presumably developed in a prehistoric hunting–gathering lifestyle and how those patterns are expressed in modern-day corporate offices (Studd & Gattiker, 1991). To shorten a complex argument, this perspective indicates that in earlier societies, the sexually promiscuous man would optimally seek many short-term sexual partners to impregnate many women and ensure reproductive success. In contrast, women evolved to be more sexually cautious and selective in their choice of sexual partners. This applies to sexual harassment because these evolutionary imperatives compel women to reject unsolicited sexual attention. Thus, men tend to seek sex in the workplace, and women to reject those overtures, resulting in the conflict we label *sexual harassment*.

In some work contexts, women in positions of power are more likely to harass men of lower status. A strictly biological and gender-based model would suggest that this would never happen. Also, the theories lack sufficient rigor to allow for differential predictions of behavior under different situational constraints. Some researchers (Barak, Pitterman, & Yitzhaki, 1995) have shown that sexual harassment occurs in generally the same ways in either traditional power structures or more egalitarian settings. These theories lack flexibility to deal with same-sex harassment, which is either sexually based or based on traditional masculine role enforcement, that is, cases in which the harasser and the target of the same gender share evolutionary imperatives.

Power-Based Theories

A number of theories are based on the observation that men have traditionally exercised more power than women in a wide range of settings. In the workplace, men's patriarchal power is abetted by their superior place in the organization's hierarchy. Catherine MacKinnon, a legal scholar whose perspective still exerts significant influence on the body of knowledge concerning sexual harassment, conceived of the origin of sexual harassment in power based on sex (MacKinnon, 1979). In this situation, men exercise patriarchal power in their treatment of women in the workplace: "men use their typically superior social, professional, familial, organizational, or educational role to exploit women to satisfy their needs for power and mastery" (Barak et al., 1995, p. 499). Others view this theory as one reflecting cultural patterns that mandate that men rule and women passively acquiesce to that rule. "According to this model, the function of sexual harassment is to manage ongoing male–female interactions according to accepted sex status norms, and to maintain male dominance occupationally and therefore economically, by intimidating, discouraging, or precipitating the removal of women from work" (Tangri, Burt, & Johnson, 1982, p. 40).

This perspective is challenged by research that indicates that much workplace sexual harassment is initiated by people who are not superiors but coworkers of the harassment target (Bastian et al., 1996; Gutek, 1985; U.S. Merit Systems Protection Board, 1981, 1988, 1995). As noted earlier, a study of people in the military revealed that the majority (54%) of people who reported harassment experiences indicated that the harassers were either of the same or of inferior rank (Bastian et al., 1996).

In the same vein, data reflecting *contrapower sexual harassment*, or harassment by one of lower organizational status, may argue against traditional organizational power theories (Rospenda et al., 1998). One explanation for this counterintuitive paradigm centers on the additional power given to harassers by advantages inherent to race and class. Even if harassers have nominally less power, their gender, race, and economic status may prompt them to engage in harassing behaviors. A review of data from the first USMSPB study determined that minority status and power differentials, even when taken together, did not account for the variance in patterns of sexual harassment (Fain & Anderton, 1987). Although power-based theories may account for these data, they encounter difficulty with same-sex harassment. Neither harassment based on enforcing male stereotypes nor homosexual same-sex harassment can readily encompass a theory that suggests that men have no reason to harass other men. After all, in both situations, both the harasser and harassed are inheritors of patriarchal prerogatives. Finally, power-based theories do not account well for data concerning workplace romances. The idea that a person of less power will enter into a special relationship with a person of greater power motivated by romance rather than the power of the supervisor is not addressed by these theories.

Organizational Models

Another prominent theory centered on culturally defined sex roles, sex role spillover theory, is similar to the power theories outlined in the preceding discussion (Gutek, 1985; Gutek & Morasch, 1982; Nieva & Gutek, 1981). In work situations, men and women are supposed to fill work roles defined by the needs of the organization and the skills and preferences of the worker. Outside of work, men have traditionally been considered to be sexually aggressive and assertive and to assume leadership positions, whereas women have been viewed conventionally as sex objects and expected to behave in generally helpful, nurturing, and unassertive ways. Sex role spillover occurs when the culturally defined sex roles *spill over* or are inappropriately assumed to exist in or apply to the workplace. This happens most obviously when women move into jobs previously held only by men. Women in traditionally male-dominated jobs often experience more focus on characteristics related to their gender than do women in occupations in which men and women are more equally represented (Gutek, 1985). In the latter situation, the incidence of sexual harassment is generally lower (Sheffey & Tindale, 1992).

College undergraduates who reviewed sexual harassment scenarios in the context of traditionally male-dominated occupations were less likely to define instances of sexual coercion as sexual harassment than they were to define similar conduct as sexual coercion in occupations traditionally held by women (Burgess & Borgida, 1997a, 1997b). A main effect associated with the gender of the observer emerged, with men less likely to view an event as harassment than women. These studies suggest that observers are likely to form stereotypes of women in nontraditional settings; these women are often seen as *iron ladies*, who are tough and able to stand up to all that comes their way. In contrast, women in traditionally female-dominated occupational settings are seen as more vulnerable and weak. In many cases, men who harass women in nontraditional settings are more readily attributed motives of "only joking" or wanting to help the woman "fit in" or to "feel like one of the guys" (Burgess & Borgida, 1997a, p. 306).

Another perspective suggests that the increased rates of sexual harassment in traditionally male-dominated occupations is more a function of the basic odds: When there are few women and many men in the workplace, women are likely to have daily contact with many more men than are their counterparts in more gender-balanced settings (Gutek, Cohen, & Konrad, 1990). This possibility was explored in a municipal setting. In contrast to the expectations generated by the contact hypothesis, the rates of reported sexual harassment among women in jobs with highly skewed gender ratios were similar to those in jobs with more gender balance (Ragins & Scandura, 1995). Rates of harassment appeared to be related to the type of occupation pursued: In blue-collar, highly physical jobs, such as fire fighting, harassment was a greater problem than it was in white-collar occupations, such as accounting.

Overall, support exists for the sex role spillover theory (e.g., Gruber, 1998), which accounts for much of the unprofessional ambience and sexualizing of the workplace encountered in gender-skewed, male-dominated workplaces (Stockdale et al., 1999). Sex role spillover theory can also account for the enforcement of traditional masculinity in such workplaces and for sexual harassment of men by women in workplaces dominated by women. Data from the 1995 DoD Study (Fitzgerald, Drasgow, & Magley, 1999) confirmed that harassment in the military decreases as the gender mix in a work group approaches parity.

Individual Theories: Person × Situation Models

A number of researchers have attempted to bring together variables related to individuals and the environments in which they work. A four-variable model to account for sexual harassment based, in part, on the work of Finkelhor (1984) lists the necessary preconditions for harassment as (a) the harasser has to be motivated to engage in such behavior; (b) the harasser has to overcome internal inhibitions against harassing others; (c) the harasser must overcome external inhibitions to harassing, including adverse organizational consequences for harassment; and (d) the harasser must overcome the victim's resistance (O'Hare & O'Donohue, 1998). The last variable is inversely related to the target's vulnerability to harassment. Research supports only one of the four preconditions: the element related to organizational consequences. The absence of grievance procedures for sexual harassment, an unprofessional work atmosphere, and the existence of sexist attitudes in the workplace were the most salient predictors of sexual harassment (Pryor et al., 1995).

Research using a similar model produced a similar result. In work situations in which women had capable *guardians* to support and protect them from harassment, the rates of harassment were lower than were those in contexts in which women were isolated (DeCoster, Estes, & Mueller, 1999). The most likely targets of harassment were not women who lacked organizational power or were otherwise ostensibly weak but women who had ventured into traditionally male preserves. It is ironic that the antidiscrimination policies that encouraged these women into the workplace also placed them in positions in which they were likely to be targets of harassment.

Significant research has been conducted on the harasser and the organization in which he works (Pryor et al., 1995; Pryor & Whalen, 1997). These findings suggest "that whereas certain dispositions may create a readiness to sexually harass in some men, these dispositions are only likely to affect behavior when the social climate condones or accepts such behavior" (Pryor et al., 1995, p. 81). That is, not every man sexually harasses and those who do differ in significant respects from those who do not. Even men high in LSH are unlikely to engage in those behaviors in situations in which they face serious sanctions from their employers.

One strength of this theoretical model is its flexibility according to the propensities of the individuals and the climate of the organization. To date, the research has focused primarily on men who harass women and not on men who harass other men or on women harassers. Given that the theory has identified ways in which these relatively rare forms of harassment could be parsed, it is likely that the Person × Situation model can encompass them.

Comprehensive Theories of Sexual Harassment

The foregoing theories each focus on a different aspect of sexual harassment: the underlying biological, political, or organizational features or the proclivities of individuals that predispose them to harass. Not one of these theories integrates what is known about organizational climates with individual target and harasser variables. Louise Fitzgerald and her colleagues at the University of Illinois at Urbana–Champaign attempted to fill this theory vacuum (Fitzgerald, Drasgow, et al., 1999), taking into account observations about the interrelationship between three different kinds of sexual harassment:

1. *Gender harassment* includes *sexist hostility*, or hostility directed toward the target's gender, and *sexual hostility*, or sexually related conduct such as telling dirty jokes or displaying sexual materials in the workplace.
2. *Unwanted sexual attention* includes attempts to get dates, writing love notes, and other activity.
3. *Sexual coercion* includes attempts on the part of the harasser to make the target engage in some sort of sexual activity.

The model envisions sexual harassment arising as a result of three variables: (a) job level (or rank in the military), (b) the organization's tolerance for sexual harassment, and (c) the degree to which women are integrated in the workplace. The consequential impact of sexual harassment is measured in two ways. First, workplace outcomes such as employment satisfaction, coworker satisfaction, supervisor satisfaction, organizational commitment, and work productivity are affected. Second, the individual's reactions to the harassment have an impact on the target's health and psychological well-being.

The data indicate that an organization's tolerance for sexual harassment is the most important variable in increasing the occurrence of sexual harassment and exerts a direct, adverse effect on the person's satisfaction with coworkers, supervisors, and the job itself. Sexual harassment has an adverse effect on (in order of effect size) psychological well-being, coworker satisfaction, supervisor satisfaction, health satisfaction, and work satisfaction. All of the work-related satisfaction variables affected organizational commitment with work satisfaction having the greatest contribution. This model has been cross-validated in cross-cultural settings (Fitzgerald, Gelfand, & Drasgow, 1995) and refined through a series of studies in different work settings (Fitzgerald, Drasgow, Hulin, Gelfand, & Magley, 1997; Fitzgerald, Drasgow, & Magley, 1999; Glomb, Munson, Hulin, Bergman, & Drasgow, 1999; Hesson-McInnis & Fitzgerald, 1997).

Sexual Harassment as a Technology of Sexism

A legal scholar reviewed the psychological research and traced the legal history of sexual harassment in the courts (Franke, 1997) with the goal of understanding why sexual harassment is outlawed. She was unconvinced that any extant theories accounted for why some individuals sexually harass others. Rather, she concluded that sexual harassment is to sexism what Jim Crow laws and lynching are to racism; namely, sexual harassment is the *technology of sexism*. Sexist beliefs are pervasive and are expressed by way of sexual harassment of both men and women (Franke, 1997). It is the means whereby a widely held set of beliefs about women and their relationships to men are played out in the workplace. In this view, a hostile work environment is a tool to prevent women from reaching their full potential in the workplace; quid pro quo harassment is a way of keeping women *in their place*. What makes sexual harassment sex discrimination is "not the fact that the conduct is sexual, but that sexual conduct is used to enforce or perpetrate gender norms and stereotypes" (Franke, 1997, p. 734). Her analysis demands attention from behavioral scientists, but few researchers have tested this theory empirically. One researcher who did, Margaret Stockdale, proposed and tested the approach–rejection theory of sexual harassment.

The Approach–Rejection Theory of Sexual Harassment

The approach–rejection theory of sexual harassment "posits that sexual harassment is a function of sexism, which operates to maintain a system of masculine dominance and feminine subordinance" (Stockdale, 2004a). Rejection-based sexual harassment is conduct to humiliate, punish, or otherwise drive away the target. This conduct may enforce heterosexist, hypermasculine gender role norms and behavior. Thus, this theory takes into account that male dominance and hegemony remain the causes of sexual harassment for both men and women. Men who engage in gender harassment may do so to bolster their masculine image among others (Quinn, 2002). Preliminary research supports this model (Stockdale, 1998).

SUMMARY

Considerable social psychological research has helped to identify who does the harassing and in what contexts the harassment is likely to occur. Extensive research has refined subtypes of sexual harassment. However, theories have lagged somewhat. Because harassment is perpetrated by both coworkers and supervisors, simple theories of power fail to account for the diversity of harassment experiences. In the same way, many theories do not account for the strong influence of context on the incidence and nature of harassment. These situational variables interact in complex ways with target and harasser. Same-sex harassment provides an example of a common phenomenon over which many theories stumble. The pervasiveness of workplace romances and their contribution to the phenomenon of sexual harassment have gone largely unremarked by theorists. Only recently have sexual harassment theories begun to focus on the consequences of sexual harassment. Fitzgerald's integrated theory speaks to this question by exploring the impact of organizational climate on the work life, health satisfaction, and psychological outcomes of the worker. Issues of vulnerability and attribution are not straightforward. For example, it may be that the experience of depression causes a worker to perceive that a common workplace experience of harassment, which had heretofore been unpleasant but tolerable, is now unbearable. Investigations supportive of the new, integrated approach–rejection theory of sexual harassment are under way.

3

THE LEGAL FRAMEWORK IN SEXUAL HARASSMENT CASES

In any forensic work, psychologists require an understanding of the underlying legal principles and law in the area in which they practice (Melton, Petrila, Poythress, & Slobogin, 1997). The importance in sexual harassment cases is underscored because legal definitions often color what the psychologist does. For example, the definition of *reasonableness*, as crafted in *Harris v. Forklift Systems, Inc.* (1993) is the basis for much research by psychologists on liability (Goodman-Delahunty, 1999; see chap. 5). Opinions concerning causation of injury are shaped by definitions of proximate cause (Goodman-Delahunty & Foote, 1995). The available legal remedies may shape recommendations for treatment. Familiarity with these elements fosters more comprehensive forensic evaluations and a better informed discussion of findings and issues with lawyers and judges.

The legal contours of sexual harassment cases have been shaped by constitutional, statutory, and case law. Case law is a constantly changing landscape and requires the psychologist to keep up with new decisions from state courts of appeal and supreme courts as well as federal circuit courts and the U.S. Supreme Court. In this chapter, we outline the legal bases for liability and damages that can be claimed following an allegation of workplace sexual harassment. The chapter begins with a discussion of the forums in which sexual harassment claims are filed. Then, we review legal prohibitions against sexual harassment and how federal and state civil rights and tort law prohibit sexual harassment. We trace the development of federal law in sexual harassment cases over the past 40 years, including the legal treatment of sexual orientation and same-sex harassment. Next, we review the standards for evaluating liability along with affirmative defenses that employers can mount in sexual harassment cases. In addition, we examine the range of recoverable damages from make-whole relief to punitive damages. The last portion of the chapter deals with the law in relation to expert testimony in sexual harassment cases.

WHERE SEXUAL HARASSMENT CLAIMS ARE LODGED

Claims Under Federal Laws and Statutes

Cases brought under federal law (e.g., alleging violations of rights under the U.S. Constitution or the Civil Rights Act of 1964) may be filed in federal district court. These cases proceed to trial before a federal district judge or magistrate. Juries of 6 to 12 persons are permitted on certain issues. Claims against federal government agencies or contractors proceed before EEOC administrative judges. Plaintiffs who exhaust their claims administratively may proceed in federal district court.

Claims Under State Laws and Statutes

Claims under state antidiscrimination statutes or tort law are typically filed in state court, for example, superior court. The two types of allegations are often included in the same complaint. Typically a jury of 12 decides these cases. Many state agencies have administrative provisions that must be exhausted before parties may proceed in state court, for example, prior to commencing litigation against state universities.

LEGAL PROHIBITIONS AGAINST SEXUAL HARASSMENT

Some laws prohibiting discrimination derive from federal or state constitutional guarantees of equal protection. Others are statutory at the federal, state, or local level. Although a number of federal civil rights laws relate to these issues (e.g., Title VII of the Federal Civil Rights Act of 1964 and sections 1983 and 1985 [3] of the Civil Rights Act of 1991), the Civil Rights Act of 1964, particularly Title VII, is the cornerstone of federal protection against discrimination and retaliation. This body of law is the most influential regarding sexual harassment claims. State courts look to the federal cases and models of analysis for guidance when interpreting and applying state law. Title IX extends the antidiscrimination coverage to educational institutions.

Title VII forbids employers with more than 15 employees from discriminating on the basis of race, color, national origin, religion or sex. The relevant portion of the act reads as follows:

> Sec. 2000e-2.—Unlawful employment practices
> (a) Employer practices
> It shall be an unlawful employment practice for an employer—
> (1) to fail or refuse to hire or to discharge any individual, or otherwise to discriminate against any individual with respect to his compensation, terms, conditions, or privileges of employment, because of such individual's race, color, religion, sex, or national origin; or
> (2) to limit, segregate, or classify his employees or applicants for employment in any way which would deprive or tend to deprive any individual of employment opportunities or otherwise adversely affect his status as an employee, because of such individual's race, color, religion, sex, or national origin. (Title VII of the Civil Rights Act of 1964)

Title VII provides two general bases for a legal action. The first occurs as a result of a conjunction between two things: (a) membership of the plaintiff in a protected class, as indicated by that person's sex in a sexual harassment case, and (b) actions of the employer to hire, fire, or alter the conditions, terms, compensation, or privileges of the worker's employment. That is, discrimination occurs when the employer does something to the employee because the employee is, for example, a woman.

The second basis under Title VII for a legal action occurs if an employer retaliates against an employee who participates in protected antidiscrimination activity, such as complaining of sexual harassment, filing an EEOC complaint or a lawsuit, or speaking out or reporting something about discrimination that the employer would rather remained undisclosed. Once an employee complains of sexual harassment, whether to the harasser, to human resources personnel, to supervisors, or formally to state or federal agencies, this assertion is often followed by negative consequences for the employee. If the target can show that adverse employment consequences are causally linked to earlier protests about perceived harassment or statutorily protected speech, this comprises unlawful reprisal or retaliation. Reprisal or retaliation claims have traditionally been easier for a plaintiff to prove than claims of harassment because these claims force the employer to prove that the firing, demotion, or transfer of the worker had a non-pretextual basis. That is, the employer must prove that there was a lawful and reasonable reason to initiate the negative job action.

OTHER SOURCES OF PROTECTION AGAINST SEXUAL HARASSMENT

In rare cases, if the complainant becomes disabled by the harassment and is not accommodated, sexual harassment claims may involve disability issues subject to disability statutes such as worker's compensation or the Americans with Disabilities Act.

Section 1983 (42 U.S.C. § 1983) of the Civil Rights Act of 1871 implements the Fourteenth Amendment's Equal Protection Clause of the U.S. Constitution, which outlaws discrimination on the basis of gender. This statute may be used independently of Title VII as a basis for a civil rights suit by an aggrieved public employee against a state or local government for violations of federal constitutional and statutory laws (Lindemann & Kadue, 1999, p. 191).

Common Law and Tort Theories

Common-law tort actions were more widely used in sexual harassment cases before the federal law permitted recovery for pain and suffering and punitive damages (Civil Rights Act of 1991). Torts are civil wrongs that occur between parties for which the legal system provides a remedy. In many instances, attorneys file complaints that include multiple causes of action, that is, tortious violations of a duty to the employee in addition to statutory violations. Popular tort claims include negligent or intentional infliction of emotional distress, invasion of privacy, assault and battery, defamation, false imprisonment, wrongful discharge, failure to maintain a safe workplace, negligent hiring, negligent supervision, and negligent retention.

Elements of proof in a case brought under common-law tort theories differ from those required by federal law. For example, to establish intentional infliction of emotional distress, a plaintiff must show that the defendant employer acted intentionally or recklessly by extreme and outrageous conduct to cause severe emotional distress to the plaintiff. Some courts have held that sexual harassment is not outrageous enough to state a cause of action for intentional infliction of emotional distress (*Gebers v. Commercial Data Center, Inc.*, 1995; *Prunty v. Arkansas Freightways, Inc.*, 1994).

Other legal bases for the claim of sexual harassment may include state contract law, for instance, based on an allegation that sexual harassment violates public policy or an express or implied contact to avoid discrimination. Sexual harassment may also comprise the basis for a workers' compensation claim or criminal charges of rape, unwanted touching, stalking, or vandalism.

Variations in the elements of proof required by different legal claims or causes of action can affect the case outcome. An advantage of proceeding under tort law is that a tort plaintiff may prevail when the proof does not rise to the level of a violation under Title VII or state antidiscrimination statutes, which are often more exacting and detailed (*Clark v. World Airways*, 1980). For example, tort claims do not require the plaintiff to prove that the harassing conduct is unwelcome.

Another difference between a cause of action under statute versus tort involves the proof of injuries sustained by the plaintiff. Under tort law, to lodge a claim, a plaintiff must show that harms or injuries were sustained. By contrast, under Title VII, the focus is on the objective detriment to the work environment of the plaintiff caused by the conduct of the harasser. Harm or injury to the plaintiff is not a prerequisite for liability but may be considered as a factor during the liability phase (*Harris v. Forklift Systems, Inc.*, 1993). Under state tort laws, individual liability may be imposed on the harasser. Federal circuit courts are split as to whether a supervisor may be held personally liable under Title VII.

The EEOC and Fair Employment Practice Acts

The EEOC developed regulations to implement Title VII and published a series of guidelines, which provide definitions of key terms (U.S. Equal Employment Opportunity Commission, 1999). In addition to Title VII, each of the 50 states has laws that offer analogous civil rights protection. These laws are designated in different ways in the various states, but are often referred to as Fair Employment Practice Acts (FEPAs). A plaintiff may prefer to proceed under the FEPA if a state's antidiscrimination law affords the plaintiff a speedier trial or more generous damages than the federal statute.

Time deadlines are often critical in processing civil rights claims, and practitioners should check local practices. If a worker files a claim under the FEPA and a state–federal work-share agreement provides for this, copies of the claim filed with one agency are deemed filed with the other for deadline and other formal purposes. An investigative officer requires the employer to answer the worker's complaint and evaluates witness statements and supportive documentation. After some investigation, a preliminary finding is submitted both to the complaining party and the respondent employer and attempts are made to resolve the dispute by mediation. The EEOC or the state agency may sue the employer if a meritorious claim is not resolved. A party who wishes to file a private lawsuit in state or federal court must obtain a Notice of Right to Sue from the EEOC or state agency.

THE DEVELOPMENT OF FEDERAL LAW IN SEXUAL HARASSMENT CASES

The major thrust of the civil rights laws was to end discriminatory termination of employment based on race. The language of Title VII does not contain any prohibitions against sexual harassment, only against discrimination based on sex. The U.S. Congress conducted hearings on sexual harassment in 1979 and commissioned a study of sexual harassment the following year (U.S. Merit Systems Protection Board, 1981). After legal scholars began defining and commenting on the existence of sexual harassment (MacKinnon, 1979), courts at times appreciated that this social problem begged for redress but saw no effective way to address it through existing legal mechanisms (Lindemann & Kadue, 1999). The grounding of sexual harassment in the sexual desire of harassers was reflected in the legal decision making of a number of courts that dealt with early sexual harassment claims (Franke, 1997). In these cases (e.g., *Corne v. Bausch & Lomb, Inc.*, 1975), the courts saw the unambiguously sexually harassing behaviors of the defendants as examples of unusual personal behaviors and largely exempt from legal action because such behaviors were out of the realm of control of the employer.

In her groundbreaking book, Professor Catherine McKinnon established use of the term *quid pro quo* and distinguished that form of harassment from harassment that was a *persistent condition of work*, that is, a *hostile work environment* (MacKinnon, 1979, p. 32). Regulations promulgated by the EEOC containing definitions of prohibited conduct that comprise harassment based on sex adopted these views. Guidelines to employers on providing a workplace free from harassment, intimidation, or insult were first issued by the EEOC in 1980, mandating that an employer take affirmative steps to eliminate workplace harassment on grounds that harassing conduct interfered with the terms, conditions, and privileges of employment. Claims based on this legal theory of discrimination are known as *hostile workplace environment claims*. The core elements are that (a) the conduct at issue must be based on sex or gender and (b) the conduct must interfere with the terms, conditions, and privileges of employment to the degree that it creates a hostile and abusive work environment.

In 1986, 22 years after the Civil Rights Act of 1964 was implemented, a case on which Professor MacKinnon was legal counsel was appealed to the U.S. Supreme Court. The facts of *Meritor Savings Bank, FSB v. Vinson* (1986) remain compelling. In 1974, Sidney Taylor, a vice president of what later became the Meritor bank, hired Michelle Vinson. She rapidly rose from the entry-level job of teller to serve as assistant branch manager. In September 1978, she took sick leave, and Taylor fired her on November 1, 1978, ostensibly for abuse of sick leave. Following her discharge, Vinson filed a civil rights claim against Taylor and the bank, claiming that during her first 4 years of employment, she had "constantly been subjected to sexual harassment" by Taylor. In her complaint, she alleged that Taylor had taken her to dinner and initiated a series of some 50 sexual encounters. Vinson claimed that during this time, Taylor fondled her in front of other employees and even forced her to have sex with him against her will. Vinson never complained to supervisors for fear of losing her job.

The case was dismissed on a motion for summary judgment by the bank because the court determined that Vinson had voluntarily participated in the relationship. The trial court was also convinced by the bank's argument that Title VII was mainly designed to deal with economic disadvantages stemming from race. The case proceeded on appeal and eventually reached the U.S. Supreme Court. The Court used this occasion to extend a concept of hostile work environment. In *Meritor*, the court adopted language penned by the Eleventh Circuit Court in *Henson v. Dundee* (1982): "Sexual harassment which creates a hostile or offensive environment for members of one sex is every bit the arbitrary barrier to sexual equality at the workplace that racial harassment is to racial equality. Surely, a requirement that a man or woman run a gauntlet of sexual abuse in return for the privilege of being allowed to work and make a living can be as demeaning and disconcerting as the harshest of racial epithets" (*Meritor Savings Bank, FSB v. Vinson*, 1986). The Court noted that it did not matter if Vinson participated in the sexual intercourse voluntarily but whether the plaintiff welcomed her boss's sexual overtures. In sexual harassment cases, plaintiffs must demonstrate that the sexual behavior at issue was not welcome. After *Meritor*, the two legal theories of sexual harassment were incorporated in the case law and became widespread. The Court also held the bank liable for Taylor's actions, even though the bank claimed it did not know or approve of Taylor's conduct. The Court noted that employers are not always liable and that common-law principles of agency would apply on a case-by-case basis, thus affirming the legal principle of *respondeat superior*. In subsequent decisions, the U.S. Supreme Court applied this rule more broadly.

Early cases of sexual harassment recognized by courts involved bargaining for sexual favors (*Barnes v. Costle*, 1977; *Barnes v. Train*, 1974/1977). Quid pro quo cases involve harassment because of sex in which some employment benefit is contingent on sexual favors, for example, an offer of a bonus or promotion in exchange for sex or sexual touching. Most often, quid pro quo cases involve harassment by a supervisor or manager who has some control over tangible employment benefits. When harassment culminates in a tangible employment action such as hiring, firing, denial of promotion, reassignment with significantly different responsibilities, or a decision causing a significant change in benefits, the employer is vicariously liable, and no affirmative defense is available. A quid pro quo case can produce a hostile work environment for the target. An example of this type of harassment is provided in the paragraph that follows:

> On a work-related trip Anna's supervisor, Jason, keeps talking about sex and rubbing her shoulders and neck. When she doesn't respond, he tells Anna to loosen up. Later, Anna asks him about opportunities in the company for promotion. He says that he's not sure she's ready and tells her, "You'll need to loosen up and be a lot nicer to me before I can recommend you." He puts his arms around her waist, adding "Remember, I can make your life very easy or very difficult here."

The second major type of sexual harassment does not involve any exchange of benefits for sexual favors and is purely a claim of a hostile work environment. Thus, the worker need not suffer a tangible job detriment, but the conditions of employment must be altered to a significant degree by the sexually related actions of the employer. Usually, this derives from gender-based hostility. For example, men in a traditionally male-dominated workplace, such as a coal mine, a shipyard, an engineering plant, a police force, a fire fighting department, or a financial services institution, may resent the intrusion of women who perform nontraditional work and may verbally or physically harass the women, who are perceived as outsiders. An example of this type of harassment is provided in the paragraph that follows:

> Anna is the only female employee in her department. Her coworkers mock her if she makes a mistake. They say, "There's no way you're gonna get this right, sweetie. It's a man's job. You don't belong here." They never include her in their conversations. She overhears them telling crude jokes about her. Some of them jostle her in the hallways. She complains to her supervisor. He says they're "just being friendly" and tells her to get used to their humor.

A hostile workplace environment claim may also be based on sexual attraction, such as constant unwanted attention from persistent requests for dates or sexual comments and touching. Most typically, it arises when an employee who refuses sexual advances by a coworker or superior is consequently subjected to negative and disadvantageous conduct, such as ostracism, denials of promotions, or unpleasant comments. Most courts have rejected claims of sexual discrimination based on a supervisor's preferential treatment of a paramour, in cases in which the relationship rather than the gender of those involved was the basis of the employment decision (*Becerra v. Dalton*, 1997; *DeCintio v. Westchester County Medical Center*, 1986, 1987). However, in some instances, a prima facie hostile workplace environment was established by showing that preferential treatment was given to employees who submitted to sexual advances, and employees who refused advances were adversely treated by comparison (*Broderick v. Ruder*, 1988; *King v. Palmer*, 1985).

RESPONSIBILITIES OF WORKERS VERSUS RESPONSIBILITIES OF EMPLOYERS

As in *Meritor*, the U.S. Supreme Court was reluctant to make employers uniformly responsible for the conduct of their employees in sexual harassment cases. In complementary cases, the U.S. Supreme Court evaluated and delineated the responsibilities of workers and of employers (*Burlington Industries, Inc. v. Ellerth*, 1998; *Faragher v. City of Boca Raton*, 1998). The first case involved Kimberly Ellerth, a salesperson for Burlington Industries, a large retailer. She alleged that during her employment "she was subjected to constant sexual harassment by her supervisor, Ted Slowik." Ellerth contended that Slowik intimated that she had to submit to his sexual advances or face retaliation. In response to this and other harassing conduct by Slowik, Ellerth quit. Significantly, she never complained about Slowik's conduct to anyone, despite knowledge of Burlington's policy against sexual harassment.

The second case involved a college student, Beth Ann Faragher, employed by the city of Boca Raton, Florida, as a lifeguard for the summers between 1985 and 1990. She had three immediate supervisors, two of whom "created a 'sexually hostile atmosphere' at the beach by repeatedly subjecting Faragher and other female lifeguards to 'uninvited and offensive touching,' by making lewd remarks, and by speaking of women in offensive terms" (*Faragher v. City of Boca Raton*, 1998, p. 9). Faragher alleged a pervasive, sexualized working environment plus repeated statements on the part of one of her supervisors that her work duties depended on her willingness to date him. She sued the city of Boca Raton on grounds that the allegedly offending supervisors were agents of the city.

In this case, the lifeguards working at the Boca Raton beaches were organized according to a paramilitary pattern with military titles like lieutenant to denote the chain of command. Although the city of Boca Raton developed a policy prohibiting sexual harassment in 1986 and revised it in 1990, the policy was never disseminated to Faragher or her supervisors. She used the chain of command and reported the harassment to her immediate supervisor, but he never took any action in response because his supervisor was the primary harasser. Thus, Faragher was working in an environment in which there was no effective sexual harassment policy and one in which reasonable complaints on her part would have had no effect.

The Supreme Court majority held that

> An employer is subject to vicarious liability to a victimized employee for an actionable hostile environment created by a supervisor with immediate (or successively higher) authority over the employee. When no tangible employment action is taken, a defending employer may raise an affirmative defense to liability or damages, subject to proof by

a preponderance of the evidence. The defense comprises two necessary elements: (a) that the employer exercised reasonable care to prevent and correct promptly any sexually harassing behavior, and (b) that the plaintiff employee unreasonably failed to take advantage of any preventive or corrective opportunities provided by the employer or to avoid harm otherwise. (*Burlington Industries, Inc. v. Ellerth*, 1998, pp. 29–30)

In other words, the employer must develop, promulgate, and enforce a policy against sexual harassment. At the same time, employees must use any existing mechanisms to address complaints.

The *Ellerth* and *Farragher* decisions eliminated the distinction between quid pro quo and hostile work environment claims. The Court determined that the distinction between the two forms of harassment was more academic than functional. Thus, elements of proof in a sexual harassment claim are those to establish a hostile work environment.

SEXUAL ORIENTATION AND SAME-SEX HARASSMENT

Federal courts have held that sexual orientation discrimination is not within the purview of Title VII, even though research on discrimination against gay men, lesbians, and bisexuals indicates that they are subjected to more intense or extreme forms of harassment at higher rates than are heterosexual men and women (Herek, Gillis, Cogan, & Glunt, 1997). Over time, the requirement that harassing conduct must be sexual in nature was broadened to include hostility resulting from conduct other than explicit sexual advances (*Andrews v. City of Philadelphia*, 1990; *Hall v. Gus Construction Co.*, 1988). Thus, actionable claims of gender-based harassment encompass some forms of discrimination against homosexuals, for example, for failure to conform to stereotypical hypermasculine gender norms. State and local antidiscrimination statutes may include prohibitions against discrimination based on marital status or sexual orientation.

For much of the history of sexual harassment law, courts assumed that men could not be sexually harassed by men nor women by other women (Foote & Goodman-Delahunty, 1999). That is, sexual harassment was presumed to consist of sexually based conduct within a heterosexual frame of reference, that is, perpetrated by a person of one gender upon a person of another gender. In 1998, the U.S. Supreme Court resolved inconsistencies between U.S. Federal Circuit Courts on this issue in the case of a Joseph Oncale, a young man hired to work as a roustabout on an oil derrick in the Gulf of Mexico. Soon after he boarded the rig, Oncale became the object of intense sexual attention and assaults by three members of the eight-man crew. Two of the men threatened to rape him, and on several occasions, one coworker physically subdued him while another worker rubbed his penis on the young man. While in the shower, Oncale was subjected to an attempted rape and his assailants pushed a bar of soap into his anus (brief for National Organization on Male Sexual Victimization, Inc., 1998). Oncale complained to his supervisor, who confided that he himself had been the recipient of similar intimidation and assaults by the same men and would do nothing to stop them. Oncale quit the job.

The Fifth Circuit Court reviewed the case and held that "Mr. Oncale, a male, has no cause of action under Title VII for harassment against male coworkers" (*Oncale v. Sundowner Offshore Services, Inc.*, 1996). The unanimous U.S. Supreme Court reversed the Fifth Circuit, noting that two decades earlier, in *Casteneda v. Partida* (1977), the Court had determined that a national origin discrimination claim was not defeated merely because the alleged perpetrator belonged to the same protected class as the target. In other words, a Hispanic person could discriminate against another Hispanic person on the basis of national origin. Relying on this precedent, the Court saw no reason to preclude the sexual harassment of a man by another man and noted "we hold today that nothing in Title VII necessarily bars a claim of discrimination 'because of . . . sex' merely because the plaintiff and the defendant (or the person charged with acting on behalf of the defendant) are of the same sex" (*Oncale v. Sundowner Offshore Services, Inc.*, 1998, p. 3).

Oncale followed *Harris v. Forklift Systems, Inc.* (1993) in its affirmation of the *reasonable person* test to determine whether specific conduct constitutes unlawful sexual harassment. The Court rejected concerns that Title VII would become a "general civility code" prohibiting all sexual harassment in the workplace. Rather, "the critical issue, Title VII's text indicates, is whether members of one sex are exposed to disadvantageous terms or conditions of employment to which members of the other sex are not exposed." (*Harris v. Forklift Systems, Inc.*, 1993, p. 3).

LEGAL STANDARDS FOR EVALUATION OF LIABILITY

Sexual harassment cases involve a number of unique issues, which are not typically raised in gender discrimination or other discrimination cases. Credibility determinations are pivotal and often reduce to the problem of *he said/she said*. In sexual harassment cases, credibility determinations are complicated by the fact that past research has shown that men and women may differ in their views of certain sexual behavior, especially when oral comments are contested. Courts have grappled with these issues in a number of guises. In this section, we discuss some of these issues.

Offensive Sexually Harassing Conduct

Community and contextual values do not necessarily nullify a claim for harassment. For example, courts have held that pervasive societal approval of pornography does not shield employers from liability when female employees are subjected to crude and vulgar comments in the workplace and when photographs of scantily clad or naked women are displayed in the workplace, even if many employees have no objections (e.g., *Rabidue v. Osceola Refining Co.*, 1986, dissenting opinion).

The offensiveness of conduct perceived to be sexually harassing is critical in determining whether an employee will report the harassing events (McDonald & Lees-Haley, 1995). A claimant must perceive conduct as unwelcome to bring a sexual harassment claim. Some research has confirmed that gender differences exist in perceptions of the types of conduct that are sexually harassing, and the law acknowledges such differences: "Genuine but innocuous differences in ways men and women routinely interact with members of the same sex and opposite sex" are not prohibited by Title VII (*Faragher v. City of Boca Raton*, 1998, p. 4). Thus, the legal focus is not on gender differences per se but on harassing conduct that is nontrivial, that is, more than innocuous.

The U.S. Supreme Court attempted to clarify the question of whose perspective should set the standard for liability in *Harris v. Forklift Systems, Inc.* (1993). The Court distinguished an objective and a subjective basis for perceiving a work environment as hostile. The subjective standard is taken from the plaintiff's perspective. If the plaintiff personally perceives the environment to be abusive, the subjective standard is met. The objective standard for a hostile work environment is one in which behavior that is "severe and pervasive" creates "an environment that a reasonable person would find hostile or abusive" (*Harris v. Forklift Systems, Inc.*, 1993, p. 4). Thus, "a sexually objectionable environment must be both objectively and subjectively offensive, one that a reasonable person would find hostile or abusive, and one that the victim did in fact perceive to be so," (*Faragher v. City of Boca Raton*, 1998, p. 9). Even where there is consensus that the conduct is harassing, it may nonetheless fail to rise to the legal standard or threshold of proof sufficient to state a legally viable cause of action, unless it is so abusive that a reasonable person in the position of the victim would conclude that a hostile and abusive environment existed. The objective reasonable person standard is intended to safeguard employers against claims by hypersensitive individuals and against claims based on petty slights. In other words, a subjective perception that the workplace is hostile is inadequate; only behavior so objectively offensive as to alter the conditions of the victim's employment constitutes prohibited harassment. A hypersensitive or idiosyncratic employee will not state a cause of action unless the complained-of conduct, objectively viewed, is harassing.

> The objective severity of harassment should be judged from the perspective of a reasonable person in the plaintiff's position, considering "all the circumstances." . . . that inquiry requires careful consideration of the social context in which particular behavior occurs and is experienced by its target. . . . Common sense, and an appropriate sensitivity to social context, will enable courts and juries to distinguish between simple teasing or roughhousing . . . and conduct which a reasonable person in the plaintiff's position would find severely hostile and abusive. (*Oncale v. Sundowner Offshore Services, Inc.*, 1998, pp. 6–7)

Totality-of-Circumstances Test

Ordinary tribulations of the workplace, such as sporadic use of abusive language, gender-related jokes, and occasional teasing, do not amount to a discriminatory change in the terms and conditions of employment (Lindemann & Kadue, 1999). In evaluating factors to assess whether the conduct at issue creates a hostile and abusive working environment, a *totality-of-circumstances* test applies. Usually, this assessment focuses on the severity and frequency or pervasiveness of the conduct in question. Thus, for example, in a jury trial, jurors are instructed to examine the evidence from the perspective of a reasonable person's reaction to a similar environment under similar circumstances and to evaluate the total circumstances and determine whether the alleged harassing behavior could be objectively classified as the kind of behavior that would seriously affect the psychological well-being of a reasonable person. The totality-of-circumstances test includes consideration of (a) the frequency of the discriminatory conduct in issue, (b) its severity, (c) whether it is physically threatening or humiliating or a mere offensive utterance, and (d) whether it unreasonably interferes with an employee's work performance (*Harris v. Forklift Systems, Inc.*, 1993, p. 370).

AFFIRMATIVE DEFENSES BY THE EMPLOYER

Recent developments in the case law, particularly the Ellerth and Faragher cases, permit employers to avoid liability if they can prove that they responded promptly and effectively to a complaint of sexual harassment. In other words, although sexually harassing conduct occurred, there may be no legally viable claim. Thus, great emphasis lies on the employer's conduct once on notice of a complaint about sexual harassment and, in particular, on the quality and timing of an internal investigation of the complaint (Abell & Jackson, 1996). Affirmative defenses for employers have expanded to the degree that some scholars have commented that if a company maintains a sexual harassment procedure and a plaintiff fails to report incidents of sexual harassment, courts are likely to grant summary judgment in favor of the employer (Krieger, 2001). Research has shown that regardless of harassment severity, relationships in the target's life, especially family relationships, play a pivotal role in the decision to pursue a sexual harassment complaint. Targets consider their maternal responsibilities, parental approval, and marital commitments (Morgan, 1999).

Different standards apply depending on whether the harasser is a supervisor with immediate authority over the employee or a coworker, customer, independent contractor, or other supervisor. When the harasser is a supervisor, affirmative defenses are available only when the conduct did not result in any tangible harm to the employee. Tangible harms include discharge, demotion, or undesirable reassignment. Tangible employment actions are within the special province of supervisors. Physical or psychological harm inflicted by a coworker does not qualify as tangible employment harm (*Burlington Industries v. Ellerth*, 1998; *Faragher v. City of Boca Raton*, 1998). When the harasser is a coworker or subordinate, a negligence standard applies. The employer is liable only when it knew or should have known of the conduct comprising harassment and failed to take prompt and effective remedial action.

DAMAGES

Driving much litigation is the available monetary relief. For this reason, it is important to distinguish between liability and damages evidence. Only if a party prevails in proving liability, that is, demonstrates that the antidiscrimination laws were violated, is a plaintiff entitled to damages, which may include monetary relief. Damages must be proven before any compensation can be assessed and awarded. The standard that applies is one of *proximate cause*. In other words, the plaintiff must show that the harms claimed were a direct consequence of the discriminatory conduct.

One goal of Title VII is to remedy injury to personhood and dignity and to remove barriers and obstacles to full participation at work (*Griggs v. Duke Power Co.*, 1971). Three major forms of legal relief available in sexual harassment cases are (a) make-whole relief, (b) compensatory damages, and (c) punitive damages. The precise nomenclature applicable to claims for different forms of compensation under different schemes or systems of relief varies from one jurisdiction to another, so readers are advised to cross-check the terminology applicable in any particular context. For instance, nominal special damages and general compensatory damages are traditionally distinguished in tort law. Under Title VII, special and general damages are acknowledged forms of compensatory damages.

Make-Whole Relief

Make-whole relief includes back pay, front pay, injunctive relief, reinstatement, retroactive raises or promotions, lost fringe benefits, sick leave, vacation pay, medical benefits, overtime, shift differentials pay, pensions, retirement bonuses, and travel allowances. Although the prospect of a back-pay award may serve as a deterrent to an employer, in most sexual harassment cases, particularly those involving a hostile work environment claim, the target does not suffer any loss of salary entitling a lost back-pay claim. This is because the target may remain employed or may voluntarily quit the job. If a victim can establish that he or she was forced to terminate involuntarily (constructively discharged, a standard very difficult to prove) or fired or demoted in retaliation for rejecting a sexual advance, a clear loss of income exists. Thus, in sexual harassment cases, there is often considerable focus on nonmonetary aspects of relief. For example, an employee may want performance evaluations changed, discipline rescinded, documents removed from a personnel file, a transfer, a promotion, accommodation in the form of a flexible work schedule, or restoration of leave. A plaintiff may also be most interested in nonmonetary redress, such as an apology or a determination by an external, neutral party that the conduct at issue was harassing (Shuman, 2000b).

Awards of attorneys' fees and experts' fees are available to prevailing parties if a statutory claim is brought (Civil Rights Act of 1991, section 1988 [b]). Unlike tort law, in which plaintiffs' lawyers typically work on the basis of a contingent fee agreement for a portion of the plaintiff's recovery, for example, one third of the award to the plaintiff, attorneys' fees may be recovered in full under statutory authority and often exceed the plaintiff's recovery. The availability of experts' fees to a prevailing party under Title VII means that the plaintiff may not ultimately pay these litigation costs. These potential awards must be considered in the light of the limitations on recovery in the form of the caps imposed on compensatory and punitive damages in federal court based on the number of employees. If attorneys can recover the full extent of their legal fees plus costs in the form of experts' fees and secure compensatory and/or punitive damages for the plaintiff under federal law, there might be little advantage to proceeding under state law.

Compensatory Damages

Awards of compensatory damages permit the plaintiff to recover funds to compensate for physical and psychological pain and suffering as well as for monetary or out-of-pocket losses in the past and future monetary losses. The plaintiff must produce evidence of actual injury caused by the discriminatory conduct and must establish (a) a reasonable probability that injury due to emotional distress was, in fact, sustained, (b) the extent of the actual injury, and (c) that such harm resulted from discriminatory conduct (*Gore v. Turner*, 1977). The employer bears the burden to show that the plaintiff failed to take reasonable measures to mitigate his or her losses. Compensatory damages under Title VII fall into three categories: (a) compensation for out-of-pocket expenses incurred in the past, (b) compensation for future out-of-pocket expenses, and (c) compensation for past and future psychological and physiological injury.

Causation of Harm

A major task is to establish causation of harm and to distinguish harm caused by sexual harassment from alternate causes of harm. These assessments are complicated by research that shows that assumptions about harms caused by sexual harassment may be erroneous. For instance, past research has indicated that victims of sexual harassment may suffer significant consequences after being subjected to low-level, frequent harassment (K. T. Schneider, Swan, & Fitzgerald, 1997). Discerning alternate causes of harm is complicated by the fact that sexual harassment victims experience many symptoms similar to those experienced by victims of other workplace stressors (see chap. 6). The admissibility criterion is whether the sexual harassment contributed to emotional distress the plaintiff would not have otherwise suffered, not whether the harassment was a substantial factor underlying the plaintiff's distress (*Webb v. Hyman*, 1994).

Factors that the law takes into account in determining compensatory damages have been enumerated by the EEOC as follows: (a) whether and to what extent the plaintiff was subject to overt discrimination, (b) whether and to what extent the plaintiff was subject to public humiliation, (c) whether the plaintiff sought professional assistance, (d) whether the plaintiff's testimony on damages is corroborated by other witnesses, (e) whether other factors or trauma that may have cause the plaintiff's injuries were present, (f) whether the plaintiff's susceptibility to emotional harm was reasonable (objective), (g) whether a subjective susceptibility to emotional harm existed (e.g., the existence of prior abuse or preexisting mental conditions that may have rendered the plaintiff more vulnerable to psychological harm), (h) what length of time the plaintiff suffered the harm, (i) the length of time the harm continued, and (j) the length of time between the discriminatory conduct and the manifestation of the psychological injury in question (Hemmingway, 1998).

Some psychologists have taken the position that once liability is established, some presumption of ordinary distress should follow (Fitzgerald, 2003). At present, there is no legal presumption of emotional distress once liability is established. For example, the Fifth Circuit Court of Appeals stated that emotional harm will not be presumed simply because a complaining party is a victim of discrimination (*Vadie v. Mississippi State Univ.*, 2000). The Supreme Court has held that mental distress injuries may only be compensated when actual injury is proved and that such injury cannot be presumed from a civil rights violation (*Carey v. Piphus*, 1978).

Punitive Damages

An incentive for employers to avoid liability comes from the availability of punitive or exemplary damages against employers who knowingly disregard the rights of their workers. The goal of punitive awards is to deter future discriminatory conduct. Relevant considerations include four topics: (a) the character of the defendant's act, (b) the nature and extent of harm likely to occur from the employer's conduct, (c) the nature and extent of harm actually suffered, and (d) the financial wealth of the defendant (*TXO Production Corp. v. Alliance Resources Corp.*, 1993). In a case in which a private employer acts with malice or reckless indifference to the federally protected rights of the plaintiff, the plaintiff is eligible for an award of punitive damages. Punitive damages are not awarded against federal agencies (public employers). In state court, punitive damages may be awarded against state agencies and employers. These awards can be large. The federal standard for punitive damages may be easier to meet than that of outrageous and extreme conduct, which triggers the recovery of punitive damages under tort law.

Factors to consider in determining whether the conduct at issue warrants an award of punitive damages include (a) the egregiousness of the conduct; (b) the nature, extent, and severity of harm to the plaintiff; (c) the duration of the discriminatory conduct; (d) the existence and frequency of past similar discriminatory conduct by the employer; (e) whether the employer attempted to conceal the conduct; (f) the response of the employer once notified of the conduct; and (g) the existence of threats or deliberate retaliatory action against the plaintiff. The financial status of the employer is assessed by considering (a) revenues and liabilities of the business; (b) fair market value of the employer's assets; (c) liquid assets on hand, including what the employer can reasonably borrow; (d) the employer's projected future earnings and future resale value of the employer's business; and (e) affiliation of the employer with, or status as a subsidiary of, a larger entity that could provide it with additional resources.

"Employers who adopt anti-discrimination policies and . . . educate their personnel on Title VII's prohibitions" have a defense against the imposition of punitive damages (*Kolstad v. American Dental Assn.*, 1999, p. 13). Thus, a good faith defense for employers who engage in good faith efforts to comply with Title VII may take the form of antidiscrimination policies and programs. Note that some scholars have pointed out that there is no empirical basis to assume that training or such an educational approach is effective in deterring discrimination in the workplace (Bisom-Rapp, 2001).

SETTLEMENT

Many sexual harassment cases are resolved by settlement rather than litigation. Difficulties to overcome in settlement often center on the credibility of the parties, the extent to which the actions rise to the level of actionable sexual harassment, and causation of harms claimed. Settlement may be achieved between the parties at the informal or formal stages (post-filing of complaint). Alternatively, the parties may seek the intervention of a third-party neutral to facilitate the settlement process. Many parties opt to take their claims before a private, third-party neutral, such as a mediator or arbitrator. This can occur before or after a formal suit is filed. Settlement is often driven by estimations of what is potentially available in litigation in terms of back pay and compensatory and punitive damages.

JUDGE VERSUS JURY TRIALS

Since the 1991 Civil Rights Act was implemented, virtually all employment discrimination cases have been tried to juries. Regardless whether the fact finder is a lawyer or a lay juror, the law on sexual harassment is complex and not necessarily intuitive. Despite Supreme Court guidance, behavior that constitutes sexual harassment is not clearly defined (FitzGibbon, 2000).

The assumption by many plaintiffs' lawyers that a jury trial is advantageous in a sexual harassment case is subject to challenge. There is some evidence that many jurors are ill disposed to these claims following widespread media coverage regarding trivial or bogus sexual harassment cases. Some plaintiffs' lawyers report that it is difficult to persuade jurors to take these cases seriously (Seymour, 1999). High-profile lawsuits have led some members of the public to resist limits on the regulation of sexual conduct (FitzGibbon, 2000).

As noted earlier, sexual harassment cases often turn on issues of credibility (Gazeley, 1997). Some empirical research on the outcomes of sexual harassment complaints illustrates some of the decision-making biases regarding the types of claims and credibility issues that may be unrelated legally to the merits of the complaints. Gender differences have emerged in assessments of the credibility of the sexual harassment allegations in the face of a denial. Overall, allegations of child sex abuse were seen as more credible than claims of rape or sexual harassment (O'Hare & O'Donohue, 1998). Other research demonstrated that of 81 cases filed in Illinois in a 2-year period, a favorable outcome for the plaintiff was more likely (a) when the behavior was extreme, specifically when it involved sexual assault, unwanted physical contact, or quid pro quo propositions; (b) when there were witnesses other than the complainant; and (c) when management was notified of the conduct before the plaintiff filed a charge of discrimination (Terpstra & Baker, 1992).

Jurors bring community standards to cases that may not be in tune with the law. For example, in *Rabidue v. Osceola Refining Co.* (1986/1987), the judge pointed out that community standards tolerated and even fostered discrimination. Jurors who ignore jury instructions or misunderstand them may fail to find sexual harassment even in cases in wich legal standards are met. A recent survey following a large-scale, high-profile class action sexual harassment case against Mitsubishi Motors Manufacturing in which the employer paid $34 million to settle the case revealed that although as many as 70% of respondents believed the claims were legitimate, only 33% would hold the employer liable (*EEOC v. Mitsubishi*, 1998). These results may show some resistance in the community to the legal standard or a lack of support for the reasonable woman standard (Morgan, 1999). Other research suggests that jurors may be reluctant to find sexual harassment based on confusion as to what constitutes sexually harassing behavior and ignorance about common reactions and coping styles by targets of harassment (Wiener et al., 2002; Wiener & Hurt, 1999). Claims by female targets may be dismissed based on stereotypes that women are hypersensitive and unable to take a joke. Similarly, jurors may be reluctant to find merit in claims by male targets based on stereotypical beliefs that men can withstand this sort of harassment.

Concerns that community values may not be in tune with antidiscrimination legislation led some courts (e.g., *Ellison v. Brady*, 1991) to adopt a *reasonable woman* as opposed to a *reasonable person* or *reasonable man* standard for liability, so that women entering a sexist workplace would not lose when the prevailing attitude among men in the workplace was tolerant of such conduct. However, the U.S. Supreme Court has continued to apply the *reasonable person* standard (Goodman-Delahunty, 1999).

EXPERTS IN SEXUAL HARASSMENT CASES

There are many issues affecting liability and damages determinations about which expert testimony may be relevant and helpful to the finder of fact. The roles and responsibilities of a forensic psychologist or other expert will vary depending on the particular case. On liability issues, for example, expert testimony may be proffered to address one or more of the following:

1. Presence or impact of gender stereotypes. Testimony on the impact of sex stereotypes has been used to show how failure of a woman to conform to traditional stereotypes led to a discriminatory hostile work environment (*Price-Waterhouse v. Hopkins*, 1989) and to show how a hostile workplace environment was created by pictures of nude and partially nude women, sexual comments, and sexual joking (*Robinson v. Jacksonville Shipyards, Inc.*, 1991).
2. Common female coping strategies in response to sexually harassing conduct. Expert testimony on reporting practices of victims has been admitted to shed light on the absence of a contemporaneous complaint of sexual harassment by a plaintiff (*Robinson v. Jacksonville Shipyards, Inc.*, 1991; *Snider v. Consolidation Coal Co.*, 1992/1993).
3. Why a plaintiff may remain in a harassing situation.
4. Gender differences in perceptions of sexually harassing conduct.
5. Profile of a sexual harasser. Testimony regarding the alleged harasser has been more controversial than potential testimony regarding the victim. Testimony on profiles of sexual harassers has been admitted in some cases (e.g., *Bushell v. Dean*, 1991), but excluded in others as inadmissible, improper *character evidence* under FRE 404(a) (Federal Rules of Evidence, 2000).
6. Factors that promote or inhibit workplace sexual harassment, for example, as part of a workplace climate
7. Adequacy of antiharassment policies. Testimony on the adequacy of employer sexual harassment policies and procedures is rare but may increase following *Faragher v. City of Boca Raton* (1998) and the availability of an affirmative defense on this basis. It was admitted in *Hurley v. Atlantic City Police Dept.* (1996) and *Weeks v. Baker & McKenzie* (1998).
8. Effective investigative practices on receipt of a sexual harassment complaint. This could include a discussion of effective investigative practices, such as that admitted in *Kestenbaum*

v. Pennzoil Co. (1988) regarding the hire of external experts to interview sectors of the workforce to gather objective data about what transpired and a review of the adequacy of an employer's internal investigation following receipt of a sexual harassment complaint.
9. Effect of the harasser's conduct on the psychological well-being of the plaintiff. Potential effects of sexual harassment on individual employees were admitted in *Moffett v. Gene B. Glick Co., Inc.* (1985). Testimony about the response of the particular plaintiff may be relevant in determining whether the plaintiff actually found the work environment abusive (*Harris v. Forklift Systems. Inc.*, 1993, p. 371).
10. Significance of the absence of a typical trauma-victim response. Testimony on common patterns of responses to sexually harassing conduct was admitted in *Robinson v. Jacksonville Shipyards, Inc.* (1991).
11. Common misconceptions about legal instructions on sexual harassment.

On injury issues, expert testimony is not required to prove injury to the plaintiff but is probative of injury and causation (*Bottomly v. Leucadia National*, 1995). Expert testimony often includes discussion of emotional distress, pain, and suffering that may be difficult for the plaintiff to describe. For example, in *Ramsey v. American Filter Co.* (1985), an award of $75,000 was reduced to $35,000 because few references to suffering were made by the plaintiff as a consequence of the discriminatory conduct, and no expert testified in her behalf. In some jurisdictions, courts have held that if the plaintiff only testifies about his or her emotional distress injuries, this evidence is insufficient to uphold an award of damages (*Bailey v. Runyon*, 2000; *Patterson v. PHP Healthcare Corp.*, 1996/1997).

Expert testimony may address the following aspects of injury and damages:

1. Diagnosis, treatment, and prognosis. Testimony by a treating, as opposed to an evaluating, psychologist or psychiatrist may affect the amount awarded in damages. For instance, an award of emotional distress was reduced from $500,000 to $250,000 on appeal on grounds that the award was based on the testimony of a forensic expert who evaluated the plaintiff after a meeting lasting just a couple of hours. The court held that absent a treating psychiatrist's testimony, the evidence did not support $500,000 (*Blakely v. Continental Airlines*, 2000).
2. Target behaviors and reactions. Testimony on the stressful effects of sexual harassment on women in the plaintiff's

position and on other workers was offered in *Broderick v. Ruder* (1988). In cases in which a psychological disorder is the consequence of the discrimination, an expert is crucial as lay jurors may not be aware of the disorder, its symptoms, or its consequences (*United States v. Hall*, 1996).

3. Causation of alleged psychological injury. A psychological expert may offer testimony probative of causation of harm, that is, that the harassment did or did not cause the psychological injuries sustained, for instance, regarding depression and emotional distress (*Karcher v. Emerson Electric*, 1996) or an adjustment disorder caused by workplace sexual harassment (*Hurley v. Atlantic City Police Dept.*, 1996). Typically, separating harm attributable to sexual harassment versus subsequent reprisal and retaliation is necessary when both claims are filed. For example, waitresses complained to management when a new manager touched them inappropriately, made sexually suggestive comments to them, replaced them when they protested, and threatened them with dismissal for failing to submit. While some waitresses picketed the restaurant, an electronic sign, visible from the freeway, was changed to read "Let our ladies wave you in." The picketers were fired. The sexual harassment was found to cause feelings of disgust, degradation, anger, belittlement, and frustration. Harms from the retaliatory discharge, which involved ridicule, teasing, and taunting, and distress at loss of employment were found to be extreme (*Delahunty v. Cahoon*, 1992). One expert's testimony on causation was challenged under Federal Rule of Evidence 403 as too speculative or confusing because all of the plaintiff's symptoms could have stemmed from non-work-related factors or problems, and the same symptoms could be the consequence of legitimate criticism of her performance at work (*George v. Frank*, 1991).
4. Impact of significant stress factors in plaintiff's life.
5. Factors influencing the severity of the trauma response.
6. Evidence of confabulation or malingering by the plaintiff.
7. Punitive damages. Testimony on injuries may also be pertinent to an award of punitive damages against the employer. For example, after a female materials handler complained to management that she suspected she was being watched while she showered because there were holes in the ceiling above the shower and tile fragments on the floor, the manager responded that there were no female employees that he would want to look at in the shower. An investigation revealed that a desk

was placed in a janitor's room with a chair on top of it so women could be observed in the bathroom and shower, and beer cans were strewn about the room. For a year, management took no action. The plaintiff experienced nightmares, marital strain, sexual aversion, and feelings of anger, humiliation, and embarrassment. The indifference of managers to her complaints after managers learned that male employees were able to spy on her in the shower resulted in a punitive damage award (*Manning v. Wire Rope Corp.*, 1993).

STANDARDS FOR THE ADMISSION OF EXPERT TESTIMONY

The trial judge must determine whether the expert is proposing to testify to scientific or other specialized knowledge that will assist the trier of fact to understand or determine a fact at issue. At least one court held that testimony about sexually harassing events and a hostile workplace dealt with common occurrences with which jurors were acquainted through their everyday experiences, thus expert testimony would not be helpful to the finder of fact, and therefore, it was excluded (*Lipsett v. Univ. of Puerto Rico*, 1988/1990). Thus, familiarity with the literature on common lay misconceptions about sexual harassment can be useful. For example, jurors may be unfamiliar with the potential effects of sexual harassment on individual employees (*Moffett v. Gene B. Glick Co., Inc.*, 1985).

First, the expert must have a reliable basis of knowledge and experience of his or her discipline and must establish that his or her experience, training, and education as a practitioner in psychology or psychiatry provide the necessary expertise to assist the fact finder. Exactly how to do this is not clear because there is no *litmus test* (*Wilson v. City of Chicago*, 1993). Education was not regarded as sufficient specialized experience to qualify, but passing further board, bar, and other examinations or difficult tests was required (*Lipsett v. Univ. of Puerto Rico*, 1988/1990). In some courts, a criterion of personal experience treating patients suffering from the conditions about which he or she will testify has been added as a requirement, for example, from posttraumatic stress disorder or memory disorders caused by trauma (*Isely v. Capuchin Province*, 1995, pp. 1063–1064).

Second, the expert must establish that the proffered testimony is grounded in a methodology that instills the evidence with sufficient reliability. The focus is on principles and methodology, not the conclusions they generate. Typically, experts must be prepared to meet the four criteria for reliability enumerated in *Daubert v. Merrell Dow Pharmaceuticals, Inc.* (1993), although in some states, the Frye test applies, focusing on the general acceptance of the methods used (*Frye v. United States*, 1923). The four-part inquiry under *Daubert* is as follows: (a) Has the theory been tested or corroborated, and if so, by whom, and under what circumstances? (b) Has the theory been proved under clinical tests or some accepted procedure for bearing it out? (c) Has the theory been subjected to other types of peer review? (d) Are the underlying data and studies upon which the expert relied of a type reasonably relied upon in the expert's field (general acceptance standard)? Recent research has indicated that judges and jurors have difficulty applying these standards to evaluate expert testimony in a hostile workplace case (Kovera & McAuliff, 2000; Kovera, Russano, & McAuliff, 2002).

Different courts apply these screening criteria in different ways, so there is no guarantee that because evidence was admitted in one case it will be admitted in another. For instance, in *Johnson v. County of Los Angeles Fire Dept.* (1994), expert testimony that reading *Playboy* magazine results in sex stereotyping that may result in inequitable treatment of women was proffered, relying on studies showing that films affected job interview questions. The opposing expert said the connection between *Playboy* and sex stereotyping was "just a hypothesis." Stereotyping testimony of this nature had been admitted previously, pre-Daubert (e.g., *Robinson v. Jacksonville Shipyards, Inc.*, 1991). Other courts have examined whether the underlying theory is irrefutable. If so, the testimony has been excluded (*Gier v. Educational Service Unit. No. 16*, 1994). Sexual harassment cases in which expert testimony was admitted under *Daubert* standards include *Webb v. Hyman* (1994), *Isely v. Capuchin Province* (1995), and *Faragher v. City of Boca Raton* (1998).

Third, the content of the testimony must be more probative than prejudicial, confusing, or misleading, following the guidance of Federal Rule of Evidence 403. Testimony by a psychologist on sexual harassment was excluded in one case on this basis, as more unfairly prejudicial than probative (*Snider v. Consolidation Coal Co.*, 1992).

SUMMARY

Sexual harassment claims may be filed in both state and federal court under a broad range of legal theories. In each setting, the legal standards for proving a claim vary and the testifying psychologist must be aware of these standards when conducting evaluations of plaintiffs and providing testimony in court. Sexual harassment laws evolved over a number of decades and are still evolving. For example, the law once observed a distinction between quid pro quo and hostile work environment claims; recently legal attributes of this distinction were eliminated. Sensitivity to the impact of harassment on all employees led the courts to recognize that workers may be harassed by persons of the same gender and that men as well as women are targets of sexual harassment.

The law is most clearly enunciated by standards applied to determine whether a party has established a case. For example, how a court defines whether conduct is offensive affects the admissibility of evidence on this issue and the type of injury testimony that an expert may provide. How employers defend themselves against cases creates new roles for psychologists who may testify on behalf of defendants.

Psychologists may testify about injuries suffered by a plaintiff in a sexual harassment case. Testimony about what caused the injuries is often the core task confronting the expert witness. Counteracting local biases about gender roles may be an important part of a testifying expert's job. In doing that job, the expert must comply with parameters of admissibility crafted by the U.S. Supreme Court in a series of decisions. Although many worry that these parameters limit the role of psychological testimony in sexual harassment cases, others are satisfied that higher standards result in more evidence-based expert testimony.

Interacting with the legal system is sometimes the most daunting part of the psychological expert's job. Psychologists need not have law degrees to testify competently. However, employment law is a complex arena. Familiarity with legal standards and procedures can permit the psychologist to testify in a way that assists the judge or jury to decide a case fairly.

4

THE FORENSIC EVALUATION: PRACTICAL, LEGAL, AND ETHICAL CONTOURS

The forensic evaluation process entails a sequence of events that occur in a relatively orderly fashion determined by legal or procedural requirements and the practicalities of the situation. The process begins with the retention of the psychologist by a lawyer involved in the case and ends when the case is resolved by the court or by settlement between the parties. In this chapter, we examine the legal, ethical, and professional issues relevant to each step in the process.

PRIVACY, CONFIDENTIALITY, AND PRIVILEGE

The psychologist doing forensic work must almost always address three distinguishable issues: privacy, confidentiality, and privilege. Privacy refers to the general right that individuals have to keep aspects of their life private. Courts have recognized an individual's right to privacy in relation to medical procedures (*Roe v. Wade*, 1973) and the more recent Health Insurance Portability and Accountability Act of 1996, or HIPAA, has codified these privacy rights in relation to medical and mental health information.

Confidentiality is a duty owed to the client or patient by health care providers. For psychologists, this duty has been a product of clinical experience that shows that when individuals are afforded confidentiality, therapy is more effective. The duty of psychologists to keep confidential communications from their patients or clients is codified in the APA Ethics Code (American Psychological Association, 2002), in state psychologist licensing laws and regulations, and in common law pertaining to malpractice.

Privilege is a right owned by the client or patient to prevent the psychologist or other health care provider from disclosing confidential information in legal proceedings. Privilege is usually recognized and applied by rules of evidence of a particular jurisdiction, and almost all states have rules of evidence providing for psychotherapist–patient, as well as attorney–client, clergy–penitent, and spousal privileges. Only recently has the U.S. Supreme Court acknowledged a psychotherapist patient privilege in cases brought in federal court (*Jaffee v. Redmond,* 1996). In general, the client or patient is the owner of the privilege, and the psychologist is the custodian of the privilege. That means that in the absence of a written release of information, a psychologist is required to assert privilege on behalf of the patient or client. Once a patient or client executes a release, the psychologist is compelled to release records or provide court testimony (American Psychological Association, Committee on Legal Issues, 1996). Courts often set aside privileges when they operate to keep relevant facts from consideration by the trier of fact (Shuman & Foote, 1999).

RETENTION

Legal Framework for Forensic Evaluation in Sexual Harassment Cases

In a sexual harassment case, counsel usually hires the psychologist for either the plaintiff or the defendant. In almost every case, it is preferable for the psychologist to be hired by the counsel on behalf of the party and not by the party directly. Hiring by the lawyer creates a legal relationship of agency in which the psychologist becomes the agent of the lawyer. Within the parameters of this agency relationship, the work of the psychologist may be protected under the attorney work product privilege provisions of the rules of evidence, and lines of duty are well established.

Retention may be on behalf of single or multiple parties in the case, or on rare occasions, the expert may be appointed by the court. For example, the hiring lawyer may be representing a named defendant (an employer company, a CEO, or a supervisor) or a number of defendants, each of whom is usually represented by separate counsel. In general, it is ethically desirable for the psychologist to be hired by only one defendant in a case because the case may evolve such that the interests of the parties diverge and the psychologist's work may be central to those differences.

The conduct of the initial retention phone call is important not only because of the psychologist's desire to gather information concerning the case, but to set the tone of balance and fairness that should mark the psychologist's conduct in the entire case (Shuman & Greenberg, 2003). Many lawyers use this occasion to advocate for their party's position and to orient the psychologist's attention in favor of the party they represent. The psychologist should inquire about the other side's perspective on the facts. Because this is a conversation about which the psychologist may be questioned in later depositions or open court, it should memorialized in written form. This record should reflect the psychologist's desire to hear both sides of the case, not only the worker's complaints, but the employer's defenses.

When hired by counsel for the defense, the psychologist may evaluate multiple plaintiffs in the same or separate causes of action springing from the same or related events. This may arise when it is alleged that one or more supervisors or coworkers harassed more than one individual or that the workplace was hostile for multiple employees.

In circumstances in which the psychologist is hired by the plaintiff's counsel, concerns about potential conflicts of interest are of less consequence. In some cases, evaluation of multiple plaintiffs can generate economies of scale, for example, savings in time and money that occur because the work is done in volume. Gaining knowledge of the corporate climate, the identities and activities of supervisory personnel, and events that were experienced or observed by many can save expert time and fees. The evaluation of multiple plaintiffs may provide differing perspectives that illuminate central issues in the case for the examining psychologist and corroborate the modus operandi of the alleged harasser. In cases in which the defendant harasser is the same for multiple plaintiffs, one might expect significant commonalities of experience and response.

On the negative side, the presence of multiple plaintiffs may provide an artificial consensus concerning the occurrence of harassment, lending greater credibility to all of the stories. A psychologist who hears similar stories from separate plaintiffs must bear in mind that similar stories may arise from deliberate collusion among plaintiffs or unintentional discussion among the witnesses or plaintiffs as well as from shared experience. An individualized, skeptical approach is needed for evaluation of each claim. When a single psychologist evaluates multiple plaintiffs, the psychologist's credibility may be negatively affected. If the findings and conclusions in multiple similar cases coincide, it may appear that the expert has approached the case with a *cookie cutter* and has prejudged the cases.

A psychologist is hired with a specific brief or purpose. In most cases, the task of the examining psychologist is to determine the nature and extent of psychological injury related to alleged sexual harassment experiences (Goodman-Delahunty & Foote, 1995). Other cases may call for the psychologist to provide testimony concerning the plaintiff's behavior in the workplace. For example, the psychologist may be asked to account for the plaintiff's failure to report recurring sexual harassment (Fitzgerald, Swan, & Fischer, 1995). The latter role comprises *scientific framework* testimony, which is designed to assist the judge or jury by providing information gleaned from psychological research (Goodman & Croyle, 1989).

No matter who hires the psychologist, the role of the psychologist relative to the hiring party is one of *agency* (Rogers, 1987; Shuman, 2000a). The psychologist is working for the lawyer representing a party to the case and expects to be paid by that lawyer. In turn, the lawyer expects an effort from the psychologist consistent with prevailing professional standards. Of course, the existence of an agency relationship does not abrogate the psychologist's professional responsibilities of objectivity, fairness, and truthfulness (Committee on Ethical Guidelines for Forensic Psychologists, 1991). An agency relationship implies more than the simple purchase of services. As an agent of the retaining lawyer, the examining or consulting psychologist owes a legal duty to the lawyer to keep private all communications or material related to the case until circumstances (report, deposition, or testimony) require specific facts to become public (Melton et al., 1997; Shuman, 2000a).

In this regard, the issue of privilege is important. First, this is a circumstance in which the party's expectation of privacy or confidentiality of evaluation is usually severely limited or absent. This is a forensic proceeding in which the party may have placed his or her mental condition into controversy by claiming emotional injury. Although the Federal Rules of Evidence do not include a psychotherapist–patient privilege, a recent U.S. Supreme Court decision in the case of *Jaffee v. Redmond* (1996) effectively established the privilege (Shuman & Foote, 1999). However, this decision and the rules of evidence in most other jurisdictions contain a specific waiver of psychotherapist–patient privilege once the *patient* uses his or her mental condition as a basis for a civil claim or criminal defense. Not all claims in sexual harassment cases include elements of psychological injury, and the U.S. Supreme Court has ruled that in order for a sexual harassment plaintiff to prevail, the claim need not include elements of psychological injury (*Harris v. Forklift Systems, Inc.*, 1993). In any event, the relationship between the examining psychologist and the party is not a therapeutic or treating relationship but one for forensic evaluation. As such, the party should rarely (see the discussion that follows) have an expectation of confidentiality or privacy.

With the advent of HIPAA (45 C.F.R. sections 160 and 164), nonforensic clinicians are required to notify clients about the parameters of confidentiality. Although HIPAA essentially exempts forensic evaluations from coverage under the act (Connell & Koocher, 2003), psychologists examining individuals in forensic settings are well advised to clearly notify the party that the forensic evaluation does not fall under HIPAA. In addition, requests for information and releases of information should correspond with formats mandated by HIPAA.

In many cases, the relationship of the examining expert and the party in the context of agency is one to which the attorney–client privilege may apply (Shuman, 2000a). The courts have long recognized that attorney–client privilege is critical; when the lawyer provides appropriate representation to the party, the lawyer must be able to obtain and review information that may be harmful to the party or to the party's case. This may be the situation if the plaintiff's counsel hires the psychologist to provide a preliminary evaluation of injury for the purpose of determining the value of the case or the probability of prevailing in later litigation. If the attorney decides not to have this expert testify in court, the work of that expert is generally not subject to disclosure and may fall under the protection of the "attorney work product" (Shuman, 2000a).

Whatever the arrangement concerning confidentiality or privilege, it is often advantageous for the psychologist and lawyer to have a written retention agreement. The agreement may itemize the purposes for which the psychologist is hired and the lawyer's expectations concerning privilege and confidentiality. This agreement may also include details of the financial arrangements between the psychologist and lawyer and may be generated by either the lawyer or the psychologist.

Financial Arrangements

Agency implies a financial relationship between the psychologist and the retaining lawyer. Psychologists are expected to clarify financial arrangements early in the professional relationship with the lawyer (Committee on Ethical Guidelines for Forensic Psychologists, Forensic Guideline IVA, 1991). This discussion should be part of the retention discussion and should be included in a written retention agreement. Even in situations in which the party may ultimately pay for the psychologist's services from his or her own pocket, it is advisable for all financial arrangements to be made through the party's lawyer to preserve the agency relationship and to clarify the function of the psychologist in the case.

Some psychologists prefer to receive a deposit or retainer at the onset of the case. This arrangement allows the psychologist to initiate work on a case without concern that professional fees will be paid. Once fees consume the deposit amount, some arrangements allow for subsequent deposits as the case progresses. The cautious psychologist may place these deposits in a separate bank account to ensure that any amount not consumed by fees is returned to the retaining lawyer. This *pay as you go* arrangement ensures that the psychologist is not in a situation from which it can be inferred that the psychologist's fees are contingent on the results of the evaluation.

Contingency fee arrangements are forbidden by Forensic Guideline IVB (Committee on Ethical Guidelines for Forensic Psychologists, 1991), and psychologists should avoid any circumstances functionally equivalent to such an arrangement. For example, a psychologist should not work under a *letter of protection* in which the retaining lawyer guarantees the psychologist's fees from the potential proceeds of the case. Such arrangements are often made for impecunious parties, and it is unlikely that the psychologist will be paid if the plaintiff does not settle the case or prevail in court. This arrangement gives the psychologist a direct financial interest in the outcome of the case, precisely what the contingency fee prohibition in the guidelines aims to avoid.

Clarification of Roles

The psychologist may be asked to serve in one of several roles in sexual harassment cases. Three distinct roles may be distinguished: (a) the treating psychotherapist, (b) the examining expert, and (c) the consultant. With some limited exceptions, it is critical for the psychologist to avoid assuming more than one of these roles in the same case. In this section, we offer a short discussion of these issues. For a more detailed discussion, see Greenberg and Shuman (1997); Hellkamp and Lewis (1995); Shuman, Greenberg, Heilbrun, and Foote (1998); and Williger (1995).

Treating Psychotherapist

Plaintiffs in sexual harassment cases may have a history of or current involvement in a psychotherapy relationship related or unrelated to the alleged sexual harassment events. This is appropriate given the impact of sexual harassment on some people. Because the treating psychotherapist may have knowledge concerning the emotional condition of the plaintiff, this professional may be called into court to testify about the impact of the sexual harassment on the plaintiff.

This entry of the psychotherapist into legal proceedings generates ethical issues in the form of dual-role concerns. APA Ethical Standards warn against assuming more than one role in a professional relationship when the ensuing multiple relationship appears reasonably likely to interfere with the psychologist's work or carries the risk of exploitation or harm. Specifically, Standard 3.05 states the following:

> (a) A multiple relationship occurs when a psychologist is in a professional role with a person and (1) at the same time is in another role

> with the same person, (2) at the same time is in a relationship with a person closely associated with or related to the person with whom the psychologist has the professional relationship, or (3) promises to enter into another relationship in the future with the person or a person closely associated with or related to the person. A psychologist refrains from entering into a multiple relationship if the multiple relationship could reasonably be expected to impair the psychologist's objectivity, competence, or effectiveness in performing his or her functions as a psychologist, or otherwise risks exploitation or harm to the person with whom the professional relationship exists. (American Psychological Association, 2002, p. 1065)

Forensic Guideline IVD1 (Committee on Ethical Guidelines for Forensic Psychologists, 1991) also provides guidance on this issue.

Although these standards allow for some degree of discretion concerning the assumption of more than one role in a forensic matter, many psychologists (Greenberg & Shuman, 1997; Gutheil, 1998; Shuman et al., 1998) argue that the role of a treating psychotherapist in court should be very limited. Specifically, the treating therapist should provide testimony about behavioral observations, working diagnoses, and the substance and process of the therapy. The plaintiff's needs for future treatment may also fall within these boundaries. However, the psychotherapist should probably avoid offering testimony concerning proximate cause or other critical psycholegal issues in the case.

The rationale for this limitation springs from dual-role impediments to both the therapy and the expert roles. The therapy relationship should be the primary commitment of the therapist. In assuming the role of expert or consultant, the therapist runs the risk of harming the therapeutic relationship, and in consequence, the psychotherapy client. In the expert role, the therapist runs the risk of working from an inadequate database (only what the client or patient tells the therapist) and appearing to be biased in favor of the client.

Expert

When the psychologist serves as an expert, his or her primary duty is to the court. FRE 702 provides the basis for admissibility of expert testimony. In general, lay or percipient witnesses (those who describe what they saw, felt, or heard) are not allowed to offer opinions to the court. However, a witness whom the court has allowed to testify as an expert may offer opinion testimony. FRE 702 states the following:

> If scientific, technical, or other specialized knowledge will assist the trier of fact to understand the evidence or to determine a fact in issue, a witness qualified as an expert by knowledge, skill, experience, training or education, may testify thereto in the form of an opinion otherwise,

> if (1) the testimony is based upon sufficient facts or data, (2) the testimony is the product of reliable principles and methods, and (3) the witness has applied the principles and methods reliably to the facts in the case. (Federal Rules of Evidence, 2000, p. 45)

This rule embodies changes to the FRE subsequent to the U.S. Supreme Court decisions in *Daubert v. Merrell Dow Pharmaceuticals, Inc.* (1993), *General Electric Co. v. Joiner* (1997), and *Kumho Tire Co. v. Carmichael* (1999).

In sexual harassment claims filed in federal courts, two Federal Rules of Civil Procedure (FRCP) pertain. The first, Rule 26(b) relates to the expert employed by the plaintiff to conduct an evaluation for the purpose of trial court testimony. This expert must produce a report. The rule dictates the following:

> The report shall contain a complete statement of all opinions to be expressed and the basis and reasons therefore; the data or other information considered by the witness in forming the opinions; any exhibits to be used as a summary of or support for the opinions; the qualifications of the witness, including a list of all publications authored by the witness within the preceding ten years; the compensation to be paid for the study and testimony; and a listing of any other cases in which the witness has testified as an expert at trial or by deposition within the preceding four years. (Federal Rules of Civil Procedure, Rule 26 [b] 2001)

In addition, the rule permits the opposing party (usually the defendant) to take the deposition of the expert.

The other relevant federal rule is FCRP 35. This rule allows one party, usually the defendant, to compel the other party, usually the plaintiff, to undergo a forensic evaluation. This evaluation is performed under court order. The place, duration, and scope of the evaluation may be specified by the order if the parties cannot reach an agreement. The rule states the following:

> When the mental or physical condition . . . of a party . . . is in controversy, the court in which the action is pending may order the party to submit to a physical or mental examination by a suitably licensed or certified examiner. The order may be made only on motion for good cause shown. (Federal Rules of Civil Procedure, Rule 35, 2001)

A Rule 35 evaluation is triggered when "the mental or physical condition of a party" is "in controversy." The examiner's report must include the results of all the testing conducted in the case and any diagnoses or conclusions determined by the evaluation (Shuman, 2000a). The U.S. Supreme Court held that "good cause" and "in controversy" require a showing of more than mere relevance (*Schlagenhauf v. Holder*, 1964) but provided little guidance to factors that warrant a psychiatric or psychological examination. An allegation of emotional distress on its own is typically not enough to trigger a Rule 35 examination. A claim for emotional distress plus one of five additional circumstances may be sufficient: (a) Plaintiff claims intentional or negligent infliction of emotional distress; (b) plaintiff alleges a specific mental or psychiatric injury; (c) plaintiff claims unusually severe emotional distress; (d) plaintiff plans to offer expert testimony to support the emotional distress claim; or (e) plaintiff concedes his or her mental condition is on controversy for purposes of Rule 35 (*Turner v. Imperial Stores*, 1995).

In general, a psychologist retained as an expert in a sexual harassment case operates under the APA "Ethical Principles of Psychologists and Code of Conduct" (American Psychological Association, 2002) and the "Specialty Guidelines for Forensic Psychologists" (Committee on Ethical Guidelines for Forensic Psychologists, 1991). These guidelines and the FRE and FRCP demand a high level of professional skill and performance.

Consultant Expert in a Nontestifying Role

In this role, the psychologist assists the lawyer with particular aspects of the case, such as expert witness selection and preparation; trial strategy; jury selection; review of testing and interview data from opposing experts; preparation of questions for opposing experts; review of documents to determine how they should be used; training lawyers in some aspect of psychology, psychopathology, or testing; preparing exhibits; or explaining why the opposing party is acting in a particular manner (Shuman, 2000a). Although some of these functions may also be part of the testifying expert's role, in contrast to the the therapist or testifying expert, the consultant works under the cover of the attorney work product so that none of the consultant's work is discoverable (Shuman, 2000a).

However, both the retaining lawyer and the psychologist must take care to ensure the confidentiality of this relationship. FRCP 26, which governs some aspects of discovery related to expert witnesses, indicates that an expert retained "in anticipation of litigation or preparation for trial and who is not expected to be called as a witness in trial" is not subject to discovery, absent a showing of "exceptional circumstances under which it is impracticable for a party seeking discovery to obtain facts or opinions on the same subject by other means" (FRCP 26 [b] [4] [B]). Shuman (2000a) has noted that the standard for discovery of consulting experts is high and has rarely been applied to psychological or psychiatric experts. The exceptions carved out by the courts are situations in which the consulting expert has in his possession or control evidence that is unobtainable from other sources (e.g., *Baki v. B. F. Diamond Constr. Co.*, 1976).

The most prudent practice is for the psychologist to avoid serving as a consultant and a testifying expert at the same time because the expert may encounter practical as well as ethical conflicts if both roles are assumed. However, the shift from consultant to expert may be accomplished in some circumstances. For example, it is not unusual for a testifying expert to begin work in a consulting role by reviewing records or evaluating other evidence to determine if a formal psychological evaluation would be appropriate. This may occur when the retaining party is unsure of the advisability of a face-to-face evaluation of the plaintiff. A preliminary review of the existing documentation, which may include other experts' reports, can provide sufficient information to determine if an evaluation is helpful and also assist in determining the contours of that evaluation. For example, a case that reveals a history of head injury in addition to the allegations of sexual harassment may require an evaluation by a neuropsychologist to rule out a neuropsychological basis for the plaintiff's complaints.

The shift from this kind of review to that of a testifying expert is relatively uncomplicated as long as several precautions are observed. First, the retaining party should not provide attorney work-product information to the psychologist, as this information will be discoverable following the forensic evaluation. Second, the psychologist should avoid engaging in consulting activities that would be inconsistent with the testifying expert's role. For example, the expert should avoid discussing trial strategy or tactics, the strengths and weaknesses of the plaintiff's or defendant's case, or anything else that would provide an appearance of partisanship.

Likewise, a shift from an expert to a consultant role sometimes poses problems. Primary among these is the discoverability of the expert's work following the disclosure of that expert. Even activities that are strictly advisory or consultative in nature may be subject to discovery under FRCP 26 when the expert is designated to testify.

Conflict Check

Before accepting the case, the expert must ensure he or she has no conflicts that would interfere with his or her performance of professional responsibilities. Conflicts would occur, for example, in instances in which the potential expert has had prior contact with the party to be examined or past or current psychotherapy relationships with any of the counsel. No conflict exists merely because the expert is working with the same lawyer or law firm on more than one case as long as the cases are not connected. However, if the potential expert has conducted psychotherapeutic work with any of the counsel or their families, except in unusual circumstances, such relationships constitute a conflicting dual relationship. If the expert were asked in deposition or court whether there existed a prior relationship with any of the counsel, he or she might be forced to disclose the existence of a heretofore confidential relationship.

Determination of Competence to Fulfill Role

The next step is to consider one's skills in relation to the requested services (Heilbrun, 2001). Five topics with which a psychologist anticipating practice in a particular area should have familiarity have been delineated by Melton et al. (1997). As those are applied to sexual harassment cases, the potential expert must first consider whether he or she has a working knowledge of the EEOC or FEPA system in which the case originated, whether it is filed in federal or state court, and the rules of evidence that apply to psychological testimony in that case. Second, the psychologist should also have a working knowledge of appropriate assessment instruments. In the assessment of sexual harassment cases, few specialized instruments exist, but the potential expert should have knowledge of those tools (described subsequently). Third, the psychologist should also have a grasp of the relevant legal principles. For example, the potential expert should understand the relevance of whether it is a Title VII case or is being tried under a state or federal tort theory and the elements necessary to establish a cause of action or defend it in the setting in which the case is filed. Fourth, the psychologist should have knowledge about the phenomena of sexual harassment as outlined in this volume to assist in determining how this particular case either conforms with or differs from the cases reported in the literature. Finally, the potential expert should have some assurance that if proffered as an expert, the court should have no reluctance to allow him or her to testify. In general, the psychologist who has done other forensic work and wishes to begin working in sexual harassment cases should consider consultation with an experienced colleague as a learning tool and as a basis for ensuring competence in the case in which professional services are requested.

Timelines and Deadlines

Although it may seem mundane after consideration of the complexities of multiple roles, the psychologist's next task is a consultation with the potential expert's calendar. The most critical question is the date of discovery cutoff, as this is the date by which the expert's report must be submitted and may also include the date to complete the potential expert's deposition. Examinations conducted under FRCP 26 or 35 may be on a shorter time line mandated by these rules. In order to compute whether the time available is sufficient, the potential expert should consider other ongoing commitments and should inquire about the nature and extent of available documents. In most cases, the expert will want to review available records before the evaluation of the party. The documents in many sexual harassment cases are extensive and require considerable time to review, annotate, and digest. A prudent practitioner will allocate twice the time anticipated for completing these tasks.

EVALUATION

Evaluation Standards

In general, psychologists should not render opinions about those whom they have not directly evaluated. APA ethical standard 9.01b (American Psychological Association, 2002) indicates that the information used by the expert must have a sufficient basis. In some cases, the psychologist may not be able to examine the plaintiff directly and must rely on testing done by another psychologist and on sworn statements or depositions. In those less than optimal circumstances, the expert has the abiding responsibility to advise the finder of fact of the impact of the limitations of information on the reliability and validity of the report and testimony. In addition, the expert must limit the scope of the conclusions or recommendations (Heilbrun, 2001).

As a general rule, these restrictions do not limit the provision of scientific framework testimony (Goodman & Croyle, 1989) that relates the scientific research on a topic to the case before the court. In general, the expert does not render an opinion about the parties in the case but may respond to hypothetical questions that relate to the case. Even in those cases, care should be taken to clarify the limitations or applications of such research on the party in the case.

Preparation for the Evaluation

The psychologist's preparation for the evaluation is dependent on the issues central to the lawsuit. These are framed by the plaintiff's complaint, which outlines the plaintiff's case, and the defendant's response, which details the defendant's perspective on the matter. More often than not, the specific requests of the retaining party and the issues that are relevant to the case will be within those documents. The psychologist should confine the evaluation to relevant issues, as needless deviation from that territory invades the privacy of the party and injects complicating information into the case. For example, the parties may agree about the facts of the alleged harassing events. If this is the case, there is no reason for the psychologist to assess the degree to which the plaintiff accurately evaluated those events as one might in an assessment of liability (see chap. 5, this volume). In short, the psychologist's first step is to determine the issues relevant to the case and focus the evaluation on those issues.

Record Review

A critical part of the psychologist's preparation in a sexual harassment case is to review relevant records. Although the records available in sexual harassment cases are often voluminous, it is not essential for the psychologist to review all available documents. At a minimum, the psychologist should review legal documents that explicate key elements for the litigants. The first is the plaintiff's claim or complaint, which lays out the factual and legal basis for the lawsuit. This provides a statement of what the plaintiff thinks can be proven in court. It is a necessary basis for starting the case and may be amended as the case develops to reduce or add elements. The second is the defendant's answer or response to the complaint. This document clarifies which of the plaintiff's claims the defendant believes may be controverted by evidence. The claim and response should be viewed as partisan documents and may or may not be supported by the expert evaluation or other evidence.

Lawyers often address interrogatories to the parties in a case. These are a series of written questions that focus on critical but relatively routine issues such as the identifying information related to the plaintiff (e.g., full name, social security number, and address). The plaintiff's job history, residential history, and a list of the plaintiff's health care providers are often included. In most jurisdictions, the party's counsel reviews the answers to interrogatories, and the party is required to swear that the statements made are true. Depositions consist of sworn testimony taken pursuant to a subpoena. The difference between depositions and court testimony is that a deposition is taken in a private setting, such as a lawyer's or professional's office, in the presence of the parties, their counsel, and a court reporter. Deposition transcripts may be used in later proceedings when a witness is not able to appear to provide viva voce (live, in court) testimony or as a basis for motions to the court or for impeachment of that witness at trial. A lawyer can also submit deposition excerpts or full deposition transcripts into evidence in the trial.

In sexual harassment cases, the psychologist will want to review the depositions of the plaintiff and any medical or mental health professionals who have evaluated or treated the plaintiff. The defendant(s)'s deposition should also be reviewed as well as depositions of anyone who may have observed the events giving rise to the lawsuit. If family members of the plaintiff have been deposed, these records can be useful as well as the testimony of friends or coworkers who may have witnessed changes in the plaintiff's functioning over time. Depositions of other experts may also be helpful. A review of the deposition of the opposing mental health expert is critical in preparation for evaluation, although depending on the timing of the evaluation, the other expert's report may not be available.

The expert should review the plaintiff's medical records when available. To determine causation of injury, the psychologist must determine which conditions preexisted the alleged harassment. A review of these records can provide a basis for that determination. When possible, these records should span the plaintiff's whole life and should include material from all providers, not just mental health practitioners. Mental health records are critical, including copies of testing gathered in the course of prior psychological evaluations. Because of state laws, regulations, or HIPAA, it may be necessary for the plaintiff to sign a separate release for test data, as those data should be forwarded directly from the examining psychologist to the forensic psychologist (American Psychological Association, Committee on Legal Issues, 1996) to avoid ethical concerns on the part of the releasing psychologist about disclosure to those not trained to review the material (see Ethics Code standard 9.04, American Psychological Association, 2002, p. 1071).

In addition, it is often helpful to review the plaintiff's school records from grade school through college or trade school when available. This information may be helpful to establish the presence of early behavioral problems such as attention-deficit/hyperactivity disorder or conduct disorder. Employment records from the job that the plaintiff was performing at the time of the lawsuit and from earlier employment are also useful. Performance reviews and promotion or transfer records can indicate how the employer considered the worker's performance. If the plaintiff served in the military, service records can provide a picture of how the plaintiff functioned within the constraints of the structure and discipline of that environment.

The psychologist may want to consolidate documentary information into a more accessible format. The development of lists of people involved in the case and their roles, alleged critical incidents, and comprehensive time lines can help the expert organize the material effectively. This organization can also allow the expert to reconstruct his or her work, particularly when a long interval transpires between the expert's initial work on a case and the time a deposition or court testimony is necessary. Deposition summaries and summaries of medical records are similarly useful. Although these documents may be created to help the psychologist organize the case facts, such notes are discoverable by the opposing party.

Research Review

The examining psychologist will almost always want to review the literature in the area in which he or she is conducting the evaluation. The necessity of a review is dependent on the psychologist's familiarity with the extant research in the area and the time since the last review of that literature. If it has been more than a year, it is probably critical to review the most recent literature to ensure currency with the research and that the procedures the psychologist anticipates using are up-to-date and accurate.

It may also be necessary to review the legal cases and legal literature in the area. In the era of *Daubert v. Merrell Dow Pharmaceuticals, Inc.* (1993) and *Kumho Tire Co. v. Carmichael* (1999), the admissibility of testimony using the particular evaluation procedures that constitute the psychologist's battery may be a critical issue to address before the evaluation, as the examiner may have only one opportunity to evaluate a given party. Also, an understanding of the elements of proof for a particular cause of action may be helpful (Goodman-Delahunty, 2000).

Notification and Appointment Setting

Once arrangements have been made for the party to be evaluated, the next step often involves a letter from the psychologist to the party. When the psychologist is working for the defendant, it is sensible to send the letter and enclosures to the party's lawyer, who will then pass them to the party. That way, if the lawyer has any concerns or objections to the contents, those may addressed before the evaluation takes place. For example, if the examiner plans to audiotape the interview portion of the evaluation, the consent form for audiotaping should be included. The party's counsel may object to the recording, as another record of the client's account could be used to impeach other testimony.

The enclosures sent to the party should include a number of elements: (a) a cordial but businesslike greeting and notification of the date, time, location, and anticipated duration of the evaluation; (b) a map to the location to assist the party to find the testing site; (c) a brief description of the anticipated procedures (e.g., paper-and-pencil testing, cognitive testing, and clinical interview); (d) a consent for evaluation; (e) any releases of information that the examiner wants the party to sign; and (f) an optional personal history questionnaire as a means of speeding up the later interview and systematizing the information-gathering process (Greenberg, 2004). The use of a questionnaire provided in advance to the party is a matter of differing practice among qualified forensic psychologists and is helpful to acquire information from a party. Whether someone other than the party may have input into the answers to the questions and whether the use of a questionnaire may deprive the clinical interview of spontaneity should be considered.

The Evaluation Appointment

When the party arrives at the site of the evaluation, the psychologist may want to check the party's identification. This ensures that the person being evaluated is the one referred. If the personal information form was not completed in advance, the psychologist should have the party complete it, including address, phone, number, and other relevant information.

This enables the psychologist to contact the party after the evaluation if necessary.

Early in the evaluation sequence (or even before that date), it is critical to determine if the party has been tested before. Recent testing may obviate using that same instrument because of a test–retest effect (Matarazzo, 1987).

Informed Consent

In all forensic cases, it is ethically and legally necessary to obtain written informed consent from the party prior to initiation of the evaluation procedures. Forensic Guideline IVE states the following:

> Forensic psychologists have an obligation to insure that prospective clients are informed of their legal rights with respect to the anticipated forensic service, of the purposes of any evaluation, of the nature of procedures to be employed, of the intended uses of any product of their services, and of the party who has employed the forensic psychologist. (Committee on Ethical Guidelines for Forensic Psychologists, 1991, p. 659)

Informed consent should include at minimum the following components: (a) a notification of the party for whom the psychologist is working, (b) a brief general summary of the issues to be addressed in the evaluation, and (c) the circumstances of confidentiality. If it is an evaluation conducted under the protection of attorney work product, then the party must be advised of that protection (Melton et al., 1997). If it is an FRCP 35 evaluation, the examinee should understand that all the parties will receive a copy of the evaluation report.

The confidentiality portion of the consent form provides an opportune site to advise the party of conditional disclosures (Shuman & Foote, 1999). These include the legally mandated disclosures such as child abuse and elder or disabled-person abuse (Greene, 1995; Kalichman, 1993; Levine & Doueck, 1995). In some jurisdictions, the evaluator should advise the party of a legal duty to protect others, called *Tarasoff* notifications (Appelbaum, 1985; Monahan, 1993; Treadway, 1990; Wulsin, Bursztajn, & Gutheil, 1983) or notifications related to concern about suicide.

In addition, the consent form should advise the party of the evaluation procedures, usually an interview and psychological testing. The party should be notified regarding the venues where the results of the evaluation may be presented, usually in a written report or in sworn testimony given in deposition in court or by affidavit. The party should also be advised that he or she may terminate the evaluation at any time and will have an opportunity to contact his or her attorney at any time. However, the form should further advise the party that there might be negative consequences for unilaterally terminating the evaluation. Finally, the consent form should include an expectation that the party will be cooperative and truthful.

The psychologist should discuss the consent form with the party and make sure the party understands all of the important aspects before signing (Glassman, 1998). Of course, the party must be competent to sign the consent form (Melton et al., 1997). Although it is very unlikely in sexual harassment evaluations, if the person is not competent, a psychologist must obtain written permission from the party's guardian or counsel or may conduct an evaluation under court order.

ASSESSMENT PROCEDURES

Testing

The initial consideration in testing is obtaining representative responses. If the party is experiencing pain or has a concentration problem, the examiner may schedule tests over series of sessions.

In general, the psychologist should select test instruments that strike a balance between assessing deficits and providing fair procedures in the circumstances. Most psychologists have a group of tests with which they are familiar and feel comfortable. However, in forensic evaluation other criteria may need to be considered in test selection. Heilbrun (1992) suggested that each test selected should meet seven criteria: (a) The test should use commercially available and documented both in its own manuals and in independent publications; (b) the test should be reliable, with a reliability coefficient greater than .80; (c) the test should be relevant to the legal issue or underlying psychological construct; (d) the psychologist should use standard administration for the instrument; (e) the test should be applied only to populations and for purposes for which it was designed, which should guide both the selection and interpretation of the instrument; (f) in general, objective tests and actuarial data are preferable if appropriate research data exist; and (g) response style should be assessed in the context of the evaluation to determine the extent of malingering or defensiveness.

In determining a battery for a particular party, it is appropriate to use redundant measures. These should include at least two paper-and-pencil personality measures. The Minnesota Multiphasic Personality Inventory—2 (MMPI–2; Green, 2000; Hersch & Alexander, 1990; Pope, Butcher, & Seelen, 1997) is used so universally that one would almost have to be prepared to explain why it was *not* used. Other paper-and-pencil measures, such as the Personality Assessment Inventory (PAI; Morrey, 1991) and the Millon Clinical Multiaxial Inventory (MCMI; Millon, 1994), can provide comparable data that confirm or generate hypotheses concerning the immediate and long-term sequelae of sexual harassment experiences. To assess the impact of emotional disorders on cognitive functioning, the Wechsler Adult Intelligence Scale—III (Wechsler, 1997) can provide a picture of the pattern of skills and impairments that may be related to depression or anxiety.

Some measures assess issues directly related to sexual harassment. The Sexual Experiences Questionnaire (Fitzgerald et al., 1988, 1995, 1999) was developed by Fitzgerald and her colleagues to provide a standardized method for recording the experiences of people in the workplace and the impact of those experiences on a range of functioning. The most recent version of the SEQ-DoD includes items that assess the experiences of men as well as women. This scale has not been used extensively in clinical or forensic settings (but see Fitzgerald, Buchanan, Collinsworth, Magley, & Ramos, 1999) and lacks any measures of irrelevant or inconsistent responding, or, more important, exaggeration or minimization. For this reason, the SEQ-DoD must be used with other measures of those response tendencies and may still be subject to measure-specific attempts to malinger or dissimulate. Other specific measures such as the Trauma Symptom Checklist (Briere, 1995) may provide a metric of the impact of traumatic experiences on the party.

In addition, as indicated by Heilbrun (1992), the psychologist should use measures of malingering (Rogers, 1997a; Rogers, Sewell, & Goldstein, 1994). Subscales to assess malingering are built into paper-and-pencil tests such as the MMPI–2, MCMI–III, and PAI. If there is concern that the party is attempting to simulate a psychosis or depression, the Structured Interview of Reported Symptoms (SIRS; Rogers, 1992) has proved to be an effective means of detecting such strategies. In addition, if the examiner has concerns about the party expending sufficient effort in the evaluation, measures such as the Test of Memory Malingering (TOMM; Tombough, 1997) or the Validity Indicator Profile (VIP; Frederick, 1997) may be used.

Although it is unusual to encounter such a response set in sexual harassment litigation, it is possible that plaintiffs may want to portray themselves as virtuous and fault free. Although few specific tests exist to assess defensiveness, the MMPI–2, MCMI–II, and PAI contain measures of a *fake-good* set. These, combined with interview data, can illuminate this pattern of responding

Standardized Interviews

Interview formats that follow a strict sequence or use a branching strategy can often add to the validity and reliability of the evaluation (Rogers, 1995, 1997b). In cases in which posttraumatic stress disorder (PTSD) is an issue, a measure such as the Clinician Administered PTSD Interview (CAPS; Blake, Weathers, & Nagy, 1990) provides a standardized methodology for assessment of both current and lifetime PTSD. In addition, this scale provides a measure of the intensity of symptoms.

Other measures assess general psychopathology on both Axes I and II of the *Diagnostic and Statistical Manual of Mental Disorders (DSM–IV)*. Measures related to DSM Axis I disorders include the Structured Clinical Interview for DSM–III–R Disorders (SCID; Spitzer, Williams, Gibbons, & First, 1990), the Diagnostic Interview Schedule (DIS; Robins, Helzer, Cottler, & Golding, 1989), and the Schedule of Affective Disorders (SADS; Spitzer & Endicott, 1978). In addition, the Structured Interview for DSM–IV Personality Disorders (SIDP–IV; Pfohl, Stangl, & Zimmerman, 1982; Pfohl, Blum, Zimmerman, & Stangl, 1989) is a useful measure for fleshing out personality disorders. Of these, only the SADS has been the topic of extensive research to determine the impact of response set on the responses of the examinee (Duncan, 1995; Rogers, 1988; Ustad, 1996).

Structured interviews provide two main advantages for the evaluating psychologist (Rogers, 1997b). First, the measure standardizes "(1) the form and sequencing of clinical inquiries and (2) the quantification of endorsed symptoms" (Rogers, 1997b, p. 306). In addition, from a practical forensic standpoint, the standardized interviews will encourage the examiner to ask questions (e.g., do you like to spend your time by yourself or with others?) that may otherwise not be asked. Also, if the examiner determines that an Axis I or Axis II disorder exists, it is a relatively straightforward exercise to provide the court with the specific statements made by the party that support that diagnosis.

Clinical Interviews

The psychologist will almost always conduct an open-ended or semi-structured clinical interview with the party. A record of the interview must capture with some accuracy what took place in the session (see Forensic Guideline IVB, Committee on Ethical Guidelines for Forensic Psychologists, 1991). Handwritten notes are most often employed. However, the psychologist must bear in mind that those notes may later become evidence in the case and be careful to ensure the legibility and accuracy of the record. Before initiating the interview, the examiner may consider whether to audiotape or videotape the interview. This, of course, requires the permission of the party (see ethical standard 4.03, American Psychological Association, 2002), and as mentioned previously, the examiner may also want to obtain the permission of the party's counsel before using recording techniques. In deciding whether to record the interview electronically, the examiner may consider several issues. If the party is paranoid and distrustful, as are some litigants who believe they are victims of retaliation or reprisal, the plaintiff may insist on recording the session as a measure of self-protection. Under those circumstances, the examiner should record the session to avoid being dependent on the party for the record. A related circumstance for recording the interview may occur if the party expresses a concern about the intrusiveness of the evaluation procedures. An electronic record can capture the tone of the examiner's questions. The examiner may want to record the session to demonstrate that the examiner is been fair and has not badgered or otherwise mistreated the party. Another reason to record may be triggered by concerns that the party may demonstrate qualitative aspects of conduct such as an overtly psychotic presentation that may be difficult to capture in written notes. Concerns that the party is made uncomfortable or guarded by the technique or that the mechanics of the recording interfere with the pace of the evaluation may prompt the examiner to avoid making a recording.

In conducting the interview, the psychologist should demonstrate the same balanced and fair approach taken throughout the process. A professional tone should be maintained in the interview and the orientation should be one of gathering facts that will later serve as a partial basis for professional opinions (Jensvold, 1993). Because many psychologists who do forensic work were trained as clinical psychologists, they may be tempted to use clinical techniques to establish and enhance rapport with the plaintiff. Although some degree of rapport is necessary for effective interviewing, psychologists should beware of using therapeutic techniques in the forensic interview. Not only does it blur the distinction between the therapist and forensic role (Greenberg & Shuman, 1996), but it may be later seen as an unfair method designed to take advantage of the plaintiff's emotional vulnerability.

Collateral Interviews

Interviews with people who know the party, usually family, friends, and coworkers, are recommended by a number of authorities (Fennig et al., 1994; Fuller, Lee, & Gordis, 1988; Gladsjo, Tucker, Hawkins, & Vuchinich, 1992; Heilbrun, 1990; Heilbrun, Rosenfeld, Warren, & Collins, 1994; Melton et al., 1997; Paetzold & Willborn, 1994). The purposes of these interviews include extending the findings from other sources, such as records and clinical interviews, and corroborating or contradicting facts provided by the party.

Such interviews are governed by the Forensic Guideline VIE: "When forensic psychologists seek data from third parties, prior records, or other sources, they do so only with the prior approval of the relevant legal party or as a consequence of an order of a court to conduct the forensic evaluation" (Committee on Ethical Guidelines for Forensic Psychologists, 1991, p. 661). Greenberg (2004) suggests obtaining written consent to contact informants from the client at the time of the evaluation. Although these conversations are most often conducted over the telephone, under Standard 4.02 in the APA Ethics Code, it may be appropriate to advise the collateral source about how the material will be used and the lack of confidentiality regarding what the collateral says.

When considering with whom to conduct collateral interviews, some obvious persons are the spouse, roommate, lover, coworkers, friends, clergy, and neighbors. The examiner should attempt to talk to one or two people who are not involved directly or indirectly in the lawsuit. In a sexual harassment case, the cast of informants is likely to be polarized according to whether they believe the alleged harasser or the plaintiff. In these cases, it is useful to talk to people from both camps to strike a balance and avoid an appearance of bias.

In some instances, it is not possible to obtain permission to interview collaterals. As this permission is at the party's discretion, plaintiff's counsel may determine that such interviews are unlikely to further the interests of his or her client and may forbid such contacts. Parties who do not want their involvement in litigation known to friends and family may not provide permission. In such instances, the psychologist may ask retaining counsel to subpoena collaterals for deposition. In this setting, the questions that would ordinarily be asked in the brief telephone calls will be gathered under oath and will be part of the official record of the case. In this instance, it may be appropriate for the psychologist to provide a list of questions or information to be gathered to the examining counsel so that essential information will be obtained. Care should be taken to provide questions only for essential information gathering and not for strategic reasons so that the examining psychologist does not veer into the role of a trial consultant.

Additional Record Collection

In the course of the clinical interview, the examiner may become aware of other documentary sources that can illuminate the client's case. These may include prior evaluations. As the psychologist's work may span a number of months, it is appropriate to review any other medical, legal or psychological records generated in the interval between the initial retention in the case and the time a report is prepared.

Collation and Interpretation of Data

In interpreting the data generated in the evaluation, the examiner should give appropriate weight to data gathered from all sources and entertain a wide range of hypotheses. Based on this review, the psychologist may then develop general conclusions. Once these are fixed, the expert may review the data to examine the best case for the contrary position from that adopted. For example, if the data are supportive of the plaintiff's claim, the psychologist can examine all the data that support the defense's claim and determine why those data do not guide the final conclusions (Greenberg, 2004).

Next, the psychologist must decide the extent to which the test data are critical for the conclusions. Because the interpretation of test data is always done in the context of data from other sources, these data should not be the sole basis for major conclusions but should support them. The examiner should also decide how to deal with data contradicting the conclusions.

In reviewing the data from an evaluation, the psychologist should weigh both ideographic and nomothetic data (Heilbrun, 2001). Ideographic data are case specific because they characterize the party as a distinct and unique individual. Attention to these data ensures accuracy in the analysis through the cross-checking of an individual's information from multiple sources. Nomothetic data are gathered in research with defined groups. These scientific data anchor the assessment to a body of research that adds considerably to the accuracy and validity of the expert's conclusions. Nomothetic data can be used to validate ideographic information and as a basis for predictions concerning the plaintiff. In sexual harassment cases, these predictions most likely pertain to the long-term impact of the alleged harassment.

Discussion With Retaining Counsel

Before committing the results of the evaluation to print, the psychologist will often have an oral discussion of the results with retaining counsel. In Rule 26 evaluations, this discussion may allow the retaining attorney to make a decision about whether it is advisable to have the psychologist testify. In settings in which a report is mandated, the discussion gives counsel an idea of what to expect in the final product. In conversations with counsel, it is critical for the psychologist to make it clear that his or her conclusions from the evaluation will not be shaped by the discussion with the lawyer. At this point, as in the whole process, balance and fairness are the rule.

The psychologist may consider the option of providing a draft of the written report to retaining counsel. While this option would allow for counsel to correct any mistakes of fact present in the report, it is ill advised (Babitsky & Mangraviti, 2002). Not only does this procedure create a draft report, which is discoverable by opposing counsel and a fertile ground for deposition or cross-examination, any revisions offered by retaining counsel and accepted by the expert may provide an appearance of bias. If the final report contains errors of fact, a supplementary report correcting those errors is the most efficient cure.

Report Preparation

As noted previously, a written report is mandated by FRCP 35. However, a report will also be essential in almost any setting in which the retaining attorney considers calling the examining psychologist as a witness in trial. For a report to be congruent with professional standards, it should contain a number of elements (Heilbrun, 2001). First, the writer should appropriately attribute information to the sources from which it was gathered. This attribution not only sharpens the thinking processes of the expert psychologist but also allows opposing counsel and the court to appropriately evaluate the reliability of and reasoning behind the expert's conclusions. Second, the report should avoid the use of technical jargon. Because many of those reviewing the psychologist's reports have little or no mental health training, the use of jargon has the potential to create confusion. By avoiding jargon and using lay terms to capture the psychologist's observations and opinions, the expert is using a language common to all potential readers. Third, the report should be written in sections that enhance clarity and assist the reader to understand the writer's conclusions. This kind of organization allows the report to stand alone as a document and to add to the presentation of oral testimony in deposition or trial.

The report should address what procedures were employed, upon what information the expert based opinions, and of course, the opinions themselves. This discussion should be followed with a statement concerning causation, which links the actions of defendant persons or organizations with the reactions of the plaintiff. In general, the report should be sent to the retaining counsel and that party should be allowed to distribute copies to opposing counsel and the court.

The evaluation report should demonstrate the psychologist's balanced and objective approach to the case. The report should present the information for the reader in such a way as to show bias toward neither the defendant nor plaintiff. Instead, an exploration of the data in a way that illuminates both the strengths and weaknesses of the case is desirable. Some writers (Greenberg, 2004) advocate inclusion of a section in the report that looks at the data from the perspective of the nonhiring party. If the psychologist is hired by the plaintiff in the case, at least one part of the report should highlight aspects of the data indicating that injuries may not have been attributable to the alleged harassment or that the injuries may not be serious or long lasting. By taking a balanced approach to the data, the examining psychologist not only fulfills the ethical obligation for accuracy and fairness but also is likely to fare better in later phases of the case.

DISCOVERY

Legal Basis

In the context of expert testimony, discovery is designed to accomplish two purposes for the side seeking discovery (Shuman, 2000a): to allow for effective "challenge or response to an opponent's expert, and it may identify potential expert witnesses" (Shuman, 2000a, pp. 6–19). In other words, the other side has a right in most cases to know what the psychologist is going to say and the basis for the psychologist's opinion. Because of the pivotal role of discovery in the legal process, the law provides the courts with tools to compel compliance. These differ according to the discovery procedure and are detailed in the following sections.

Subpoena

A subpoena is a request for the expert's testimony or documents under the expert's control (American Psychological Association, Committee on Legal Issues, 1996). A subpoena is usually issued following a formal request to the court clerk and is usually in one of two forms: a *subpoena*, which is a written request for a person's appearance at a specific time and place, or a *subpoena duces tecum*, which is a written request for the witness to appear and produce specific items, usually documents, notes, or other records. In most jurisdictions the court rules require written notice of at least 5 working days between issuance of subpoena and date of compliance. Subpoenas have other formal requirements and may be invalid if not in proper form.

Court Order

A court order is issued by a judge or magistrate and may be pursuant to an agreement between parties or *ex parte* (one party seeks an order from the judge without the other party's knowledge or permission). The latter are unusual in sexual harassment cases. In general, the psychologist, under pain of a contempt citation, fines, or even being placed in jail, *must* comply with a court order.

Sworn Statement or Affidavit

An affidavit is a sworn statement usually appended to a pleading or brief by a party. For example, if the defendant wishes to have a psychological evaluation of the plaintiff, it may be necessary to file a motion to show that the evaluation is necessary given the facts of the case. An affidavit from the retained psychologist may be appended to support such a motion. The affidavit is no different from sworn in-person testimony, and the psychologist should verify the accuracy of the written statements.

Deposition

As noted previously, a deposition is sworn testimony before a court reporter. From the psychological expert's perspective, the deposition of the examining psychologist is often the most important record created in the case. It is the chance for opposing counsel to ascertain the bases for the psychologist's testimony, including the database, main findings, and any limitations on the expert's opinions. Depositions also provide a record that serves as material for later cross-examination and impeachment. If the expert changes an opinion between the time of the deposition and the trial, the party taking the deposition may have a basis for impeachment. If facts relied on by the expert are contrary to other facts in the case, this may also comprise a basis for impeachment.

Depositions are usually scheduled and taken by the opposing counsel. The goal of that lawyer in asking deposition questions is to gain information and to further the case for that lawyer's client(s). This can be done by gaining concessions from the expert, causing the expert to undermine his or her own testimony or the testimony of other experts or to admit to the better qualifications or expertise of the opposing expert (Brodsky, 1991).

Before the deposition, the expert should review all of the relevant case data to clarify the data and the conclusions. During the deposition, the psychologist should keep in mind that a deposition transcript is a written document, not a spoken one. The emphasis of a point through tone or gesture may be lost on the finder of fact who may read it.

Review of Other Expert's Data and Report

The psychologist should always ask for all of the data from the other expert. This should be reviewed with an eye on accuracy, appropriateness, and completeness. If both experts use similar or identical instruments, comparisons may be made. A review of these data should allow the expert to determine if the information from that source alters already formed opinions in the case. If so, advise retaining counsel immediately.

TESTIMONY

Preparation

The psychologist should begin preparing for trial weeks before the trial date. This preparation begins with a review of all the case materials generated in the psychologist's office. The psychologist should pay specific attention to those data on which professional opinions are based. The professional should also review the material that contradicts the final opinion. Then, the expert should review the documents in the case.

If practical, about a month before trial, the psychologist should call or meet with the retaining lawyer. In this discussion, it is critical to ensure that the expert has all of the necessary documents and depositions and to obtain up-to-date legal proceedings and issues to determine if anything has emerged that could possibly alter the final opinions. As deadlines for exhibit production are usually some weeks before trial, this discussion should address whether the expert wishes to use charts or graphs as demonstrative evidence. The expert may want to prepare exhibits for the jury to illustrate critical points. These may include test profiles, time lines, sequences, or *DSM–IV* criteria.

It is usually appropriate to meet with the lawyer for whom the expert is going to testify several weeks before trial. This is the occasion to outline the testimony sequence for the upcoming trial. Also, the time available for testimony may be limited, and decisions concerning the detail of the testimony may have to be made.

In structuring testimony, it is important to deal both with the strengths and weaknesses of the retaining party's case. Not only will frank discussions of the data provide the court or jury with an awareness of the expert's fairness and balance in the proceedings but also they will allow for discussion of that material in a controlled situation that will make later cross-examination on the same material less effective. This testimony will also frame the material in a way that is congruent with the testifying expert's conclusions in the case.

On the day of the testimony, the expert should attend to what is taken to the courtroom (Daley, 1996). The expert needs enough material to refresh his or her memory but may exclude extraneous material. The main duty is to teach the fact finder about his or her findings in the case. It is critical to use lay language to discuss results and to avoid jargon (Williger, 1995). The skilled expert will make use of a number of other strategies (Brodsky, 1991, 1999) to enhance communication and clarity.

Concluding the Case

After the court testimony, it is beneficial to discuss the testimony with retaining counsel as a learning experience for the expert. In some cases, counsel may poll the jury to determine the basis for their decisions and may include questions about the expert. This can be an excellent source of feedback.

Records of the evaluation, including test protocols and interview notes, should be kept for at least 6 years and may be maintained longer, depending on the laws and rules in the jurisdiction. Many forensic psychologists keep copies of files for an indefinite period, using methods of record reduction such as microfilming or transcription onto CD-ROM. Records not generated by the expert may be destroyed or returned to retaining counsel. If the case is appealed, it is good practice to keep the entire file until the appeals are resolved.

SUMMARY

From the time of the initial retention phone call to the exhaustion of appeals, the psychologist is required to conduct professional work at the highest standards. Keeping accurate records, attending to the rights of the party and others involved in the case, and maintaining appropriate professional roles are required. Attention to fairness and balance will not only ensure the quality of the psychologist's work but also help the psychologist to develop a respected professional identity.

The legal system is a demanding venue for psychological services. Not only are the stakes high but also the translation of legal demands into psychological terms and of psychological terms into legally useful products requires a solid grasp of clinical and legal issues.

5

ASSESSING LIABILITY ISSUES

Psychological evaluations in sexual harassment cases may pertain to liability and psychological injury to the plaintiff. As indicated in chapter 4, psychologists may offer a wide range of testimony pertinent to these issues. Most of this testimony requires a clinical evaluation of the plaintiff. An evaluation of the plaintiff to determine if the defendant was to blame for what occurred in the workplace is highly controversial. Nonetheless, some courts have permitted evaluating psychologists to address certain liability issues in an examination of the plaintiff, such as whether the sexual conduct in issue was unwelcome or the extent to which the conduct at issue would offend a reasonable person. Lawyers and mental health professionals have weighed in on both the plaintiff's side (Fitzgerald, Buchanan-Biddle, et al., 1999; Streseman, 1995) and the defendant's side of the argument (Feldman-Schorrig, 1994, 1995, 1996; Feldman-Schorrig & McDonald, 1992; McDonald & Lees-Haley, 1996; Rosen, 1995b; Rosman & McDonald, 1999). In this chapter, we review legal and psychological bases for an evaluation and subsequent testimony by a forensic psychologist on liability issues for sexual harassment. First, we discuss the extent to which certain legal elements in controversy in the liability phase of a sexual harassment claim may be amenable to information from an evaluating psychologist and how FRCP 35 and FRE 412 may be applied to compel a psychological evaluation directed toward liability questions. Next, we discuss the scientific bases for psychological opinions on liability issues. Finally, we review literature concerning perceptions of harassment.

LEGAL AND PSYCHOLOGICAL PREMISES FOR PSYCHOLOGICAL ASSESSMENT OF LIABILITY ISSUES

The admissibility of psychological testimony concerning liability is not well established. Once an evaluation is allowed for damages purposes, the two issues may become blurred, and testimony concerning liability may enter *on the coattails* of damages opinions. For example, an expert whose testimony on injuries is admitted may be asked questions that stray into other areas by the examining attorney. In the guise of offering evidence on alternative causation of injuries, an expert may discuss a personality disorder or the complainant's past history as they apply to liability issues.

Evidence may be admitted at trial so long as it is relevant to issues to be determined in the case and tends to make the likelihood of discussion of a fact at issue more or less probable. During discovery, when lawyers are seeking relevant information, the standard that guides the scope of inquiry is broad, namely, whether the inquiries are calculated to uncover relevant information that the parties may later offer into evidence in court. Some limits on the scope of discovery are imposed by the federal or state common-law patient–psychotherapist privilege (*Jaffee v. Redmond,* 1996; Shuman & Foote, 1999), which places information disclosed by a patient to his or her treating therapist off limits. In certain circumstances, courts may rule that the privilege between a therapist and a client is waived in a civil case when a plaintiff places his or her mental state *in controversy*. Depending on the nature and extent of the harm suffered as a consequence of sexual harassment, a plaintiff who claims monetary compensation for emotional distress may be deemed to have placed her mental state in controversy, justifying waiver of the privilege. Consequently, the plaintiff must produce medical and therapeutic treatment records. How far back in time before the alleged harassing events or how long after the harassing events these records encompass will vary from one case to another, based in part on the length of time during which medical treatment ensued. Not all courts follow the same procedures or guidelines in determining the extent of the waiver of the privilege; thus it is important to check local case law and rules.

The Shield

Another limitation is imposed by FRE 412, which restricts the extent to which the plaintiff's sexual history can be delved into in a sexual harassment case (Curcio, 1988). This rule is analogous to rape shield laws, which often apply in criminal cases to protect rape victims from being victimized a second time by having their sexual histories made public. FRE 412 prohibits the introduction of a plaintiff's sexual history to prove that the victim engaged in other sexual behavior or to establish a plaintiff's sexual predisposition. In sexual harassment cases, evidence of this sort may be offered to rebut the plaintiff's contention that the sexual conduct at issue was unwelcome or to rebut the plaintiff's claim that particular conduct was distressing. Some commentators refer to this as the *slut* defense to liability, as it attempts to prove that the plaintiff solicited the harassment or *asked for it* (Streseman, 1995).

In general, evidence of sexual conduct by the plaintiff with persons other than the defendant is irrelevant and inadmissible. For example, if the defendant never contended that the plaintiff had flirted with her, if the plaintiff never complained about the defendant's foul language, and if the plaintiff never discussed her affair or oral sex with the alleged harasser, evidence on those issues should have been excluded at trial. Such evidence could not be considered in determining welcomeness, namely, testimony from (a) a coworker with whom the plaintiff discussed an affair she had with a previous supervisor, (b) a coworker with whom the plaintiff discussed oral sex, (c) a coworker who observed that the plaintiff was flirting with harasser, or (d) a coworker who observed that the plaintiff used profanity at work (*Socks-Brunot v. Hirschvogel, Inc.*, 1999). However, if the defendant can persuade the trial judge that the probative value of evidence about the victim's sexual history outweighs its prejudicial value, the prohibition may be set aside (Bloom, 1997).

A hearing in advance of the trial may determine the admissibility of the evidence at trial. Existing case law on the application of the rule has addressed volitional or intentional sexual behavior on the part of the plaintiff, not unintentional conduct, such as a history of child sex abuse. Thus, one difficulty for the defense when seeking to discover or introduce information at trial about a history of past sex abuse is that the plaintiff in these instances was not engaging in voluntary behavior. Courts have noted the lack of similarity between being a victim of a crime and soliciting sexual behavior in the workplace.

Compelled Evaluation of the Plaintiff

If a court finds that the plaintiff's mental condition is in controversy, pursuant to FRCP 35 or a similar state rule, the plaintiff may be compelled to submit to a mental examination. Not all plaintiffs who seek compensation for sexual harassment place their mental state in controversy, because not all plaintiffs experience negative consequences that cause them to seek treatment from a mental health care provider or to claim monetary compensation for psychological injuries following sexually harassing events. Many plaintiffs may not experience psychological or psychiatric injuries that are severe or diagnosable (Fitzgerald, Drasgow, et al., 1999; Gutek, 1985; U.S. Merit Systems Protection Board, 1981, 1988, 1994). Plaintiffs in these groups may restrict their claims to ordinary or *garden variety* damages in litigation for consequences of sexual harassment such as humiliation, embarrassment, or annoyance. One result of such a tactic is to reduce the range of monetary damages available to the plaintiff.

When the plaintiff does not place his or her mental state in controversy, courts will rarely permit a defendant to examine and evaluate the plaintiff, as the typical reason for allowing an examination of this nature is to permit the defense to look for other potential information regarding alternative causation of claimed harm, aside from sexual harassment. The important fact to bear in mind is that the stated purpose of the evaluation is centered on exploring factors related to causation of injuries, not issues related to liability. Lacking a reason to evaluate injuries, the defense-retained psychologist's inquiry into issues related to liability would be obviated. When the plaintiff seeks monetary compensation for mental distress or injury or the plaintiff's case is premised on an allegation that the defendant intended to inflict emotional injuries, or a tort claim of intentional infliction of emotional distress comprises one basis or all of the lawsuit, there is little dispute that a plaintiff has placed her mental condition in controversy, and an evaluation will typically be ordered.

Some defendants have argued that information about a plaintiff's prior history of sex abuse may be relevant to causation of harm, for example, by providing an alternative explanation as to the source of harm or injury to the plaintiff (McDonald & Feldman-Schorrig, 1994). Damages claimed may be reduced if some of the harms or injuries experienced by the plaintiff were derived from alternate causes, not sexual harassment (*Hurley v. Atlantic City Police Dept.*, 1996). Considerable research (see chap. 6, this volume) has demonstrated that a plaintiff who experienced sexual abuse in the past may be more fragile and vulnerable than other individuals and may suffer more serious consequences than others when exposed to sexually harassing conduct. Thus, the plaintiff's past sexual history may produce evidence of factors that exacerbate the injuries and increase compensation. This strategy may invoke more sympathy for the plaintiff.

Evidence That the Defendant's Conduct Was Unwelcome in the Eyes of the Plaintiff

As outlined in chapter 3, the law requires that a plaintiff demonstrate a subjective perception that conduct or behavior at issue on the part of the defendant was unwelcome. This is the only liability element that rests on subjective perceptions by the plaintiff. Once a target indicates the conduct is unwelcome, the defendant is on notice to desist. Numerous courts have pointed out that the perception of workplace conduct as unwelcome does not turn on the private sexual behavior or history of a target or her sexual naiveté or sophistication. Some lawyers and psychiatrists have expressed the view that a psychological evaluation can permit a determination that a plaintiff unconsciously incited the harassing behavior, even if he or she now claims it was unwelcome.

> For example, a forensic evaluation of the plaintiff might establish that, although she regarded the conduct as undesirable or offensive, she semiconsciously or even unconsciously incited it. This sort of evidence would tend, at least in part, to invalidate the plaintiff's claim. (Feldman-Schorrig, 1994, pp. 336–337)

The theory is that the plaintiff may have a psychological predisposition to engage in behavior that welcomes or *asks for* the harassment. In other words, a plaintiff who is seductive or who merely sends others the wrong signals about her desire for sexual conduct must have a psychological basis for this contradictory and confusing behavior.

Some employers have argued that information about a plaintiff's psychiatric history is relevant to liability determinations because it bears on whether the sexually harassing conduct at issue was welcomed by the plaintiff and whether the plaintiff is a reasonable person. The type of evidence sought by defendants on the issue of welcomeness is a diagnosis of past sexual abuse leading to repetition compulsion, which they contend permits them to demonstrate that the plaintiff invited or solicited the sexual conduct from the harasser or in some other way welcomed it. The psychological viability of this defense strategy is discussed next.

Research Support for Evidence on the Plaintiff's Views of Unwelcome Sexual Conduct

Two psychopathological processes are posited to account for why a plaintiff may appear to ask for sexual conduct in the workplace, when in fact, she finds the behavior offensive: (a) repetition compulsion and (b) personality traits and disorders (Feldman-Schorrig & McDonald, 1992).

Repetition Compulsion

The concept of repetition compulsion derives from psychoanalytic theory "that refers to the tendency of individuals to repeat past behavior despite the suffering associated with it, in an attempt to gain mastery of the original trauma that generated the compulsion" (Feldman-Schorrig & McDonald, 1992, p. 14). The theory is that individuals who have suffered severe prior trauma, particularly child sexual abuse, will initiate a sexual relationship with someone in the workplace as a way of resolving and mastering their traumatic experiences as a child. Evidence for repetition compulsion is found in the frequent observation that people who have been sexually abused as children are likely to be revictimized (Hamilton, 1989; Humphrey & White, 2000; Maker, Kemmelmeier, & Peterson, 2001). For example, women who were sexually abused as children are about twice as likely as nonvictims to become rape victims.

Surprisingly little research supports the purported phenomenon of repetition compulsion. The notion of compelled conduct is questioned as the explanatory or motivating mechanism underlying any repetitive behavior. Although evidence suggests that certain women are repeatedly victimized, no data exist to support the notion that mere repetition, or repeated occurrence, can be equated with truly compulsive activity, wherein feelings of anxiety emerge if the compulsive action is not completed or prevented from occurring (Sandberg, Lynn, & Green, 1994, p. 251). Thus, although substantial support for the phenomenon of revictimization exists, none demonstrates that child sexual abuse victims actively seek new abuse experiences as a means of mastering the childhood trauma.

Many researchers have observed that sexualized behavior is perhaps the most common childhood and adolescent reaction of children to child sexual abuse (Kendall-Tackett, Williams, & Finkelhor, 1993; Paolucci, Genuis, & Violato, 2001; Wells, McCann, Adams, Voris, & Ensign, 1995). Child sexual abuse victims engage in higher rates of sexualized behavior and consensual sexual activity than those who have not had those experiences. In childhood, the sexualized behavior often occurs in the form of precocious sexuality or inappropriate sexual behavior such as public masturbation. In adolescence and young adulthood, child sexual abuse victims are more likely to engage in consensual sexual activity such as petting or sexual intercourse at younger ages. They are more likely to have a large number of sexual partners, to enter into relationships of brief duration (Wyatt, Guthrie, & Notgrass, 1992), and to engage in prostitution (Sandberg et al., 1994; West, Williams, & Siegel, 2000; Widom & Kuhns, 1996). However, aside from the apparent paradox that individuals who were sexually victimized engage in sexual activity at higher rates than those who were not sexually victimized, these data do not support the conclusion that people with childhood sex abuse trauma histories seek or initiate unpleasant sexual conduct from others.

Considerable research has probed why child sexual abuse victims are prone to revictimization. These studies yielded support for three different mechanisms that account for child sexual abuse victims' higher rates of subsequent sexual assault: posttraumatic symptoms, interpersonal problems, and target attractiveness.

Symptoms of PTSD are frequent consequences of child sexual abuse (e.g., J. D. Ford & Kidd, 1998; Gold, Lucenko, Elhai, Swingle, & Sellers, 1999; Leitenberg, Greenwald, & Cado, 1992; Roesler & McKenzie, 1994; M. B. Stein et al., 1996; D. A. Wolfe, Sas, & Wekerle, 1994). This strong association prompted some researchers to infer that revictimization of child sexual abuse victims is causally related to the experience of PTSD symptoms (Arata, 2000; Briere & Runtz, 1987; Dansky, Roitzsch, Brady, & Saladin, 1997).

The posttraumatic symptoms may arise spontaneously or in response to events that recapitulate the original child sexual abuse. Suppose a man attempts to control or overpower a woman who was a child sexual abuse victim. She may respond to that attempt by experiencing numbing and a sense of helplessness related to the original trauma. These reactions lead to a higher probability that a second assault will occur, perhaps by delaying an adaptive or a protective response to the new threat (Wilson, Calhoun, & Bernat, 1999). Likewise, the symptom of dissociation may prime the child sexual abuse victim for repeated assault (Briere & Runtz, 1988; Martin, 2000; Sandberg et al., 1994) by causing the target to become passive while dissociating in response to the new threat. Although both kinds of symptoms appear to prime the child sexual abuse victim for subsequent revictimization, recent studies suggest that compared with dissociative symptoms, the presence of PTSD symptoms is a better predictor of revictimization (Sandberg, Matorin, & Lynn, 1999).

Interpersonal problems or impairments may promote revictimization. Impairment of interpersonal perceptions and responses caused by child sexual abuse may prevent the victims from either avoiding a dangerous situation or extricating themselves from one. Support for this hypothesis comes from research showing that child sexual abuse victims are more vulnerable than those without this history to verbal coercion or pressure from people in authority (Messman-Moore & Long, 2000). In addition, child sexual abuse victims are more likely to describe themselves as having difficulty being assertive or as overly responsible and nurturant (Classen, Field, Koopman, Nevill-Manning, & Spiegel, 2001). The same studies indicate that the social avoidance pattern in some child sexual abuse victims may predispose them as targets of predatory individuals.

Target attractiveness coincides with three characteristics often shared by child sexual abuse victims (Boney-McCoy & Finkelhor, 1995). These include an increased need for nurturance, low self-esteem, and an impaired ability to perceive threats (but see Breitenbecher, 1999). These characteristics make the child sexual abuse victim a more attractive target to the prospective offender. Ironically, the same personal attributes that attracted the original child sexual abuse perpetrator(s) may work to attract the revictimizer (Briere & Runtz, 1988).

In sum, current trauma research reveals no credible researcher who posits that repetition compulsion accounts for repeated experiences of trauma by former victims. Rather, the literature reveals a number of reasons why a child sexual abuse victim, compared to a person without that unfortunate childhood experience, may be more vulnerable to subsequent revictimization:

(a) The adult child sexual abuse victim may experience PTSD symptoms, which interfere with avoidance of or escape from dangerous circumstances; (b) interpersonal perceptions or distortions may cause the child sexual abuse victim to be more compliant in the face of demanding authority figures; and (c) increased target attractiveness may cause the child sexual abuse victim to present characteristics that raise her probability of being chosen as a focus of a predator's attention. These characteristics may occur in combination for a given individual, increasing the probability that a person with a childhood sexual abuse history will be revictimized. However, none of the scientifically validated aspects of postchildhood sexual abuse behavior support the notion that the child sexual abuse victim, actively or passively, consciously or unconsciously, seeks revictimization.

Personality Traits and Disorders

Several writers have speculated that individuals who have particular constellations of personality characteristics or those who evidence frank personality disorders may convey the mistaken impression that sexual conduct is welcome. For example, plaintiffs with personality disorders may "create situations in which they eventually become victimized" (Rosman & McDonald, 1999, p. 138). Some experts testifying in sexual harassment cases have diagnosed a large proportion of plaintiffs with personality disorders (Long, 1994). The contention is not that the plaintiff is the victim of sexual discrimination, but that "there are also numerous cases in this area in which the plaintiff is really a 'pseudo-victim,' who sets the stage, directs the show, and then blames the employer or coworkers for the unhappy ending" (McDonald & Lees-Haley, 1996, p. 57). This strategy shifts the focus from the actions of the defendant to the psychology of the plaintiff and inquires whether the plaintiff's personality traits or disorder caused the plaintiff to invite or appear to invite the sexual conduct in the workplace.

Histrionic and borderline syndromes are implicated as sources of confusion on the part of the plaintiff about seeking out sexual conduct in the workplace (McDonald & Lees-Haley, 1996). Some aspects of a Histrionic Personality Disorder may give rise to mistaken impressions that sexual conduct in the workplace is welcome. The characteristic sexually provocative dress and manner of histrionic people, along with their tendency to engage in flirtatious behavior with others, may give rise to the mistaken impression of sexual interest on the histrionic plaintiff's part. Yet, histrionic people are often unaware of the impact of their behavior on others and are surprised when people take their flirtatious behavior as an invitation to sexual activity.

People with an unstable pattern of behavior associated with the Borderline Personality Disorder tend to be manipulative and affectively mercurial (Feldman-Schorrig, 1994; McDonald, 2000). In relationships, people with borderline personality disorder may shift rapidly from nurturing and flattering to paranoid, suspicious, and rageful. Some lawyers and experts have suggested that in the workplace, a borderline employee will initiate relationships with sexualized conduct and then "suddenly change her mind and angrily accuse her colleagues of 'harassing' her" (McDonald, 2000, p. 111; McDonald & Lees-Haley, 1996).

These descriptions are derived from the diagnostic criteria for these personality disorders outlined in the *DSM–IV* (American Psychiatric Association, 2000) or the literature related to the syndromes (e.g., Millon, 1996). Plaintiffs who meet the criteria for these personality disorders may evince behaviors relevant to a clinical inquiry concerning whether sexual conduct in the workplace is perceived by the plaintiff as unwelcome and offensive. However, a preliminary issue for the forensic examiner is the extent to which these personality disorders may be implicated in a significant number of sexual harassment claims and how the psychological expert can approach an assessment of a plaintiff to determine the impact of Histrionic or Borderline Personality Disorders.

To estimate the extent to which the presence of Borderline Personality Disorder may account for complaints of a hostile work environment, the prevalence of the disorder in the general population is relevant. The *DSM–IV–TR* (American Psychiatric Association, 2000) notes that Borderline Personality Disorder afflicts about 2% of the general population, and Histrionic Personality Disorder affects a slightly higher proportion, 2%–3%. Thus, these disorders are relatively rare.

A closer look at the diagnostic criteria for general personality disorder in the text revision of the *Diagnostic and Statistical Manual of Mental Disorders* (American Psychiatric Association, 2000) is further instructive. First, an Axis II Personality Disorder is a serious, longstanding, and enduring condition that differs significantly from the expectations of the person's culture. Second, the disorder is evident in two of the following four areas: cognition, affectivity, interpersonal functioning, or impulse control. Third, the personality disorder adversely affects a number of life areas, including social or occupational functioning. Thus, similar patterns of seductiveness or confusing and destructive relationships should be evident outside the workplace. It is improbable that the first and only time that a worker complains of inappropriately initiated sexual conduct will be in the context of the current litigated case. Similar events should have occurred in other occupational or social settings. To support an opinion that the plaintiff initially instigated conduct perceived to be unwelcome, the forensic examiner should seek corroborative evidence, especially from former work settings or contemporaneous nonwork situations.

The presence of a preexisting personality disorders is typically evident in impaired functioning in a number of life areas, such as relationships, behavioral control, and work functioning, for a significant time period before the onset of the alleged hostile work environment. The number of people with preexisting personality disorders who are likely be employed and in a position to lodge a sexual harassment claim is further limited, because the impairment caused by personality disorders is often sufficiently severe to prevent those individuals from working in competitive employment. Some illustrative data come from a long-term follow-up study of 500 patients in a New York hospital and a similar study in Finland (Antikainen, Hintikka, Lehtonen, Koponen, & Arstila, 1995; Stone, 1990). All of the patients were treated as inpatients in a comprehensive program. During the follow-up period, only 33% of the men and 59% of the women were employed in full-time work. The best predictor of employment was whether the individual had a successful work history before hospitalization.

As noted in chapter 1, over half of the women in the general population report the experience of sexual harassment. This suggests that only a small proportion of sexual harassment reports derive from individuals with either of those diagnoses. Moreover, only a small percentage of those who were sexually harassed ever file suit against their employer (Fitzgerald, Swann, et al., 1995).

In sum, a review of data on the impact of personality disorders indicates that the presence of personality disorder and severely disturbed behavioral traits may account for a few cases of false or unsubstantiated sexual harassment complaints. That is, a very small proportion of people with these conditions may display behavior that provides an observer with the impression that they welcome sexual conduct in the workplace. However, these cases will be extremely rare and are easily distinguished from the more frequent experience of unwanted workplace sexual conduct because (a) the worker with Borderline or Histrionic Personality Disorder will be sexually provocative or seductive in other work contexts and in other life areas; (b) the worker will demonstrate other characteristics of the personality disorder and impairments in multiple life areas outside of work; (c) the behavior will be marked by conduct that acquaintances and coworkers define as inappropriate in the circumstances; and (d) the personality disorder will be characterized by findings on psychological tests that differentiate a worker with personality disorders from others. The forensic psychologist should assess these instances through a plaintiff interview, document review, and collateral interviews. A thorough psychological evaluation will help resolve the origins of the worker's behavior.

Evidence About a Reasonable Person Versus Plaintiff Reasonableness

As a general rule, the *reasonable person* test applies to the totality of circumstances in a sexual harassment case and addresses the conduct of the defendant, not the state of mind of the individual plaintiff. The legally relevant question is whether, ignoring and setting aside what the plaintiff thinks and feels, a hypothetical reasonable person from the relevant community and in those circumstances would regard the defendant's conduct as sufficiently severe, pervasive, or abusive to comprise a hostile workplace environment. A debate in the legal literature arose on how to define the legally relevant community, that is, whether it should be comprised of women or *reasonable women*, because women are the most frequent victims of workplace sexual harassment, or whether the relevant legal community standard should be derived from the perspective of both men and women. In *Harris v. Forklift Systems, Inc.* (1993), the U.S. Supreme Court endorsed a standard that focused on a reasonable person in the position of the victim, not a reasonable woman test, which had been adopted in one jurisdiction (*Ellison v. Brady*, 1991).

A determination that a reasonable person would find no abusive, hostile work environment existed may imply that the plaintiff, by comparison, is unusually sensitive. However, the inquiry into this issue does not center on the plaintiff. Even if a psychological evaluation indicates that the plaintiff suffers from a disorder that afflicts only a small percentage of the population, the issue is not resolved legally, as the legal issue is not how reasonable or normative the plaintiff is, but how the community standard is applied to the plaintiff's circumstances. Community standards may reflect that a defendant's conduct is hostile and abusive in cases in which the plaintiff is mentally ill or impaired, just as they may reflect no hostile and abusive determination in a case in which a plaintiff is mentally healthy. In other words, the more useful psychological research that bears on the issue of what a reasonable person or woman might think about a course of conduct comes from experimental studies of perceptions of sexual harassment, not from clinically oriented studies of individual pathologies. Evidence gathered in the course of an individual evaluation that shows that a particular plaintiff could not accurately determine the nature of others' actions and was undermined by past experiences or psychopathology cannot inform community standards regarding reasonable conduct in the workplace.

A well-known psychiatrist contended that a psychological evaluation of the plaintiff can inform the fact finder on the issue of reasonableness in determining liability:

> The requirement of reasonableness can be read unmistakably to say that if a sexual harassment plaintiff is a hypersensitive individual who, because of her psychological history or makeup, is offended by workplace conduct that a normal, reasonable person would not find offensive, such a plaintiff cannot prevail in a sexual harassment claim. (Feldman-Schorrig, 1994, p. 336)

This statement may be accurate, but the problem is that some mental health care professionals have interpreted this to warrant an inquiry into whether the plaintiff is a reasonable person, rather than an inquiry into whether a normal, reasonable person perceives the conduct to be hostile and abusive. Liability turns on the latter issue in sexual harassment cases. Nevertheless, some courts permit litigation over the plaintiff's perceptions as they pertain to liability. Some lawyers and mental health professionals who train litigators contend that such inquiries are not only legitimate but necessary as part of the fact-finding process in sexual harassment cases (Feldman-Schorrig, 1994, 1995, 1996; Feldman-Schorrig & McDonald, 1992; McDonald & Lees-Haley, 1996; Rosen, 1995b; Rosman & McDonald, 1999). The following discussion examines the scientific basis for assessing the extent to which the plaintiff's perceptions of the hostile and abusive conduct are reasonable.

Research Support for Evidence on the Reasonableness of the Plaintiff

According to some commentators, the issue of whether reasonable people in the position of the plaintiff would find the harassing conduct so abusive that a hostile work environment existed reduces to a question whether the plaintiff was for some reason hypersensitive to relatively normal workplace behavior, inclined to misperceive innocuous behavior as offensive, and inappropriately sexual. Those who advocate this notion focus on a history of child sexual abuse as the origin of hypersensitivity and distorted perceptions.

At least one legal practitioner contends that women with a history of child sexual abuse manifest a pattern of posttraumatic reactions (McDonald, 2000). Hypervigilance, a common symptom of posttraumatic reactions, is believed to translate directly into workplace hypersensitivity: "This fear and hypervigilance may be manifest as a form of hypersensitivity to perceived sexual cues in the workplace" (McDonald, 2000, p. 113).

Research on the long-term correlates of child sexual abuse (Beitchman et al., 1992; Dhaliwal, Gauzas, Antonowicz, & Ross, 1996; Paolucci et al., 2001; Polusny & Follette, 1995) delineated a number of emotional reactions to sexual abuse, including depression, sexual problems, and anxiety disorders. However, hypervigilance is rarely observed as a freestanding symptom. Although about half of child sexual abuse victims report PTSD symptoms (Polusny & Follette, 1995), there are no data concerning the proportion of those with that diagnosis who manifest a specific hypervigilence response. Current research fails to support the contention that a significant proportion of child sexual abuse victims experience hypervigilance, much less that they systematically misperceive daily interpersonal experiences on the basis of

PTSD reactions. In fact, some experimental research suggests that hypervigilant people may be better problem solvers than others (Johnston, Driskell, & Salas, 1997). More fundamentally, PTSD hypervigilance has a specific function in relation to new experiences: It leads the trauma survivor to *avoid* potentially dangerous situations, not to immerse herself in them.

Most notably, revictimization research does not suggest that trauma victims are unusually sensitive to trauma-related signals but rather that they are insensitive to them. For example, women who are revictimized "exhibit delays in the recognition and response to danger cues in sexual interactions" (Wilson et al., 1999, p. 709).

Some research directly examined the link between prior sexual victimization and sexual harassment. One study determined that women who had a prior experience of sexual victimization were no more sensitive to sexual harassment scenarios than were those who did not (M. E. Reilly, Lott, Caldwell, & DeLuca, 1992). Other researchers indicate that soldiers who reported a prior experience of child sexual abuse were more likely to report less severe sexual harassment than were those who were physically abused, who were more likely to report more severe harassment (L. N. Rosen & Martin, 1998). This finding would support the notion that child sexual abuse victims are more sensitive to gender harassment and unwanted sexual attention and respond actively to sexual harassment. In another study involving female college students, half of the participants had prior experiences of child sexual abuse (Fitzgerald et al., 1999). The experimenters exposed both groups to a range of sexually harassing behavior on videotape. The results indicated that both groups had similar reactions to the harassment depicted on film. When asked how they would respond in the same situations, both groups responded similarly. In short, this study provided no support for the notion that child sexual abuse victims become hypersensitive.

In sum, the available research indicates that a psychological assessment aimed at commenting on the reasonable person standard is fraught with difficulty. There is no support for the notion that the experience of child sexual abuse on the part of the plaintiff makes him or her misperceive workplace experiences as sexual harassment when others similarly situated view the behavior as innocuous. This is the critical differential applicable to the legal standard of a reasonable person. There is no scientific basis to assume that a significant number of people who have experienced child sexual abuse are hypervigilant in relation to social sexual stimuli. Some research on the relationship of child sexual abuse to workplace sexual harassment suggests that child sexual abuse victims are more likely to report lower levels of workplace harassment than those who lack that experience. A heightened tendency to report workplace sexual harassment does not imply a tendency to misperceive sexual harassment where none exists. It may well reflect a more coherent, mobilized response to sexual harassment on the part of child sexual abuse victims compared with those who "ignore milder forms of sexual harassment, and only answer positively if they have experienced coercion, or more frequent occurrences of gender harassment and unwanted sexual attention" (L. N. Rosen & Martin, 1998, p. 280).

Research on Perceptions of Sexual Harassment

Extensive social–psychological research has addressed normative perceptions of sexual harassment, how people perceive workplace sexual behaviors in particular, and the elements of the overall context that contribute to the perception that behavior is harassing. These findings, which include a number of meta-analyses, are relevant to what constitutes a reasonable woman or a reasonable person (Blumenthal, 1998; Gutek & O'Connor, 1995; Gutek et al., 1999; Rotundo, Nguyen, & Sackett, 2001; Wiener et al., 1995; Woody, Viney, Bell, & Bensko, 1996). More important, from the perspective of the forensic psychologist, this research provides an empirical basis for understanding factors that enter into the perception of events as harassing.

Early research on sexual harassment asked workers about a broad range of interpersonal experiences in the workplace and separated the issue of whether the worker experienced the activity from whether the activity was perceived as harassing or unwanted. This study showed that the prevalence of potentially harassing behavior on the job was high: Three quarters of women reported experiences of nonsexual touching, and about one third reported sexual touching in the workplace. However, fewer than 4% of women saw the nonsexual touching as harassment, and only 24% regarded the sexual touching as harassment (Gutek, 1985). Similar findings (e.g., Barak, Fisher, & Houston, 1992; Hemmasi, Graf, & Russ, 1994; Jaschik-Herman & Fisk, 1995; Powell, 1986; Pryor, 1995; Pryor et al., 1997; Stockdale & Vaux, 1993) prompted a large body of research on variables that affect people's perception of whether an event constitutes sexual harassment. Four factors emerged as important in determining how people evaluate those events: *Actions* on the part of an *alleged harasser* occurred in a particular *context* and related in some way to a particular *target*.

Actions

Sexual behaviors in the workplace have been scaled along a continuum of severity (Baker, Terpstra, & Larntz, 1990; Blakely, Blakely, & Moorman, 1995; Cochran, Frazier, & Olson, 1997; Ellis, Barak, & Pinto, 1991; Fitzgerald, Gelfand, et al., 1995; Lees-Haley, Lees-Haley, Price, & Williams, 1994; Loredo, Reid, & Deaux, 1995; Pryor, 1995; C. W. Williams, Brown, Lees-

Haley, & Price, 1995). For example, Rotundo et al. (2001) discerned the following seven categories of social sexual conduct: (a) sexual coercion, such as sexual bribery or threats if sexual favors were not granted; (b) physical sexual contact, such as kissing or stroking the target; (c) physical nonsexual contact, such as a congratulatory hug; (d) sexual propositions, such as explicit requests for a sexual encounter or affair; (e) unwanted dating pressure, such as persistent requests for dates after the target refused; (f) derogatory personal attitudes or conduct, such as belittling the target's gender and obscene telephone calls; and (g) derogatory impersonal attitudes or conduct, such as sex-stereotyped jokes or comments and obscene gestures.

Some conduct is perceived as more serious and inappropriate than others. Most observers label behavior as sexual harassment when it involves sexual coercion and other overt attempts on the part of a harasser to link some condition or benefit of employment with sexual favors. This definition corresponds most closely with the legal standard for quid pro quo harassment. Men and women alike view behavior that involves sexual propositions, seduction, sexual bribery, or coercion as sexually harassing (but see Dougherty, Turban, Olson, Dwyer, & LaPreze, 1996; Stockdale & Vaux, 1993). At the other end of the spectrum, behaviors that are benign, such as a supervisor's paying for a subordinate's meal, a supervisor's helping a subordinate perform a physically arduous task, a supervisor's opening a door for a subordinate, or hugging a coworker (physical, nonsexual contact) are not seen as sexual harassment (Blakely et al., 1995). Behavior between those two extremes is where some individuals disagree. Cases at either end of he spectrum often settle out of court or are dismissed for failing to meet standards for a prima facie claim (Goodman-Delahunty, 1999). Thus cases in the middle ranges of the continuum may constitute many litigated allegations.

Severe or blatant forms of harassment are often seen to reflect malevolent intent on the part of the harasser (Ellis et al., 1991; Henry & Meltzoff, 1998). Other data (e.g., Pryor, 1985) indicate that to the extent a given behavior is pervasive or consistent, both over time and in relation to people who are similarly situated in the organization, it is likely to be viewed as harassing. Variables related to the actor, context, or target have a reduced or negligible impact when the act itself is a violation of the accepted rules of civil behavior (Blumenthal, 1998; Bursik, 1992; Cochran et al., 1997; Gutek, 1995; Gutek & O'Connor, 1995; Rotundo et al., 2001). Thus, for those extreme or severe instances, the analysis may terminate at this level. In the view of most people, a worker who was raped, groped, or fondled in front of coworkers or who was forced to have sex with a supervisor to keep her job would prevail in establishing that the conduct was unwelcome and that a reasonable person in the position of the plaintiff would find it comprised a hostile and abusive work environment.

The Actor

A number of characteristics of the person who allegedly engaged in harassment are relevant to the perception that the event constitutes harassment. The status of the alleged harasser is a potent variable (Blumenthal, 1998; Bursik, 1992; Dougherty et al., 1996; Ellis et al., 1991; Hendrix, Rueb, & Steel, 1998; Katz et al., 1996; Lester et al., 1986; Loredo et al., 1995; Marks & Nelson, 1993; Reilly et al., 1982; Stockdale, Vaux, & Cashin, 1995; Summers, 1996; Tata, 1993; Wiener, Hurt, Russell, Mannen, & Gasper, 1997; C. W. Williams et al., 1995). The status of the harasser can moderate gender differences in perceived harassment. Men and women are more likely to agree that conduct is sexual harassment when the perpetrator is a supervisor than when the perpetrator is a peer or a coworker (Rotundo et al., 2001).

Researchers commonly assume that the power of the alleged harasser is correlated with his or her status. The higher the rank of the alleged harasser, the more power that person may wield. It is the unfairness in that exercise of power that marks behavior from a powerful person as sexual harassment (Dougherty et al., 1996). A person with more power in an organization is expected to use that power in a benevolent manner. When the power is used malevolently, it is seen to violate expectations associated with the responsibility that accompanies the more powerful role (Dougherty et al., 1996; Pryor, 1985).

However, a power differential is not a prerequisite for the perception of harassment. A recent study (Wayne, 2000) indicated that even when those with less power engage in sexual workplace behavior, it is nonetheless regarded as harassment. A corollary of power is age because older workers are more likely to assume leadership positions in organizations or may possess seniority. There is limited support for the proposition that the behavior of older workers may be seen as more harassing than the same behavior from a younger person (Hendrix et al., 1998).

Interestingly, attractiveness of the alleged harasser has proved to be a relatively robust variable (Hendrix et al., 1998; Popovich et al., 1995; Pryor, 1985, 1995). Unattractive men are seen as more harassing. This finding counters predictions based on feminist or power theories, which posit that the power relationship between the alleged harasser and the target is the most potent variable. The fact that the attractiveness variable is so influential supports the notion that perceptions of harassment are premised in part on commonplace stereotypes about romance (Pryor, 1995; Summers & Myklebust, 1992; K. B. Williams & Cyr, 1992). That is, women may be more likely to view sexual advances from an attractive man as invited because those sexual advances may be viewed through a lens of a potential romantic relationship. For the same reason, married men are more likely to be seen as harassing (Pryor, 1995).

The Context

The context in which the harassment occurs influences perceived harassment. For example, the identical behavior may be tolerable in private but considered harassment in public (Rhodes & Stern, 1995). Workers expect others to act in professionally in work settings. Behavior that violates professional norms is seen as harassing (Pryor, 1995). If the behavior is seen to have an adverse impact on the work group, it may be seen as more harassing (Pryor, 1995). Larger context variables, such as culture, affect perceptions of harassment (Pryor et al., 1997). For example, Brazilian subjects were much less likely to view a given scenario as harassment than were U.S., British, or German participants.

The Target

Several factors related to the alleged target of harassment have been identified. The gender of the target or the person evaluating the alleged harassment has been the focus of numerous studies (Baird, Bensko, Bell, Viney, & Woody, 1995; Blakely et al., 1995; Blumenthal, 1998; Burian, Yanico, & Martinez, 1998; Eisenman, 1995; Gervasio & Ruckdeschel, 1992; Henry & Meltzoff, 1998; Lester et al., 1986; Loredo et al., 1995; Tata, 1993; Wiener et al., 1995). See Blumenthal (1998), Gutek (1995), Gutek et al. (1999), and Rotundo et al. (2001) for reviews. With some exceptions (Dougherty et al., 1996; Marks & Nelson, 1993), women are more likely to rate a given behavior as harassment than are men. This is a highly consistent finding, but many (Blumenthal, 1998; Gutek, 1995; Gutek & O'Connor, 1995; Gutek et al., 1999; Rotundo et al., 2001) have observed that the gender-based differences are small and often overrated. Men and women tend to agree that behavior at the severe or mild extremes of the sexual harassment continuum does or does not constitute sexual harassment. It is in the ambiguous middle-range scenarios that gender differences emerge.

Within genders, individual perceptions are often correlates of other variables. One potent determinant is age. In general, younger people tend to regard a narrower range of behaviors as harassing (Barak et al., 1992; Gutek, 1995; Gutek & O'Connor, 1995). This finding is not universal (Blumenthal, 1998; Ford & Donis, 1996) and may be related to underlying variables that have an impact on perceptions. For example, with few exceptions (cf. Saperstein, Triolo, & Heinzen, 1995; Stockdale, O'Connor, Gutek, & Geer, 2002), older women who have had more experience with sexual harassment than younger women tend to see more behavior as harassing.

It is this personal experience with harassment, and not necessarily age, that causes the older women to view a broader range of actions as harassment (Barak et al., 1992; Blakely et al., 1995; Malovich & Stake, 1990; Mazer & Percival, 1989). Women who claim a strong religious affiliation are more likely to view a given act as harassing (Gutek & O'Connor, 1995; Terpstra & Baker, 1986). Political liberalism has been shown to correlate positively with sensitivity to sexual harassment (Baker, Terpstra, et al., 1990; Malovich & Stake, 1990).

Not much research has focused on the contribution of personality variables to the perception of potentially harassing events. A need for social approval has been shown to decrease sensitivity to harassment. Similarly, women who feel more attractive compared with other women tend to be less sensitive to harassment (Malovich & Stake, 1990), possibly because these women are more accustomed to uninvited sexual attention.

The general attitude of the worker toward sexual harassment has not been shown to play a significant role in the perception of sexual harassment. As part of a large study concerning the impact of sexual harassment on women in both academic and nonacademic settings, researchers administered a measure of attitudes toward harassment (K. T. Schneider et al., 1997). These data indicate a small and statistically nonsignificant inverse correlation between the severity of reported sexual harassment on the SEQ and the scores on the attitude questionnaire.

SUMMARY

In most cases, the court will not allow evaluation or testimony about the plaintiff's perception about liability, avoids the issue of whether the plaintiff's judgment was impaired, and focuses on whether the alleged harasser's behavior was, to objective, reasonable people, sufficient to create a hostile and abusive workplace (Fitzgerald et al., 1999). Some courts may admit expert testimony about liability derived from a psychological evaluation of the plaintiff, regarding whether the plaintiff in some way misperceived otherwise innocuous actions, in some way invited sexual behavior from others in the workplace, or is a reasonable person. In cases in which a court does allow such inquiry, for the forensic psychologist the issue of the plaintiff's perception arises only after an analysis of the objective facts related to the workplace events. A review of the depositions of the plaintiff, defendant, and other people present at the time of the alleged workplace events is the starting point. In most cases, some events are uncontroverted; others are in dispute. A detailed inquiry into the events perceived by the plaintiff will reveal the individual's perspective on what transpired. In certain cases, the events that occurred may be in dispute. For example, the plaintiff may contend that the alleged harasser deliberately touched her breast, and the alleged harasser may contend that no such touching occurred. In other cases, the parties may agree about the events, but disagree as to whether the behavior was a form of sexual harassment.

In the first circumstance, an assessment of the plaintiff's perceptions may be critical as a way of explaining the disparity between the two accounts. If the plaintiff's perceptual capacities are functioning normally, then the inquiry may shift to the defendant or to issues of credibility. But, inquiry into the plaintiff's sexual history is unlikely to enlighten the fact finder about these perceptions. First, the above review indicates that nothing about a history of child sexual abuse alone would account for gross perceptual disturbances sufficient to cause a plaintiff to imagine that an event happened when it in fact did not. Gross misperceptions would be the product of a serious mental disorder

Facts in contention in the current case and the plaintiff's reaction to specific events can be compared with the normative reactions of participants in past studies of social sexual conduct. This comparison may provide a basis to determine some parameters of responses of a reasonable person if placed in the position of the plaintiff. For example, the research suggests that a 45-year-old, politically liberal, churchgoing woman will be more likely to view a given event as harassment than will a 22-year-old, politically conservative, religiously unobservant woman. In a case in which individuals fitting these descriptions observed the same events, some of their differences in assessing the situation may be attributable to differences in the age, political, and religious affiliation. These observations may help the finder of fact to understand differences in testimony among workers regarding allegedly harassing events and the extent to which they are perceived as offensive and abusive.

6

EVALUATION OF DAMAGES

Forensic conclusions concerning plaintiffs in sexual harassment cases should meet four specific goals to be useful from a forensic and clinical standpoint. First, the evaluation should facilitate the integration of data from disparate sources such as interviews, work records, depositions, and psychological testing. Second, the evaluation procedures should permit an individualized approach to the case. The forensic examination should illuminate a picture of the party that is unique, respecting that person's strengths, vulnerabilities, and experiences. Third, the evaluation should acknowledge that many aspects of psychological reactions following workplace events are dynamic. A sexual harassment complaint is very rarely based on a single event. Most hostile work environment claims require a persisting pattern of conduct on the part of the harasser (*Clark County School Distric v. Shirley A. Breeden*, 2001). Thus, the interaction among the target, the harasser, the organization, and other sources of stress must be taken into account. Fourth, the evaluation should address the legal issues. In sexual harassment cases, those usually center on the causal nexus between the actions of the defendants and the reactions of the plaintiff. Many cases also require the determination of the long-term impact and cost to the plaintiff of reactions attributable to unlawful conduct on the part of the defendant. An impaired ability to work, a necessity for retraining or relocation, or a need for psychotherapy may be considered as part of the damages award in these cases.

A useful strategy is to capture a description of the condition of the plaintiff at three times: before the alleged harassment began, during the alleged harassment, and following the cessation of the alleged harassment. These three phases require addressing separate issues, which may interact in complex ways over the course of the plaintiff's life. The following sections focus on these three phases. Although the topics are divided in this manner, the reader should assume that an issue raised in one phase may very well apply to other phases.

An examination of the impact of disparate factors is critical to determine the causal nexus between the alleged harassment and the alleged damages. First, if a life problem is caused by earlier life events and has continued through the time of the evaluation, that problem may be mistaken for a symptom resulting from the alleged sexual harassment. For example, suppose a victim of a rape reports difficulty in social situations with others. That problem could be a continuing symptom of the rape or a reaction to the alleged sexual harassment. Second, the life problem may serve as a vulnerability factor in causing a symptom resulting from sexual harassment to be experienced more profoundly. A plaintiff with a preexisting fragility, known as a plaintiff with an *eggshell skull,* may complicate the analysis of the impact of the alleged sexual harassment. For example, a plaintiff who has experienced a severe battery may react with extreme symptoms to an incident involving uninvited touching. Third, an ongoing problem may be exacerbated by alleged sexual harassment. If a plaintiff has a preexisting panic disorder, sexual harassment may cause panic attacks to be triggered by work-related stimuli.

In the first portion of this chapter, we review the research on target responses to sexual harassment, particularly the likelihood to report the problem and the coping styles adopted. The impact of sexual harassment on the plaintiff's psychological well-being, general health, and outcomes in the workplace is outlined. Next, we review factors most relevant to the assessment of the condition of the worker before the alleged harassment commenced. These factors include details of the impact of historical factors such as a history of prior physical or sexual trauma, preexisting psychopathology, and the effects of ongoing job stress. Finally, we examine the impact of postsexual harassment events, including reprisal and discharge.

RESPONSES TO SEXUAL HARASSMENT

Targets who perceive that they have been sexually harassed engage in continua of behaviors ranging from passive to active and internal to external (Barling, Rogers, & Kelloway, 2001; DuBois et al., 1998; Gruber, 1998; Gutek & Koss, 1993; T. S. Jones & Remland, 1992; Malamut & Offerman, 2001; Terpstra & Baker, 1989). Some may simply cope with the harassment without considering any action to stop it (Gruber, 1989). Others may deal with the harassment in their own, private ways (Magley, 2002). Some targets may attempt to avoid the harasser or to diffuse the harassing behavior by making jokes or stalling the harasser. The target may seek social support from friends and coworkers. A more active target may negotiate with the harasser or ask the harasser to stop. Finally, the target may seek outside help by consulting experts outside of the work situation, going up the chain of command to confront the problem with an immediate or higher level supervisor, or using an organizational system for registering complaints, such as a company's human relations or equal opportunity office.

A robust research finding is that targets of sexual harassment are unlikely to report the events to anyone (Gutek & Koss, 1993). One survey revealed that fewer than one in five (18%) women who had been harassed reported the sexual harassment incident to someone in authority (Gutek, 1985). An even smaller proportion of women (10%) and men (3%) took formal action against their harassers (Knapp, Faley, Ekeberg, & DuBois, 1997). Similar findings have been replicated in a number of settings (Fitzgerald, Swan, & Fischer, 1995; Gruber & Smith, 1995; Gutek & Done, 2001). Most workers attempt to ignore the first few harassment incidents. Behavior may initially appear ambiguous, and the harasser's intent may be unclear absent the larger context that may become evident only later. Women who are subject to repeated harassment are more likely to acquiesce, reflecting a tendency to give up and become passive rather than to resist unavoidable unwanted sexual contact (Thacker, 1996).

The seriousness of the events influences the likelihood that they will be reported. For example, a female worker is five times as likely to report efforts of a supervisor to engage in quid pro quo harassment (sexual bribery) than to report offensive gestures (Gruber & Smith, 1995). This same study showed that the proportion of workers who reported very serious events such as sexual assault (17%) was similar to the proportion who reported inappropriate pressure for dates (15%) and offensive jokes (11%).

Recent research (Magley, 2002) reviewed data from eight studies that examined the coping strategies of workers in both civilian and military settings. The intent of the study was to extract factors that represent the major ways that workers cope with on the job harassment. Four clusters of two behavioral and two cognitive strategies emerged from this research: (a) *Behavioral engagement* included responses that were directed toward solving the problem, such as telling a supervisor; (b) *behavioral disengagement* was more passive and avoidant in nature, and included staying away from the offending worker; (c) *cognitive engagement* included coping strategies in which the target took responsibility for the harassment, engaging in self-blame and recrimination; and (d) *cognitive disengagement* responses were internal avoidance activities, such as minimizing or denying the existence of the harassment. One implication of this research is that much of the time, the fact that a sexual harassment target is reacting to the job circumstances is not always readily observable based on the coping strategy that individual has chosen. These approaches are not mutually exclusive, but are dynamic. In many cases, a target may use one method (e.g., cognitive disengagement) before another (behavioral engagement) is tried.

The data generally indicate that women who were more active after they determine that they have been sexually harassed actually had more negative outcomes than those who were less active (Bergman, Langhout, Palmieri, Cortina, & Fitzgerald, 2002). In large part, the nature of the reaction to reporting is, as one might expect from studies reported in chapter 2, related to organizational climate. Reporting occurs earlier in the sequence and more frequently if the employer has a well-publicized formal and informal complaint process, allowing affected employees options as to how they report the conduct, and if the employer has made it clear that sexual harassment will not be tolerated (Offerman & Malamut, 2002).

Even when no report is made, other coping strategies are used. For example, the data from a large study involving 553 men and 1,782 women showed that people who experienced more severe harassment were more likely to use assertive coping strategies such as institutional complaints (Stockdale, 1998). These people also experienced the most negative outcomes in the form of negative views of both themselves in their jobs and the people with whom they worked. They took leave from work more often and were more likely to transfer from or quit their current jobs. Similar results were obtained in a review of the files of a number of sexual harassment complaints (Coles, 1986) and in a study of university employees (Bingham & Scherer, 1993). Men were especially likely to experience the negative consequences of reacting most actively to the harassment (Bingham & Scherer).

Seeking and receiving social support are important responses to sexual harassment. For example, one study found that women were much more likely than men to respond to sexual harassment by talking to family or friends (Bingham & Scherer, 1993). However, this response did not contribute to greater satisfaction for the sexual harassment target. Dealing directly with the harasser can be a positive means of coping with sexual harassment (Bingham & Scherer, 1993; Gruber & Smith, 1995; Livingston, 1982) and was the most common response reported by women in several studies (Gruber & Smith, 1995; Pryor, 1995).

EVALUATION OF THE PSYCHOLOGICAL IMPACT OF SEXUAL HARASSMENT

Psychological harm is not a universal reaction to sexual harassment. For example, a survey of students, staff, and faculty at Southern Illinios University revealed that although sexual harassment (as assessed by the SEQ) was experienced by a high percentage of men and women in the various samples, the majority of participants who provided details about their "most personally distressing" incident experienced no strong negative emotions (44%–60%) and no negative work impact (65%–89%) as a consequence (Vaux, 1993). Outcomes such as embarrassment, humiliation, pain and suffering, and even severe distress have been termed ordinary or "garden variety" damages, as opposed to more egregious consequences, which comprise psychological injuries, disorders, or disabilities (*Cody v. Marriott Corp.*, 1984; Marcus, 1993; *Tyler v. U.S. District Court*, 1997). The severity of the target's response may vary as a function of the personal vulnerability of the target.

In addition, negative reactions to harassment vary as a function of a number of contextual variables related to the harassment itself, such as the identity of the harasser or the duration of the harassing conduct. For example, in research on military women, the harasser's status (i.e., rank) in relation to the sexual harassment target was an important variable; victims of higher ranking personnel suffered greater psychological injury (Pryor, 1995). Likewise, extended duration of the sexual harassment had a major negative impact on productivity, attitudes toward the organization, and emotional reactions (Thacker & Gohmann, 1996).

Information about the psychological sequelae of sexual harassment has been gathered from diverse sources, such as individual case studies, reports of focus groups for victims of sexual harassment, empirical studies, and research reviews. In the past decade, several comprehensive reviews evaluating research on the effects of sexual harassment have been published (Charney & Russell, 1994; Fitzgerald, 1993; Gutek & Done, 2001; Gutek & Koss, 1993; Sbraga & O'Donohue, 2000; Welsh, 1999). These sources reveal that impairment of life functions, psychological symptoms, and emotional disorders are common consequences of sexual harassment in some targets. For example, women who came to the Working Women's Institute for assistance after their work performance was impaired by sexual harassment answered a questionnaire (Crull, 1982). Psychological stress symptoms were reported by 90% of the women in this sample. Another study focused on the symptoms of women who sought group therapy following experiences of sexual harassment. These women presented identifiable stages of reactions to sexual harassment: confusion and self-blame, fear and anxiety, depression and anger, and, finally, disillusionment (Salisbury, Ginorio, Remick, & Stringer, 1986).

Early studies on the consequences of sexual harassment have been the target of some criticism. Major weaknesses of the research are factors related to (a) participant selection, (b) the operational definitions of sexual harassment and of various job and psychological outcomes, and (c) the extent to which alternative explanations were acknowledged or controlled (Goodman-Delahunty, Shanahan, & Charlson, 2003). For example, researchers have been inconsistent in their definitions of sexual harassment, making it difficult to compare studies and to derive general principles from the body of research (McDonald & Lees-Haley, 1995). Some researchers operationally defined sexual harassment in their own way; few used legal definitions disseminated by the EEOC. The research has not accounted for the reactivity of measures of both harassment and its purported consequences (Lengnick-Hall, 1995). Measures of psychopathology have been crude, and the presence of psychopathology in those who report sexual harassment is often used as a basis for assuming that the alleged harassment caused the pathology, without exploring other sources of the pathology (McDonald & Lees-Haley, 1995). Only very recently have researchers systematically gathered longitudinal data to assess changes in sexual harassment consequences over time (e.g., Glomb et al., 1999; Munson, Hulin, & Drasgow, 2000).

Although initially much knowledge about the consequences of sexual harassment was derived from anecdotal accounts, nonrepresentative samples, and self-identified victims, more recently, researchers have mounted large-scale studies using increasingly sophisticated methods to assess the impact of sexual harassment (Dansky & Kilpatrick, 1997; Fitzgerald, Shullman, et al., 1988; Fitzgerald, Gelfand, et al., 1995; Lancaster, 1999). Several studies have been conducted with stratified samples (e.g., Glomb et al., 1999; Munson et al., 2000), including random samples (e.g., Goldenhar, Swanson, Hurrell, Ruder, & Deddens, 1998; Piotrkowski, 1998; K. T. Schneider et al., 1997; Vaux, 1993). Some researchers have undertaken to distinguish effects and consequences of sexual harassment by subtype of harassment, that is, whether the conduct experienced was sexually coercive or whether the complainant was subjected to a hostile workplace environment (e.g., Cochran et al., 1997; Crocker & Kalemba, 1999; O'Connell & Korabik, 2000). Others have examined the impact of target coping style upon consequences (e.g., DuBois et al., 1998). More sophisticated analyses have been conducted, using structural equation modeling (e.g., Glomb et al., 1999) and controlling for other work stressors (e.g., Fitzgerald et al., 1997; Munson et al., 2000; K. T. Schneider et al., 1997).

The precise nature and extent of the impact of sexual harassment remain debated (e.g., Avina & O'Donohue, 2002). For some time, sexual harassment has been associated in the literature with negative psychological, health, and work-related outcomes. Notwithstanding criticisms of research on the consequences of sexual harassment, the body of research is sufficiently valid and diverse to provide some guidance for psychologists examining sexual harassment plaintiffs. We discuss the psychological, health, and work-related outcomes of sexual harassment in turn.

NEGATIVE PSYCHOLOGICAL AND SOMATIC OUTCOMES OF SEXUAL HARASSMENT

In many instances, the injuries sustained following sexual harassment are temporary and include psychological and somatic symptoms such as distress, disappointment, and anxiety. In other instances, the observed psychological consequences of sexual harassment include more severe symptoms such as generalized anxiety and depression (Amaro, Russo, & Johnson, 1987; Meyer, 1995; Williams & Williams-Morris, 2000), decreased life satisfaction (Birt & Dion, 1987; Utsey, Ponterotto, Reynolds, & Cancelli, 2000), lower self-esteem (Utsey et al., 2000), feelings of lack of control (Birt & Dion, 1987), and social withdrawal (Curry, Hassouneh-Phillips, & Johnston-Silverberg, 2001).

Much research on the psychological impact of sexual harassment fails to distinguish feelings such as unhappiness and discomfort from more serious problems such as symptoms of depression and anxiety. One of the difficulties is the lack of any commonly understood measure of the severity of injury. There have been few attempts to equate psychological outcome measures with any standard of clinically significant impairment or distress, and the methodologies used to measure psychological distress, well-being, or adjustment vary widely. The lack of consistency in measuring and assessing sexual harassment, and in particular psychological sequelae, has made it difficult to identify common patterns or reactions to sexual harassment (McDonald & Lees-Haley, 1995). Conversely, researchers have noted that "empirical documentation of the psychological impact of harassment is difficult to obtain because the symptomatology is multiply determined" (Gutek & Koss, 1993, p. 30).

The psychological impact and health consequences of sexual harassment among a stratified sample (with oversampling in nontraditional occupations) of women (N = 357) in a large utility company were examined (Fitzgerald et al., 1997). The psychological outcomes measured included general psychological distress and subjective well-being. The former was assessed using the Mental Health Index (MHI; Veit & Ware, 1983) and an abbreviated version of the Crime-Related Posttraumatic Stress Disorder Scale (CR–PTSD; Saunders, Arata, & Kilpatrick, 1990), and the latter using the Satisfaction With Life Scale (Diener, Emmons, Larsen, & Griffin, 1985). Higher levels of sexual harassment were associated with more negative psychological outcomes. When discrimination is chronic, as may be the case for some sexual harassment victims, it may produce more severe symptoms of anxiety and depression, such as emotional numbing (Dunbar, 2001), feelings of helplessness (Uomoto, 1986), paranoid guardedness (Newhill, 1990), panic attacks, and sleep disturbances (Dunbar, 2001). Correlations of about .37 were reported in one study between the experience of high-frequency harassment and negative psychological outcomes (K. T. Schneider et al., 1997). These findings were replicated employing essentially the same methodology as Fitzgerald et al. (1997) and controlling for other work stressors in two independent samples of female private-sector employees and female university faculty and staff (K. T. Schneider et al., 1997). Even at low frequencies, sexual harassment affects women's psychological well-being.

A number of studies have been conducted in public and private-sector workplaces. In research concerning female firefighters, 80% of women who said they experienced sexual harassment reported job stress compared with 60% of nonharassed women. In this sample, 23% of harassed women were afraid to come to work, although only 9% of the nonharassed women had such fears (Rossell, Miller, & Barber, 1995). Another study of government employees in1987 and 1994, revealed that approximately 7%–12% said they would have found medical or emotional help beneficial and 2%–3% actually received medical and emotional help (U.S. Merit System Protection Board, 1994). The extent of seven types of sexual harassment, ranging from being exposed to sexually explicit comments to being subjected to a serious sexual assault, in a British sample of policewomen (*N* = 1,802) revealed that the vast majority of women had been subjected to either sexually explicit comments or comments on their own or other women's appearance; 30% had been touched or pinched; 19% received persistent requests for unwanted dates; and 6% reported being subjected to a serious sexual assault. Sexual harassment was associated with an increase in symptoms of psychological distress, as measured by the General Health Questionnaire (J. Brown, Campbell, & Fife-Shaw, 1995).

A study that examined the prevalence and impact of sexual harassment on a sample (*N* = 186) of male and female residents in medical training showed that 93% of the sample reported experiencing one or more incidents of sexual impropriety and transgression, ranging from sexist jokes and sexual comments (the most common) to unwanted sexual contact and sexual bribery. Among the residents, 38% had no emotional reaction to this sexual harassment. Embarrassment, anger, and frustration were reported most often (by over 20% of respondents), followed by anxiety (16%), feelings of violation (11%), helplessness (7%), feeling threatened (7%), and depression (6%; Cook et al., 1996).

Mental health correlates of sexual harassment were assessed in a large sample (N = 2,492) of university students, faculty, and staff (Richman et al., 1999). Outcomes included depressive symptomatology, anxiety, and hostility (measured by seven items from the Center for Epidemiologic Studies [CES] Depression Scale, the anxiety factor of the Profile of Mood States, and the hostility dimension of the Symptom Checklist—90 [SCL–90–R], respectively). In addition, respondents provided data on a variety of measures of alcohol and prescription drug use. For both men and women, sexual harassment was significantly related to all the above measures of symptomatic distress. For women, sexual harassment was also related to increased frequency of drinking, escapist drinking motives, drinking to intoxication, and prescription drug use. For men, sexual harassment related to heavy episodic drinking and prescription drug use. The researchers concluded that it was not possible to determine whether sexual harassment predicts deleterious mental health outcomes or whether individuals with mental health problems are differentially prone to either evoke problematic workplace interactions or to perceive such interactions as harassing.

Researchers in a recent study (Richman, Shinsako, Rospenda, Flaherty, & Freels, 2002) conducted telephone interviews with employees at a large midwestern university. The two interviews, conducted a year apart, used the SEQ and other measures to assess sexual harassment experiences and alcohol consumption over the year interval. The goal was to see how sexual harassment unfolded as a dynamic process, that is, to examine how harassment experiences occurring over the year interval could be seen as a variable that might change alcohol consumption patterns, the baseline of which was established in the first interview. The results indicated that individuals who experienced sexual harassment over the interval were more likely to abuse alcohol. The more severe the harassment, the more likely were the targets to abuse alcohol. Psychological distress proved to be a mediating variable, with those who were more distressed being more likely to use alcohol as a means of reducing this distress.

An analysis of a portion of the data from the 1995 DoD Sexual Harassment Study indicated that for women, the negative impact on health satisfaction was directly related to the frequency of sexual harassment, with a somewhat more pronounced negative effect at higher levels of harassment. Even low frequencies of sexual harassment generated a high number of emotional and physical health problems (Magley et al., 1999). When combined with the more severe quid pro quo harassment, hostile work environments can be adverse to the target's psychological condition (Thacker & Gohmann, 1996). Psychosocial outcomes experienced as the result of workplace sexual harassment in a large sample of female U.S. military personnel were examined (Pryor, 1995). Of those who experienced at least one form of uninvited and unwanted sexual attention, 58% experienced emotional distress (loss of self-esteem, lesser opinion of the opposite sex, and deterioration in emotional and physical condition), and 8% experienced less favorable relationships with their spouses and other family members. Like other studies, this research confirmed that more severe forms of harassment, such as pressure for dates or sexual favors, had the greatest influence on emotional reactions (Pryor, 1995).

Posttraumatic Stress Disorder and Depression

Questions about PTSD have attracted the attention of sexual harassment researchers. Studies applying clinical criteria related to diagnosable psychological disorders are a recent feature of sexual harassment research. A low degree of association has been determined in most of this work, with one study finding correlations between .17 and .19 between sexual harassment and symptoms of PTSD (Fitzgerald et al., 1997; K. T. Schneider et al., 1997). One study of a group of 56 women who were forensically evaluated in the context of sexual harassment litigation revealed that 75% of the plaintiffs had some history of trauma, and among those, one third reported a history of child sexual abuse. Approximately equal proportions of plaintiffs with a history of child sexual abuse (71%) and those without any such history (64%) reported a pattern of symptoms congruent with PTSD. The presence or absence of a history of any trauma did not predict the presence of PTSD symptoms. The researchers did not attempt to distinguish between PTSD symptoms related to prior trauma from PTSD related to the alleged sexual harassment (Fitzgerald et al., 1999). On the basis of this and other research, some scientists have concluded that events that commonly occur in quid pro quo and hostile work environment cases are of sufficient severity to trigger posttraumatic reactions and thus argue that PTSD is an appropriate diagnosis in sexual harassment cases (Avina & O'Donohue, 2002).

From another perspective, many events classified as sexual harassment would not be classified as sufficient to trigger PTSD. Simon (1995) argues that the severity criteria for PTSD must be strictly observed. The *DSM–IV–TR* states the following:

> A. The person has been exposed to a traumatic event in which both of the following were present: 1. the person experienced, witnessed, or was confronted with an event or events that involved actual or threatened death or serious injury, or a threat to the physical integrity of self or others; 2. the person's response involved intense fear, helplessness, or horror. (American Psychiatric Association, 2000, p. 467)

If these criteria are not appropriately applied, behavioral scientists and forensic practitioners may dilute or overextend the scope of the PTSD diagnosis. In sexual harassment cases, most triggering incidents simply do not constitute life-threatening events. Although some workplace harassment involving sexual coercion, unwanted touching, or even circumstances involving humiliation before coworkers may fit within the scope of the current PTSD diagnostic criteria, it is probably inappropriate to apply the PTSD diagnosis to most sexual harassment cases. Overuse of the PTSD diagnosis in this context adds no diagnostic precision and does little to advance the understanding of the finder of fact of the plaintiff's emotional reactions. Those are better described by a review of changes in the plaintiff's ability to engage in day-to-day activities or to function in essential life roles. In addition, the use of PTSD may make diagnosis a focus for legal argument, whereas a more descriptive approach diverts the emphasis from diagnosis to injury.

Work-Related Problems

The most widely and consistently reported form of injury related to sexual harassment is found in behaviors and attitudes about the job itself (Fitzgerald, Swann, et al., 1995, 1997; Gutek, 1985). For example, a British study found that 10% of sexually harassed female police officers reported that their work was adversely affected by sexual harassment (J. Brown et al., 1995). Another study noted that 38% of women who had experienced sexual harassment reported negative feelings about their jobs and that 28% complained of negative sexual harassment effects on workplace relationships (Gutek, 1985).

Subsequent research demonstrated a strong relationship between sexual harassment and job-related outcomes (Gutek, Cohen, & Tsui, 1996; O'Connell & Korabik, 2000; Piotrkowski, 1998; K. T. Schneider et al., 1997). One study determined that the severity of sexual harassment was correlated with the negative impact of sexual harassment on both how women approached their work-related tasks (absenteeism, tardiness, and behaviors generally viewed by management as negative) and their tendency to leave the job (K. T. Schneider et al., 1997). Even relatively low levels of harassment are sufficient to create a hostile work environment and produce significant negative job-related outcomes (Munson et al., 2000; O'Connell & Korabik, 2000; Piotrkowski, 1998).

Sexual harassment also has an effect on job satisfaction, with a specific adverse affect on satisfaction with supervisors and coworkers. Data from a study that followed a sample of women over a 3-year period showed that in addition to reporting impaired relationships within the workplace, women who experienced sexual harassment withdrew from work-related activities (Glomb et al., 1999). In a large-scale government study, 14%–21% of sexual harassment targets experienced a decline in productivity (U.S. Merit System Protection Board, 1994). In a sample of female U.S. military personnel who reported experiencing sexual harassment, 42% experienced productivity problems (diminished quality and quantity of work, less favorable attitude toward work, and less reliable time and attendance), and 60% reported less favorable attitudes toward their colleagues and the organization (Pryor, 1995).

Sexual harassment was correlated with negative job-related outcomes such as aspects of both job satisfaction (specifically, satisfaction with work, coworkers, and supervisors) and organizational withdrawal (e.g., a decrease in productivity or quality of work, absenteeism, thoughts about quitting; Magley et al., 1999). These outcomes were better predictors of employees who had been harassed than psychological outcome variables (K. T. Schneider et al., 1997). The SEQ was used to examine the relationship between two forms of sexual harassment, gender harassment and unwanted sexual attention, and several job-related outcomes in a sample of working women (*N* = 538) drawn from the United States and China (Shaffer, Joplin, Bell, Lau, & Oguz, 2000). Gender harassment predicted turnover intentions, and unwanted sexual attention predicted job satisfaction. Neither form of harassment was significantly related to work commitment or life stress.

Not surprisingly, the role and status of the harasser in the workplace can influence the degree to which the targets experience negative consequences in the workplace. One study showed that consequences of sexual harassment depended primarily on the perpetrator–target relationship: The more formal power the harassers held over their targets, the more likely the targets were to report experiencing negative outcomes. In the case of sexual harassment by a higher level man, only gender harassment was associated with negative outcomes such as work-related negative mood, perceived stress, turnover intentions, decreased satisfaction with supervisor, and increased stress with supervisor. For sexual harassment by equal-level men, gender harassment and unwanted sexual attention were related to higher levels of perceived stress and turnover intentions. Sexual harassment by lower level men was found to have no significant negative consequences for the target women despite the fact that gender harassment is prevalent in this situation (O'Connell & Korabik, 2000). Table 6.1 provides a list of the consequences of sexual harassment that have been observed in research in three different outcome areas: psychological, physiological, and work related.

EVALUATION OF PREHARASSMENT STATUS

History of Child Sexual Abuse

Individuals are exposed to a wide range of adverse childhood experiences that cause them to function less effectively as adults. In the context of evaluations of harm caused by sexual harassment, the most controversial

TABLE 6.1
Negative Outcomes Observed in Victims of Sexual Harassment

Psychological	Physiological	Work related
Fear and anxiety	Sleep disturbances	Impaired concentration at work
Depression	Nausea	Increased absenteeism
Confusion	Dizziness	Decreased confidence in relating to coworkers
Feeling helpless, powerless	Headaches	Decreased work satisfaction
Decreased self-esteem	Tiredness/fatigue	Negative feelings about work
Anger and bitterness	Ulcers	Decreased commitment to the organization
Decreased life satisfaction	Tremors	Increased job turnover
Feeling stressed	Weight loss	
Social withdrawal	Increased physiological reactivity	
Feelings of loneliness or isolation	Dental problems	
Irritability	Increased frequency of respiratory and urinary tract infections	
Self-blame	Decreased sex drive	
Increased suspiciousness		
Emotional numbing		
Disruption in relationships		
Difficulties with sexual relationships		
Disturbed body image, over- or undereating		
Increased use of cigarettes, alcohol, or illicit drugs		
Uncontrolled crying		
Recurrent nightmares		

is the experience of child sexual abuse. Significant research indicates that not all children who are sexually abused experience major negative consequences (Kendall-Tackett et al., 1993; McMillen, Zuravin, & Rideout, 1995; Rind, Bauserman, &Tromovitch, 1998). Individuals who are less severely affected may have experienced less severe abuse, may be more psychologically robust, or may have had more social resources (Conte & Schuerman, 1987; Runtz & Schallow, 1997). Nonetheless, some legal and mental health professionals have concluded that child sexual abuse is a source of a number of emotional problems that may be mistaken for reactions to sexual harassment (Feldman-Schorrig, 1994, 1995, 1996; Feldman-Schorrig & McDonald, 1992; McDonald & Kulick, 2001; McDonald & Lees-Haley, 1996; Rosen, 1995b; Rosman & McDonald, 1999). McDonald (2000) stated the following:

> Prior sexual abuse can cause a whole range of chronic psychopathology later in life that the abuse victim may misattribute to more contemporary events, such as workplace harassment or discrimination. Thus, although a sexual harassment plaintiff may exhibit genuine symptoms or workplace events, it must be determined whether an alternative explanation of the causation of these symptoms is more plausible. (p. 82)

Researchers who have examined the contention empirically concluded that the experience of child sexual abuse is largely irrelevant to the process of determining causation of harm from sexual harassment: "There is no scientific evidence for broad claims concerning the characteristics of survivors involved in sexual harassment litigation and their appeals to empirical findings misread both theory and data" (Fitzgerald, Buchanan-Biddle, et al., 1999, p. 732).

In this section, we apply the relevant literature on child sexual abuse to the functioning of adults in the workplace. Our goal is not to provide a comprehensive review of the extensive child sexual abuse literature, but to provide a basis for the examining psychologist to determine if the plaintiff demonstrates sufficient persistent behavioral residue of child sexual abuse to affect the assessment of the impact of alleged sexual harassment.

The child sexual abuse literature reveals some consistent findings. First, child sexual abuse is a relatively frequent occurrence in the lives of both female and male children. A criterion that the child sexual abuse involve direct physical contact between the perpetrator and victim yields a lifetime prevalence rate from 2.8% to 17.3% among men (Fromuth & Burkhart, 1987; Urquiza & Capra, 1990) and from 6.8% to 28.1% among women (Finkelhor, Hotaling, Lewis, & Smith, 1990; J. A. Stein, Golding, Siegel, Burnam, & Sorenson, 1988). Second, large review studies indicate that people with a history of child sexual abuse experience a range of abusive events (Beitchman et al., 1992; Dhaliwal et al., 1996; Paolucci et al., 2001; Polusny & Follette, 1995). Children who experience child sexual abuse are most likely to be boys between the ages of 7 and 11 and girls between the ages of 7 and 14. For both boys and girls, the average duration of abuse ranges from 2 to 6 years. Up to half of child sexual abuse victims experienced sexual intercourse, with equal numbers reporting oral intercourse. Fondling is a more frequent event, reported by as many as 92% of people with a history of child sexual abuse (Hunter, 1991; Kendall-Tackett & Simon, 1992). Most studies indicate that about half of people with a history of child sexual abuse experience more than one abusive incident. Men are more likely to be perpetrators for both male and female victims. However, in some samples, the majority of men were abused by women (Fritz, Stoll, & Wagner, 1981; Fromuth & Burkhart, 1989). Between one tenth and one half of child sexual abuse victims were abused by family members (Dhaliwal et al., 1996).

Third, the research indicates that people with a history of child sexual abuse, especially intrafamilial child sexual abuse, often come from homes in which there is serious disruption, which may be reflected in domestic violence directed toward the child or a parent (G. R. Brown & Anderson, 1991; Levitan et al., 1998; Mulder, Beautrais, Joyce, & Fergusson, 1998; Roesler & McKenzie, 1994; M. B. Stein et al., 1996). In some cases, researchers have determined that the impact of physical abuse exceeded or equaled the impact of sexual abuse (G. R. Brown & Anderson, 1991). In other cases, the combination of physical and sexual abuse proved to have a more devastating impact than the simple addition of their adverse effects (Mulder et al., 1998). The implication of these findings is that the evaluation of sexual harassment plaintiffs should be broad ranging and not focused on the issue of child sexual abuse. Other family trauma, including spousal violence and child physical abuse, should be included in the inquiry. In some cases, the existence of a child sexual abuse history may serve as a marker for other family-related problems that could manifest as symptoms similar to those seen in sexual harassment targets. For example, if a child was raised in a home in which the father engaged in violence against the mother and children, the child may have learned that staying away from other people during times of conflict was an adaptive strategy. In a sexual harassment case, this voluntary social isolation may be seen as a reaction to workplace events.

Fourth, the literature reveals that people with a history of child sexual abuse experience an increased risk for a range of negative adult outcomes such as psychopathology and impaired capacities for functioning in critical life areas. Specific kinds of psychological maladjustment observed more frequently in samples of people who have experienced child sexual abuse compared to those who have not are outlined in the following paragraphs.

In general, people with a history of child sexual abuse are less well adjusted than those who were not abused (G. R. Brown & Anderson, 1991; A. Jacobson & Herald, 1990; Paris, Zweig-Frank, & Guzder, 1994; Roesler & McKenzie, 1994; Rohsenow, Corbett, & Devine, 1988). A number of studies have implicated child sexual abuse as an element in the histories of people suffering from physical illnesses. Research in both community and patient samples indicates that people with a history of child sexual abuse have an increased risk for a diagnosis of depression (Polusny & Follette, 1995). Likewise, suicidal ideation and behavior have been observed more frequently in child sexual abuse populations (Saunders, Villeponteaux, Lipovsky, Kilpatrick, & Veronen, 1992). In general, the number of suicide attempts in a child abuse patient population is about twice that of similar self-destructive acts in non-child-sexual-abuse patients (Briere, Evans, Runtz, & Wall, 1988; Briere & Zaidi, 1989). People who have experienced child sexual abuse are also at significantly higher risk for substance abuse problems (Polusney & Follette, 1995; Rohsenow et al., 1995), although this may not be true for men (G. R. Brown & Anderson, 1991; Dhaliwal et al., 1996).

Anxiety disorders and particularly PTSD appear to be common consequences of child sexual abuse (Briere & Runtz, 1988). Compared to controls, people with a history of child sexual abuse had a threefold increase in risk for agoraphobia, a fivefold increase in risk for social phobia, a fourfold increase in risk for simple phobia, and a fourfold increase in risk for panic disorder (Polusny & Follette, 1995). A diagnosis of PTSD is common in people with child sexual abuse histories (G. R. Brown & Anderson, 1991; Pribor & Dinwiddie, 1992; Roesler & McKenzie, 1994).

The prevalence of personality disorder diagnoses is higher among people with a history of child sexual abuse (Paris et al., 1994; Silk, Lee, Hill, & Lohr, 1995; Weaver & Clum, 1993). In general, research indicates that the more severe the sexual abuse (i.e., penetration as compared to fondling) and the longer the duration of the abuse (i.e., multiple incidents over multiple years), the more likely that the child sexual abuse victim will be diagnosed later with Borderline Personality Disorder. As Silk et al. (1995) noted: "Perhaps repetition of abuse and not abuse itself fertilizes the soil from which future symptoms and behavior of Borderline Personality Disorder grow" (p. 1062). However, while child sexual abuse may be sufficient as a cause of Borderline Personality Disorder, it is not a necessary one. About one third to one half of Borderline Personality Disorder patients did not experience child sexual abuse (Silk et al., 1995).

However, some writers suggest that virtually all child sexual abuse victims are eligible for the diagnosis of Borderline Personality Disorder (McDonald & Lees-Haley, 1996). People with Borderline Personality Disorder make up a very small proportion of individuals with a history of child sexual abuse. As noted previously, about 25% of the female population has experienced child sexual abuse in contrast with the *DSM–IV–TR* estimate of a 2% lifetime prevalence of Borderline Personality Disorder (American Psychiatric Association, 2000). Thus, the best generalization would be that a substantial portion of people with a diagnosis of Borderline Personality Disorder are likely to be victims of sexual abuse, but only a small proportion of those who were sexually abused as children meet the criteria to warrant such a diagnosis.

Preexisting Psychopathology

A plaintiff claiming damages in a sexual harassment case is at some risk of having a preexisting diagnosable psychiatric disorder. Some defense lawyers and experts submit that the prevalence of preexisting disorders among sexual harassment plaintiffs is high (Feldman-Schorrig, 1994, 1995, 1996; Feldman-Schorrig & McDonald, 1992; McDonald & Lees-Haley, 1996; Rosen, 1995b; Rosman & McDonald, 1999). In this section, we assess the prevalence of these disorders in the general population and discuss how those disorders may be taken into account in the assessment of damages in sexual harassment cases.

Based on the nature of observed psychological injuries in sexual harassment cases, in this section we concentrate on depressive and anxiety disorders, particularly PTSD. A comprehensive study of the prevalence of mental disorders in North America is detailed in a well-respected Ecological Catchment Area Study (ECA) that provides an estimate of the prevalence and impact of mental disorders in the general population (Robins & Regier, 1991). The ECA data on affective disorders indicate that the lifetime prevalence of major depression is 5%, and the lifetime prevalence of dysthymia (a milder form of chronic depression) is 3% (Weissman, Bruce, Leaf, Florio, & Holzer, 1991). Women are more than twice as likely to report depressive episodes as men. In general, employed people are less likely to be depressed (2%) than are unemployed people (3%). For those who are chronically unemployed, the rates of depression are more than three times the rates among those who are employed. This correlation may indicate that unemployed persons are likely to become depressed or, more likely, that the chronically depressed are less likely to function in the workplace. Substantial data indicate that unemployment causes depression (Ginexi, Howe, & Caplan, 2000), but other research indicates that the onset of serious depression predicates later unemployment (Jayakody, Danziger, & Kessler, 1998).

Panic disorders occur less often, with a lifetime prevalence of 1.57% (Eaton, Dryman, & Weissman, 1991). Women are twice as likely to report a panic disorder as men. Although employment statistics were not provided in this study, the data indicate that the prevalence of panic disorder among those who are financially dependent on welfare or social security is fourfold for men and threefold for women as compared the occurrence of this disorder among those who function independently.

Generalized anxiety disorder is often comorbid with depression or other anxiety disorders. One-year incidence rates for generalized anxiety disorder as a comorbid disorder are 3.76%, but as a freestanding disorder, there is a lower incidence of 1.72% (Blazer, Hughes, George, Swartz, & Boyer, 1991). Severity of this disorder is inversely related to occupational and income levels.

At a lifetime prevalence of 1%–1.3%, PTSD is relatively rare in the general population (Davidson & Fairbank, 1993). However, in populations of people who have experienced trauma, such as the survivors of the Mt. St. Helens eruption, the rates of PTSD were three times higher. For people who have experienced crime victimization, the rates are significantly higher. High PTSD lifetime prevalence rates occur among rape survivors (35%) and individuals who experience sexual molestation (23%), aggravated assault (39%), or the homicide death of a family member or friend (24%; Kilpatrick & Resnick, 1993). Similar data emerged in a national study of over 4,000 women (Resnick, Kilpatrick, Dansky, Saunders, & Best, 1993). This study indicated that the exposure to a major life stressor sufficient to meet Criterion A as defined by the *DSM–IV* was 69%. Severe or chronic PTSD is rarely the only symptom the trauma victim experiences and usually occurs as a comorbid disorder (Greene, 1995). Most commonly seen with PTSD is depression, but dissociative disorders are also comorbid with PTSD (Briere, 1997; Chu & Dill, 1990). Substance abuse disorders often occur in the context of PTSD (Dansky et al., 1996; Rohsenow et al., 1988). Following trauma, the victim may use drugs or alcohol to self-medicate the anxiety, depression, and emotional numbing of PTSD (Keane, 1995). Because of this high incidence of comorbidity, the psychological examiner must be alert to the presence of other diagnosable disorders or to the possibility that the symptoms that may be attributed to PTSD instead arise from another disorder. For example, the social isolation, sleep disturbance, and concentration impairment seen in PTSD are also symptoms of a major depressive episode.

Because of the many problems associated with PTSD, it is not surprising that trauma victims sometimes experience difficulty in the workplace (Storzbach et al., 2000; J. Wolfe et al., 1998). In general, people with PTSD are less likely to be gainfully employed than those who are no so afflicted. In a study of military veterans, the unemployment rate of veterans with PTSD was four times that of those without that diagnosis (Zatzick et al., 1997). Another study showed that men who had experienced sexual abuse as children and had posttraumatic symptoms also experienced severe disruption of their work life (Little & Hamby, 1999). Of course, if the patient has a comorbid substance abuse or depressive disorder, the impact of the trauma can be multiplied by work problems (attendance, performance, reliability) associated with those disorders.

Nonharassment Job Stressors

For the forensic psychologist to determine that alleged sexual harassment caused observed emotional disorders, the presence of other sources for those same symptoms must be ruled out. Research on the impact of preexisting job stress may provide an explanation for the observed psychological status of the plaintiff. Considerable psychological research has illuminated how a job itself and job loss can affect men and women. Some sexual harassment researchers view sexual harassment as a form of job stress (e.g., Fontana & Rosenheck, 1998; Rosell et al., 1995; K. T. Schneider et al., 1997). This perspective allows the examining psychologist to apply findings from job stress research to sexual harassment situations, if appropriate, and to view sexual harassment as another occupational stressor. Alternatively, the stresses arising from the sexual harassment may add to the stresses already inherent in the plaintiff's workplace. In order to examine these issues, we review research on stress related to vocational contexts.

Job Stress Reactions

Job-related stress has been implicated as a cause of a number of negative reactions among employees. Extensive research has established a relationship between various measures of job stress and morbidity and mortality (Barsade & Wiesenfeld, 1997; National Institute for Occupational Safety and Health, 2000; Northwestern National Life Insurance Company, 1991, 1992; Princeton Survey Research Associates, 1997; Vagg & Spielberger, 1998). For example, the Northwestern National Studies showed that 40% of American workers describe their job as "stressful or extremely stressful." The same study indicated that 69% experienced reduced work productivity caused by stress, and 14% reported that job stress had resulted in resignation or job change. One extensive study showed that workers related negative health outcomes to job stressors more than to other life stressors (Northwestern National Life Insurance Company, 1992; St. Paul Fire and Insurance Company, 1992). About 5% of employees are at any one time under work-related strain severe enough to warrant professional help (Warr, 1982). Vagg and Spielberger (1998) have summarized as follows:

> Numerous studies have linked stress to impaired performance in the workplace due to such factors as health problems, absenteeism, turnover, industrial accidents, the use of drugs and alcohol on the job, and counterproductive behaviors such as spreading rumors, doing inferior work on purpose, stealing from employers, purposely damaging property, equipment and products, and various kinds of white collar crimes. (p. 294)

Work-related stress can cause a host of physiological and emotional reactions: increased incidence of physical health complaints and visits to health care centers (Beehr & Bhagat, 1985; Repetti, 1993); fatigue (Repetti, 1993); headaches (Repetti, 1993); increased incidence of heart attack and stroke (Siegrist, 1996); higher levels of hypertension and atherogenic lipid levels (both indicative of subclinical heart disease; Siegrist, 1996); ulcers (Beehr & Schuler, 1982); skin disorders (Berg & Bengt, 1996); increased levels of the stress hormones adrenalin, noradrenalin, and cortisol (Frankenhaeuser, 1991); and increased lower back pain (Feuerstein, Sult, & Houle, 1985). Other research has shown that work stress can cause a range of clinical psychiatric effects: anxiety disorder symptomatology (Driscoll, Worthington, & Hurrell, 1995) and depressive symptomatology (Dormann & Zapf, 1999; Driscoll et al., 1995; Wang & Patten, 2001).

Work stress has also been shown to have an impact on psychological well-being that may not rise to the level of clinical syndromes. For example, work stress has been associated with the following: decreased self-esteem, although this is mediated by factors such as gender, age, and social support (Driscoll et al., 1995); negative mood (Repetti, 1993); distracted thoughts

(McLain, 1995); fear and anxiety (Driscoll et al., 1995); poorer general psychological well-being and symptoms of general psychological distress (Cortina, Magley, Williams, & Langhout, 2001); marital stress (Repetti, 1993); emotional exhaustion (Taris, Peeters, Le Blanc, Schreurs, & Schaufeli, 2001); depersonalization (Taris et al., 2001); feeling a lack of accomplishment (Taris et al., 2001); increased cigarette use (Conway, Vickers, Ward, & Rahe, 1981); increased coffee consumption (Conway et al., 1981); poor interpersonal relations (Newman & Beehr, 1979); and substance abuse (Newman & Beehr, 1979).

Work stress has been shown to cause decreased effectiveness in performing the job (Beehr & Bhagat, 1985). Work stress has also been shown to have an impact on employees' attitudes toward their job and the workplace itself. For example, research demonstrated the negative impact of work stress by the following: decreased job satisfaction (Cortina et al., 2001; Driscoll et al., 1995), decreased importance of career (Cortina et al., 2001), decreased commitment to the organization (Armstrong-Stassen, 2001), increased retaliatory behaviors toward the organization (Aquino, Tripp, & Bies, 2001; Cortina et al., 2001), increased intentions to change jobs and incidence of actual retirement or resignation (Cortina et al., 2001; Gupta & Beehr, 1979), increased proneness to industrial accidents (Hirschfeld & Behan, 1966), and increased absenteeism (Gupta & Beehr, 1979).

Two major theories have emerged to account for the origins of work stress: the person–environment fit model and the demand–control model.

Person–Environment Fit

One source of job stress is poor fit between the characteristics of the person occupying the job and the requirements of the job. Considerable research has been done on this topic and has resulted in the person–environment fit (PEF) model (Edwards & Harrison, 1993; French, Caplan, & Harrison, 1982). This model posits that a lack of fit can occur in two ways (Gutierres, Saenz, & Green, 1994). First, it may occur at the level of the individual's needs and preferences vis-à-vis the organization's ability to provide rewards or resources to meet those needs. Second, there may a lack of fit between the person's work style or ability and organizational requirements or demands. This latter gap may occur because of poor management practices or inadequate training for employees.

The research indicates that the incongruence between the individual and the organization results in failures to attain goals and in stress reactions among employees. These stress reactions have long been related to physical health measures (Kasl & Cobb, 1970); psychological reactions such as depression, tension, and job dissatisfaction (French et al., 1982); and behavior such as substance abuse and absenteeism (Newman & Beehr, 1979).

Although the bulk of the research on the PEF model has focused on men in managerial positions, recent research (Gutierres et al., 1994) suggests that the model also predicts stress reactions among women and minority groups. In this study, stress resulting from lack of fit resulted in negative health outcomes. Although minority status (e.g., whether the worker was non-Hispanic or Hispanic) did not predict job stress, the research revealed that non-Hispanic White workers among a majority of Hispanic workers experienced greater stress than did Hispanic employees when they were in the minority.

Demand–Control Model

Another influential model of job stress focused primarily on the physiological impact of job stress, particularly on the impact of job conditions on cardiovascular health (Karasek, 1979; Karasek & Theorell, 1990; Landsbergis, Schnall, Schwartz, Warren & Pickering, 1995; Theorell & Karasek, 1996). Health outcomes to various combinations of job demands are related to the ability of the worker to make job-related decisions.

In this model, shown in Table 6.2, if the worker has a job with low demands and high control, low strain results. Correspondingly, in contexts with high job demands and low job control, high strain results. In situations in which the control is high and demands are high, the worker is forced to take an active role, whereas the low demand and low control combination forces the worker into a passive mode (Kohn & Schooler, 1973).

Considerable research has established a clear relationship between stress and jobs in which the worker faces high demands armed with few ways of controlling the job (Theorell & Karasek, 1996). One large-scale study of work stress in the United States showed that workers who had jobs characterized by high demands and low control reported four times the level of depression reported in those working at jobs with high control and low demands (Piltch, Walsh, Mangione, & Jennings, 1994). Researchers have explored the demand–control model mostly in the context of cardiovascular

TABLE 6.2
Demand–Control Model

	Demand	
Control	Low	High
Low	Passive role	High strain
High	Low strain	Active role

Note. From "Job Strain, Hypertension, and Cardiovascular Disease: Empirical Evidence, Methodological Issues, and Recommendations for Future Research" (p. 98, Figure 1), by P. A. Landsbergis, P. L. Schnall, J. E. Schwartz, K. Warren, and T. G. Pickering, 1995. In S. L. E. Sauter and L. R. E. Murphy (Eds.), *Organizational Risk Factors for Job Stress,* Washington, DC: American Psychological Association. Copyright 1995 by the American Psychological Association. Adapted with permission.

disease. They have not focused on the impact of these variables on psychological or job-related outcomes, which is a strength of the person–environment fit research. As Gutierres et al. (1994) note, the demand–control model complements the person–environment fit model.

For the forensic psychologist, the value of these models is fourfold. First, the job stress literature indicates that a substantial number of workers suffer physiological, psychological, and social consequences of job stress. Second, the individual impact of this stress may be substantial. Third, although some jobs are clearly more inherently stressful than others, this stress is not absolutely related to the job itself. Fourth, how stressful a given job is for a given individual requires an evaluation of both the person and the job.

Gender Differences in Job Stress

Recently, job stress research has examined the relationship of the worker's gender to job stress. The social roles in which women commonly find themselves may intensify job stress (Trocki & Orioli, 1994). For example, women have traditionally borne the responsibility for child care and have carried the bulk of the workload at home (Chapman, Ingersoll-Dayton, & Neal, 1994; Cherry, 1984; Crosby, 1987; Pleck, 1985). This *second shift* places increased demands on women and potential for role conflicts.

One wide-ranging study of gender differences on work stress as compared to stress from other sources indicated that women experience more stress-related symptoms than men, but that these symptoms are strongly tied with stress arising from family and personal pressures (Trocki & Orioli, 1994). Among men and women, stress from work and stress from other sources tend to be cumulative. On the job, men react more to stress generated by the ambiguity of their work roles and by work-related competition. In contrast, women experience more stress-related job duties.

Another recent study examined the conflict between the roles of women as caretakers for children or for elder relatives and women's roles as workers (Chapman et al., 1994). As might be expected, absenteeism and stress were directly related to the number of others for whom the female worker was responsible. Basically, the women were caught in a time crunch: The demands of work competed with demands from people in the worker's home.

Other research found gender differences in job stress on several dimensions (Vagg & Spielberger, 1998). Women rated stress arising from inadequate salary, having to cover for another employee, and inadequate time as the most significant stressors. In contrast, men rated being left out of policymaking decisions, conflict with other departments, and negative attitudes toward the organization as their major sources of stress. Other research, however, has shown no similar gender-based differences (Cherry, 1984).

In short, men and women experience job stress from an array of sources. Because of culturally defined roles, women more often experience stress from conflicts between the demands of home and family with the demands of work than do men.

Impact of Social Support on Job Stress

Although job stress has been implicated in both physical and psychological dysfunction, the correlation between stressful events and symptoms has rarely exceeded .40 (Thoits, 1983). This modest effect suggests that even stressful occupations do not make all workers sick.

The exceptions have generated keen interest in factors that could moderate or buffer the impact of stress on the worker (House & Wells, 1978). The most widely studied moderator variable is social support. Anyone in the worker's social environment may provide support. Support from a marital partner reduces depressive symptoms and perceived stress levels (Monroe, Bromet, Connell, & Steiner, 1986). People outside of work as well as supervisors and coworkers reduce the impact of stress on workers (House & Wells, 1978). Goldenhar et al. (1998) looked at both sources and buffers of stress among female construction workers. These women indicated that in addition to the deleterious impact of sexual harassment, having responsibility for the safety of others had a negative impact on psychological well-being. Social support from supervisors had a positive impact on the women's job satisfaction.

Within the constraints of the demand–control model, social support may increase the person's perception of control in a given situation (Theorell & Karasek, 1996). For women, the conflict between the demands of work and home was a major source of stress. The buffering effect of social support is greatest among women and men in blue-collar occupations. Social support was critical in buffering the impact of high-stress jobs (Piltch et al., 1994).

A longitudinal study evaluated the impact of stress on working married women who had at least one child at home. The primary sources of stress were a lack of authority and influence on the job, sex discrimination, heavy workload, work imposing on relaxation, family imposing on relaxation, and conflict between the home and work roles (Reifman, Biernat, & Lang, 1991). For this sample, however, social support did not produce a buffering effect. On the contrary, for those who experienced high-job-related stress, greater social support was associated with more symptoms. The researchers concluded, "the benefits of interpersonal relationships may be attenuated by the obligations and responsibilities they entail or by social conflicts" (Reifman et al., 1991, p. 443).

The extent to which workers find jobs that match their skills and personality characteristics varies widely. People who are in the wrong job suffer increased morbidity, stress reactions, depression, and behavioral symptoms that may adversely affect their work performance. The forensic psychologist must assess the plaintiff's job stress reactions as part of a competent evaluation in a sexual harassment case. To the extent that job stress reactions are caused by a lack of fit or reduced control at work, they are not attributable to incidents of sexual harassment or to a sexually hostile work environment.

EVALUATION OF EVENTS AND REACTIONS FOLLOWING SEXUAL HARASSMENT

Workers who experience sexual harassment may initiate job actions or face employer sanctions that affect their status in the organization. A common circumstance is that there are costs associated with voicing a complaint. Once an employee complains about sexual harassment, whether formally or informally, the employer often treats that individual less favorably because of the complaint and engages in retaliation or reprisal against the complaining employee. In some cases, this adverse reaction by the employer may culminate in the discharge or firing of the employee. Alternatively, work conditions may worsen, even if the harassment abates, and the complaining employee may be ostracized and decide to quit his or her job. In the next section, the research on whistle-blowing and how that phenomenon may manifest itself in sexual harassment contexts is addressed. Next, the psychological impact of involuntary discharge, a common outcome for targets of sexual harassment, is reviewed.

Whistle-Blowing

Research indicates that between 40% and 62% of women who reported sexual harassment experienced retaliation (Loy & Stewart, 1984; Parmerlee, Near, & Jensen, 1982). In this section, we review the literature on this topic.

Whistle-blowing is defined as "the disclosure by organization members (former or current) of illegal, immoral, or illegitimate practices under the control of their employers" (Miceli & Near, 1992, p. 15). Much of the research on the topic has concerned who makes such complaints (Brabeck, 1984; Dozier & Miceli, 1985; Miceli, Dozier, & Near, 1991; Miceli & Near, 1984, 1988, 1992; Miceli, Near, & Schwenk, 1991) and why those people make the complaints (Elliston, 1982; Greenberger, Miceli, & Cohen, 1987;

D. A. Johnson & Pany, 1981; Keenan, 1990; Micheli & Near, 1985; Miceli, Roach, & Near, 1988; Perrucci, Anderson, Schendel, & Trachtman, 1980).

Of most interest to the forensic psychologist in a sexual harassment case is, however, the impact of retaliation on whistle-blowers. Compared with people who are recipients of retaliation following sexual harassment complaints, whistle-blowers usually do not have a history of sexual harassment preceding the retaliation. Thus, studies of this population allow an examination of the impact of retaliation as a specific phenomenon, divorced from the stress or trauma related to consequences of sexual harassment. Complaints in sexual harassment cases may involve multiple legal allegations or causes of action, such as quid pro quo harassment, hostile work environment, constructive discharge, and retaliation. In the course of litigation, some of those allegations may be determined by the court to lack sufficient merit and may be eliminated by way of summary judgment. If a fact finder determines that there is no liability on the part of the employer for the sexual harassment claim, a complaint for retaliation may be the only element for which psychological injuries are considered. In these circumstances, an evaluating psychologist may be asked to separate consequences of retaliation from those attributable to alleged sexual harassment.

First, it should be noted that although slightly fewer than one half (43%–45%) of workers have observed situations that would prompt a complaint, of those, fewer than one third actually blow the whistle on their employers (Miceli & Near, 1989; Miceli, Rehg, Near, & Ryan, 1999). Of those who do report, between one quarter and one half are subject to retaliation (Miceli & Near, 1992; Near & Miceli, 1987). Whether they are targets of retaliation depends on a number of factors, including the lack of support from supervisors and management, the seriousness of the wrongdoing, and whether the worker chose a channel for disclosure that was outside of the organization.

Retaliation by the employer affects workers in many ways. Their work performance suffers and many are fired or involuntary transferred (MacNamara, 1991; Near & Miceli, 1986). As a result of retaliation, many whistle-blowers become more likely to repeat the reporting behavior in other settings (Miceli & Near, 1992). In short, retaliation for reporting sexual harassment may result in a number of negative consequences for the worker, and many of these consequences my result in psychological injuries.

Paranoid Reactions

The experience of retaliation in the workplace is likely to involve feelings that supervisors and coworkers are conspiring to make the worker's life miserable. In true cases of retaliation, this is exactly the case. The worker is the focus of the actions of others in the workplace to deprive the worker of status, opportunities, a comfortable workstation, or even a safe workplace. For the worker who is the recipient of retaliation, the workplace may become hostile indeed, and the worker may start to feel as though the job site is a place in which the worker is disliked and perhaps even in some peril. Thus, it would be likely that personality measures such as the MMPI–2 and the PAI administered to plaintiffs who claim retaliation would show evidence of suspiciousness and fear of threat. These would be most evident in elevations on scales measuring clinical paranoia.

From another perspective, a worker who is already prone to paranoid reactions may view others' behavior in the workplace as being more personal and inimical than it really is. For example, consider the worker who complained of sexual harassment in the workplace and then has a change of office or duties, which had been scheduled before the complaint. A paranoid worker might, nevertheless, view the changes as retaliation, even though a more rational person would view the actions as benign.

This raises an issue of differential diagnosis for the examining psychologist. The presence of elevations on paranoia scales in the plaintiff's testing may, on the one hand, represent injuries caused by unlawful retaliation. On the other hand, those elevations may represent a gross misperception of the intentions of others and actually go to the legal issue of liability (see chap. 5, this volume). In this case, as in situations in which borderline or hysteroid syndromes are in question, the examiner's job is to develop a detailed history of the plaintiff's relationships both on and off the job. If it is a case in which the paranoid thinking was part of a preexisting pattern, the examiner should find evidence of suspiciousness, inability to trust others, and pathological jealousy, among other symptoms. If the evidence indicates that the paranoid symptoms began only after the on-the-job harassment, attributing these symptoms to retaliation may be more appropriate.

Impact of Involuntary Discharge

In some situations, allegations of sexual harassment precede the discharge or resignation of the employee (Coles, 1986). Whether the discharge has its origins in substandard work by the complainant or is a form of retaliation for the claimant's formal or informal complaint about sexual harassment is often a point of contention in sexual harassment lawsuits. As noted in chapter 3, when a worker resigns in the midst of work circumstances that he or she believes to be untenable, the resignation may amount to a *constructive discharge*. Often, it is the forensic examiner's job to determine if the worker exhibits emotional reactions related to the discharge per se. If the discharge is determined to be unlawful or wrongful, those reactions may constitute part of the emotional damages claimed by the plaintiff. If the court determines that the discharge was lawful, then the reactions from the discharge must be separated from the worker's reactions to events for which the defendant may be held liable (Goodman-Delahunty & Foote, 1995).

To understand the impact of job loss, it is helpful to examine importance of work itself. Warr (1982) identified six benefits of having a job: (a) Financial gain is the most obvious benefit of work, as paid employment is the principal source of income for most people; (b) work provides a setting in which the worker engages in physical activity, which expends mental and physical energy and allows for the development of personal skills; (c) a job provides variety, especially in contrast to the relative sameness of a domestic environment; (d) a job allows people to structure their time over the course of the day because work usually has fixed starting hours, breaks, and quitting times; (e) most jobs require social interactions and enlarge the worker's interpersonal environment from family and friends; and (f) work provides identity and social status, and for many, you are what you do.

Correspondingly, the loss of those benefits can result in particular psychological reactions to unemployment. The loss of all these things together may be greater than the simple addition of the reactions to the loss of the benefits. For example, given what is known about the buffering impact of social support, the loss of social networks associated with work may exacerbate the emotional reactions related to the worker's loss of identity and financial problems (D. Jacobson, 1987; L. P. Jones, 1991). For some, loss of the benefits associated with work stimulates a process like mourning (Finley & Lee, 1981; Schlossberg & Leibowitz, 1980).

Prolonged unemployment can adversely affect not only the psychological status but also the health and family relationships of workers (Liem & Rayman, 1982). For many workers, the immediate reactions to job loss are increased depression, anxiety, and somatic symptoms (Kasl, 1979). The families of workers may also experience stress, with spouses of unemployed workers reporting the greatest stress (Kasl & Cobb, 1979). However, even in job loss situations, social support can play a big role. Social support was a significant buffer to depression for both unemployed and employed women. Functioning and rewarding intimate relationships are a significant buffer against stress related to job loss (Schwarzer, Hahn, & Fuchs, 1994).

SUMMARY

When a psychologist conducts a forensic evaluation of a sexual harassment plaintiff, it is reasonable to assess the plaintiff's condition at three intervals: before the harassment, during the harassment, and after the harassment. Assessment of the plaintiff's status at these three times is part of the process of record review and allows for the formation of inferences from clinical and collateral interviews. The construction of a chronology of events can assist in focusing on these three time frames. This chapter first reviewed the available research on the impact of sexual harassment on targets. During the interval when sexual harassment is alleged, the most relevant concern is the impact that sexual harassment has on individuals. The research indicates that compared with people whose workplace is characterized by few reports of sexual harassment, people who report sexual harassment are more likely to experience an adverse impact on their lives from that harassment. Their ability to function in the workplace is decreased by reduced desires to be at work, less satisfaction with the job, and increased chances of leaving that workplace. They are less likely to be comfortable with supervisors and coworkers. They experience more work-related stress and more medical problems. In addition, they are more likely to have symptoms of depressive and anxiety disorders.

This chapter also reviewed the data on the impact of prior events. In evaluating the plaintiff's condition before the harassment, it is critical to determine if the plaintiff experienced childhood trauma or other life experiences that account for the symptoms experienced after the alleged workplace experiences. The research indicates that the lives of adults who were abused as children are often very different from the lives of those who had more benign childhoods. The long-term impact of such abuse varies widely, depending on the nature, severity, duration, and source of the abuse. Additionally, the availability and provision of social support from critical family members or others can have a substantial impact on the recovery of a person who experienced child abuse. A number of psychological disorders exist with some incidence in the general population and can be expected in populations of sexual harassment plaintiffs. To perform a competent forensic evaluation of a plaintiff in a sexual harassment case, a psychologist must determine the presence of preexisting psychopathology. Evaluating the plaintiff's personal, medical, and psychiatric history is essential for this task. Likewise, a review of appropriate medical and mental health records allows for substantiation of the presence or absence of preexisting disorders. Collateral informants can provide a picture the plaintiff's pre-sexual-harassment functioning, which may reflect ongoing symptomatology arising from preexisting disorders. As noted in chapter 5, evidence of these preexisting conditions should be present before the events that give rise to the sexual harassment complaints.

Although a range of responses to harassment are available to sexual harassment targets, most do not react directly to initial, mild, and ambiguous instances of harassment. Rather, most people will *get along and go along* and ignore the behavior or avoid the harasser. More severe harassment generally predicts more assertive responses. These assertive responses often have an unfortunate result: The workers get less satisfaction from the job and are more likely to quit.

Loss of employment produces a cascade of other losses for the discharged worker. Not only does the worker lose pay and the things that money can purchase but also a significant social milieu, resources for future job hunting, and a source of social support. The impact of unemployment may spread to members of the discharged worker's family. Social support plays a significant role in moderating the impact of discharge.

The evaluating psychologist usually examines the plaintiff some months or years after the alleged harassment incidents. Thus, it is important to take the natural history of emotional reactions into account. Research on the long-term impact of hostile work environments indicates that these reactions tend to become worse as a function of the length of time that the worker is exposed to those stressful events. An accrual of stress symptoms over time, including increased sleeplessness, social isolation, physical symptoms, and impaired concentration is expected. Conversely, once the target is out of the hostile workplace, these symptoms should abate with time unless other factors enter into to the equation to maintain these symptoms. For example, if the plaintiff experienced very traumatic events such as a battery or rape, PTSD or other trauma-related symptoms are likely to be most severe in the days or weeks immediately following the harassing events and to diminish as a function of time after the events. A claimant who says that symptoms are becoming increasingly severe as time passes merits a close examination to determine if other events following the alleged harassment contributed to the exacerbation of symptoms.

7

ALTERNATE DISPUTE RESOLUTION IN SEXUAL HARASSMENT CLAIMS: NEUTRAL FACT-FINDING, MEDIATION, AND ARBITRATION

Resolution of sexual harassment claims informally outside of court has been encouraged since the inception of Title VII through the procedural requirement for conciliation in the form of negotiations between the parties to attempt to resolve the issues before litigation. The 1991 Civil Rights Act specifically authorized and encouraged the use of alternate dispute resolution to resolve Title VII disputes. Congressional intent to promote conciliation rather than litigation was reaffirmed by the U.S. Supreme Court in *Burlington Industries, Inc. v. Ellerth* (1998). This endorsement flows in part from recognition that the volume of sexual harassment cases filed exceeds the capacity of the EEOC and the courts to process these claims efficiently.

Although resolution of a sexual harassment claim can occur by means of negotiations between the employer and the employee, one drawback to this process is that the employer has responsibilities to both the accused and the target and may have difficulty remaining impartial. For example, if the alleged harasser is a senior employee or someone friendly with managers and supervisors and the target is relatively new to the workforce, the latter is unlikely to trust the employer sufficiently to engage in meaningful informal negotiations. In these situations, the intervention of a third-party neutral who can appraise the situation from a more objective, arm's length perspective can be valuable in assisting the parties to achieve a resolution. Third-party neutrals are often involved in the informal resolution of sexual harassment claims.

Mediation and arbitration are the two most common forms of alternate dispute resolution in which third-party neutrals are sought in employment cases. In this chapter, we review aspects of informal resolution of sexual harassment claims outside of traditional litigation channels. We begin with a discussion of neutral fact-finding, a less well known form of third-party neutral intervention, and then review uses of mediation and arbitration in sexual harassment cases.

SUITABILITY OF SEXUAL HARASSMENT CASES TO INFORMAL THIRD-PARTY INTERVENTION

Potential advantages and disadvantages in sexual harassment cases of third-party informal resolution such as mediation and of other more formal means of alternate dispute resolution such as arbitration have been the topic of much debate recently. Proponents of mediation emphasize the fact that this process can meet the interests of all of the parties, the target, the accused, and the employer, as well as some public goals or interests. The potential of arbitration to circumvent the interests of the complainant and public goals of antidiscrimination legislation has been controversial (*Duffield v. Robertson Stephens & Co.*, 1998; Harkavy, 1999; *Wright v. Universal Maritime Service Corp.*, 1998).

In situations in which a target files an internal complaint at the workplace, operations and productivity are often disrupted. Consequences are often negative whether a claim is meritorious or frivolous. Targets are often concerned that once they become known for having filed a complaint, their accusations will be met with disbelief and skepticism, their reputation at work will be negatively affected, and they will be regarded unfavorably as disloyal by employers (Fitzgerald, Swann, et al., 1995).

By law, employers must take prompt action to investigate the complaint, and a thorough investigation has to go beyond a discussion with the accused harasser to seek corroborative information from potential witnesses. Within days, information about the investigative interviews and rumors spread among employees. In some situations, the target and the harasser are placed on administrative leave or temporarily transferred pending the outcome of the investigation. Their lives are disrupted. Other employees are often polarized or split in their opinions and loyalties to the target and the alleged harasser and may take sides, creating schism in departments. Follow-up interviews of coworkers and potential witnesses are disruptive. In some instances, the claim is accompanied by unwelcome publicity, and the employer may become very defensive.

Once the employee files a claim with a state or federal agency and initiates administrative processing of the complaint, that agency will begin on-site visits, conduct additional interviews, and request information. This process may ensue for 6 months, until the employee obtains notice of his or her *right to sue*. This formal step ends the federal EEOC process and entitles the worker to proceed with his or her own private litigation. The administrative investigation may become protracted and last up to 2 years or more. Little can be done to reverse the impact of unfavorable publicity. While an investigation or litigation is pending, suspicion hangs over participants. The participants and coworkers who may be friends, allies, and witnesses often become hostile, accusatory, or overly defensive. The careers of the target and the harasser may be interrupted. The time until trial may be lengthy, lasting several years after the events in issue. The outcome of litigation can do little to restore the good name and career progress of a complainant or a falsely accused harasser. Thus, alternatives to litigation that may allow the parties to preserve their relationship for the future and to avoid further deterioration or aggravation of the situation are attractive.

NEUTRAL FACT-FINDING INVESTIGATION ON RECEIPT OF A COMPLAINT

A practice that is increasing is use of a third-party neutral by an employer on receipt of a sexual harassment complaint. This practice is unrelated to mediation or arbitration but flows from the employer's obligation to investigate the allegations promptly and thoroughly and to take prompt action to intervene to prevent harm from increasing. An employer's obligation to prevent harassment is scrutinized most closely once the employer has notice of a potential claim. Retention of a psychologist as a neutral fact finder can assist the employer in fulfilling the obligation and usually has the benefit of facilitating a prompt resolution of the case without litigation.

A suitable fact-finding investigator is someone familiar with the legal and psychological aspects of sexual harassment. Psychologists who are acquainted with the sexual harassment laws and research and skilled at interviewing individuals about topics that may be difficult to discuss are well qualified for the job. In certain situations, depending on the scope of the claim, a team of two persons can best perform the investigation. Sometimes a team comprising a man and a woman is recommended, particularly in sexual harassment cases in which employees may feel more comfortable and forthcoming responding to inquiries posed by a person of their own gender. However, this practice increases the costs to the employer.

Usually, no lawyer is present during the fact-finding interviews, nor is any employer or management representative in attendance. Employees are typically reluctant to disclose what they may have observed or experienced to any employer representative from either management or the human resources or personnel department as they fear this will impact their relationships with the employer, and in particular, their chances for promotion and advancement. For this reason, investigations conducted in house are often unsuccessful at uncovering what really transpired in the workplace.

Thus, the neutral fact-finding process is successful in part because the investigators are outsiders, impartial, and professional. Structuring the situation to maintain this objectivity and to reduce the impact of the financial aspects of employment in these contexts is essential. The interviews may be recorded and transcribed for the sake of accuracy; however, this process may be too intimidating for some witnesses and interviewees. Of course, the APA ethics code (American Psychological Association, 2002) requires written permission from the interviewees before the interview. A structured interview format is recommended. The advantages include the absence of lengthy depositions, court-reporting fees, and other costs of formal discovery and speed. Within 7 to 14 days, an employer can obtain a picture of interactions and issues and be in a position to take informed action. If, for example, the investigation tends to support the claim of harassment, the employer may need to terminate the harasser or transfer the target or take other appropriate disciplinary action. If the investigation fails to confirm the allegations, the employer is in a position to share the findings with the employee, to confirm that a thorough in-depth examination of all the issues has been conducted, and perhaps to end the matter by conducting some on-the-job training on harassment for all affected employees.

Given the complex array of potential outcomes related to the investigation, the psychologist filling this role is obligated to provide accurate and written informed consent to those interviewed (Committee on Ethical Guidelines for Forensic Psychologists, 1991). As noted in chapter 4, this informed consent should include the purpose of the interview and how the information may be used at the end of the process. For example, if one outcome of the investigation is that a harassing worker may be terminated, all potential interviewees should be advised of this possibility. If the information from the interviews is unlikely to be shared with the workers at the end of the process, they should be so informed at the outset. Informed-consent forms may have to be crafted for each situation. Assistance from a lawyer skilled in employment law should be helpful in developing these forms.

The investigators interview the target, the harasser, and any related witnesses such as coworkers, supervisors and managers, or members of the public who interact with those employees and may have relevant information tending to support or rebut the claim. In some cases, for example, it may be appropriate to interview past employees who have nothing at stake with respect to the current employer to shed additional light on the conduct of a purported harasser. This may reveal a pattern, a modus operandi, or may serve to exonerate the accused from the allegations. For instance, in one such investigation, women who had been harassed to the point that they left their jobs as long as 14 years before the events at issue were contacted, and their stories corroborated the claims of the current female targets by establishing a pattern and practice perpetrated by an upper management executive who routinely preyed on younger vulnerable female employees.

Extreme care must be taken by the neutral fact finder to assure employees who are interviewed that their comments will remain confidential and that they will not face reprisal or retaliation for disclosing risky information about the employer, that is, for whistle-blowing activity (Miceli et al., 1991). One option is for the employer to agree that certain information may be shared with legal counsel but not with line supervisors of the interviewees. The investigator may have to withhold certain information from interviewees' reports to protect their identify and disclose it in a form that ensures that the identity of the employees can not be discerned. Permission to make these decisions must be negotiated by the investigator before the interviews commence and should probably be part of a written contract that clearly states the roles and obligations of the investigator(s).

The investigators typically prepare written summaries for the employer, the employer's legal counsel, or the parties (claimant and alleged harasser) reporting on their findings. These findings are not usually covered by the work-product privilege and will be available at trial. They can be made available to any mediator or arbitrator in an informal dispute resolution setting in an effort to foster settlement discussions. Alternatively, the investigators may proceed to serve as mediators. In such situations, it is best if the parties confirm their agreement to this extension and change in the role of the investigator in writing. The psychologist should take care, as noted in chapter 4, that this change in role does not generate an ethically problematic dual role. Consultation with colleagues is advised in such circumstances.

MEDIATION

Mediation is a form of third-party neutral intervention in which the parties meet and explore options to resolve the issues over one or two sessions, depending on the complexity of the case. If successful, the mediation concludes with an outline of points to include in a settlement agreement between the parties. If the mediation fails, it is often nonetheless useful in narrowing issues, educating the parties, and advancing the case in a more cost-effective and less adversarial fashion than formal discovery.

Mediation offers a forum for the target to assert and confront the harasser and for the harasser to explain or deny the conduct in issue. However, the procedure is sufficiently flexible and adaptable that if the mediator determines that it is counterproductive for the parties to confront each other, mediation may still proceed without them ever being present in the same room or meeting face-to-face. This is sometimes called *shuttle diplomacy* (Gadlin, 1991) and allows each party to hear the other party's side without having to confront the other party. In sexual harassment cases, a disparity of power between the alleged harasser and the target often exists. By separating the parties, the person with less power may be better able to state a case and work toward a solution in an atmosphere absent intimidation.

This process is attractive because it allows the parties to retain control over the outcome, as there is no externally imposed solution. Thus, mediation can achieve personal empowerment and recognition that does not occur in litigation and avoid the revictimization of complainants that may occur through protracted litigation or through pubic disclosure of the target's past sexual behavior and medical history (Fitzgerald et al., 1999; Streseman, 1995). Among the major advantages of mediation are that emotions can be productively directed, and the relationship between the parties and their employer can be preserved. An early settlement offers advantages to all. In an informal setting, no credibility findings are made, thus damage to both parties is avoided. Much of the information may remain confidential, and negative publicity may be contained. Treatment of a traumatized target can proceed more quickly. A harasser can be disciplined faster. Preventive action can be taken to minimize future disruption to all and diversion from the employer's business. Fewer hard feelings result.

Another major consideration is that mediation offers very flexible options to tailor solutions to address the problems, including solutions that may not be available through litigation. Two notable examples are the option to provide either the target or the accused with a transfer and the opportunity to include a written apology to the target in the proceedings (Shuman, 2000b). Other remedies that are common include education or retraining at a local or company-wide level, counseling, discipline, separation of the parties, letters of reference to future employers, and job modifications. Because the process is confidential, much of the damaging disparagement in the workplace that accompanies litigation can be avoided. An attraction to the target is that he or she secures a certain, immediate outcome such as monetary compensation or a transfer. Employers may avoid high damages from jury awards.

Opposition to and Disadvantages of Mediation

Despite congressional support for the process, some employers perceive a willingness to mediate as a concession of weakness. There are other more substantial criticisms of mediation as a means to resolve sexual harassment cases. Some commentators have noted that this process obfuscates acceptable and unacceptable behavior in the workplace because there is no fact finder who can delineate such conduct with bright lines (Irvine, 1993). In other words, the precedent-setting value of the cases is lost. Conversely, it has been argued that the adversary system has trouble with gradations of sexual harassment. Although it is difficult to know precisely what sort of cases proceed to litigation and what sort of cases are settled informally, the idea has been propounded that if only the hard cases are litigated, meaning those about which the law is unclear, the development of a coherent body of sexual harassment jurisprudence is hindered by widespread use of mediation. Of course, more than 90% of all civil cases settle out of court. There is also some reason to believe that some hard cases are strong candidates for settlement rather than litigation precisely because the risk of uncertain outcomes deters the parties from proceeding to trial. Some commentators have pointed out that most of the disputes in sexual harassment cases center on interpretations of the evidence regarding the conduct at issue rather than whether the conduct occurred.

Other detractors highlight the fact that mediation risks trivializing the seriousness of harassment and can make the workplace more inhospitable to women. If the community is deprived of knowledge of what occurred because the events are kept confidential, the deterrent function of Title VII is not well served. Rather than offering public vindication by a neutral third-party adjudicator or jury, some aspects of the mediation process may imply that sexual harassment targets share responsibility for the illegal conduct of the harasser (Gadlin, 1991; Irvine, 1993). As noted in chapter 2 of this volume, many are prone to view sexual harassment as an activity committed by a *perpetrator* on a *victim*. Entering into a process that places these two parties at the same level and assumes that a compromise is possible between the two perspectives risks losing sight of the fact that a wrong has been committed and that one of the parties has to bear blame for that wrong. In sum, most concerns about mediation are focused on public goals and issues rather than the interests of the parties in a particular case.

Psychologists as Mediators

Psychologists have increasingly been called on to serve as mediators (Roberts, 2003). This role is one that flows naturally from the psychologist's role as therapist, especially as one working with groups or families. However, there are some aspects of the mediation role that are foreign to the conventionally trained psychologist. Roberts (2003) provided a capsule description of the mediator's role:

> Consider the behavioral expectations for professional mediators. During work, mediators are supposed to maintain strict neutrality, yet demonstrate emotional compassion. They are supposed to facilitate creative solutions and yet use a limited number of verbal techniques for doing so. They need to split their focus fairly evenly between what is going on with the parties involved, what the mediator is processing internally, and what is going on with their co-mediator. They typically expend a great deal of emotional and intellectual energy in facilitating a positive outcome for the participants, but are supposed to be just as accepting if no agreement can be reached.

Many aspects of mediation differ from the roles that clinical or forensic psychologists are asked to fill, thus it is appropriate for psychologists to obtain additional training in mediation before entering this arena. Legal considerations, the demand for neutrality (Spratlen, 1997), the range of available legal outcomes, and other aspects of mediation should all be part of the psychologist's knowledge base before entering the field.

ARBITRATION

Arbitration is a more adversarial form of dispute resolution than mediation and one in which the neutral party issues a decision on the merits of the case. In recent years, there has been considerable debate as to whether arbitration should apply to statutes designed to further important social policies, such as antidiscrimination statutes that prohibit sexual harassment (Buehrer, 1998). This debate has focused on whether the goals of antidiscrimination are controverted by mandatory arbitration by pointing to cases in which employers require employees at the time of hire to enter into a contract that provides that all disputes over the terms and conditions of their employment will be decided by arbitration rather than litigation. In other words, on signing this contract, the employee waives his or her right to a jury trial in the event that he or she later has a sexual harassment claim against the employer. Contractual provisions such as these, known as *mandatory arbitration clauses*, are regarded as more favorable to employers than to employees because arbitral awards are often lower than jury awards if the plaintiff prevails in the claim and because many arbitrators may lack a thorough understanding of the intricacies of the sexual harassment laws.

The argument reduces to the point that at the time the contract is formed the employer has more bargaining power than the employee who wants the job. Courts have noted that Congress intended that alternate forms of dispute resolution should supplement the remedies available under Title VII, which now include the right to a jury trial. The issue has been whether sexual harassment targets should be allowed to waive their rights to a jury trial by signing contracts with employers that all workplace disputes over sexual harassment will be arbitrated. In other areas of the law, such as commercial contracts that provide for compulsory arbitration, federal courts have held that arbitrator's awards are enforceable. Predispute arbitration agreements cannot be set aside simply because the parties had unequal bargaining power (*Alexander v. Gardner-Denver Co.*, 1974; *Gillmer v. Interstate/Johnson Lane Corp.*, 1991). Various commentators have noted that the resolution is for employers to offer safeguards, such as providing potential employees with access to legal representation at the time of contract formation, for instance, by paying their attorney's fees, by allowing employees to participate in the selection of mediators and arbitrators, and by taking steps to avoid situations in which the employer becomes a *repeat player* in front of one particular mediator or arbitrator or one firm of mediators or arbitrators. In other words, if fair process standards are implemented at the time of contract formation and a large pool of potential arbitrators is accessible, these concerns are allayed (FitzGibbon, 2000). Some federal courts have determined that Title VII rights must be treated differently from other federal rights regarding mandatory arbitration; others have concluded that arbitration is an important remedy for discrimination (*Duffield v. Robertson Stephens & Co.*, 1998; *Wright v. Universal Maritime Service Corp.*, 1998).

The debate over mandatory arbitration clauses must be distinguished from controversies arising under grievance arbitration procedures. A long tradition in unionized workplaces has been to offer employees and employers the option to engage in bargaining and negotiation to resolve their differences. When an employee files a claim against an employer in the form of a grievance and the matter progresses to arbitration, an arbitrator may ultimately issue a decision that affects a claim of sexual harassment in the workplace. For example, in some cases, when an employer has terminated the service of a harasser following an investigation, the harasser has lodged a claim of unfair dismissal through the grievance process. If the arbitrator overturns an employer's decision to fire a harasser, there may be concern that this outcome is contrary to public policy interests in eliminating sexual harassment form the workplace. The Federal Arbitration Act (1925) governs grievance arbitration decisions. The standard for setting aside an arbitral decision is that the decision represents "a manifest disregard of law."

Numerous cases have been cited in which grievance arbitrators who are often not lawyers have reinstated a harasser on grounds that termination was a penalty too severe for the conduct at issue. In these proceedings, the target is not a party.

SUMMARY

The psychologist serving the role of investigator should have a grasp of the dynamics of sexual harassment, the role of the law in harassment cases, and how corporate cultures may inhibit or contribute to the incidence of sexual harassment. This role is distinct from the usual role of the psychologist in evaluating injuries, and therefore, increased concern about ethical issues is warranted. The impact of agency and financial arrangements may be significant and should be acknowledged. The necessity of informed consent from those interviewed may slow the process somewhat but is critical to make sure that the procedures are fair to all involved. How the information from the interviews will be used should be clear to both the employer and those interviewed, and the parameters of discretion for the psychologist to keep confidential some information and identities must be clearly understood by all parties.

Satisfaction with mediation processes as contrasted with litigation is well documented (Tyler & Lind, 2001). Neutral fact-finding, mediation, and arbitration offer the target options to put a stop to offensive conduct, to continue working without stigma, and to obtain some prompt redress for past injuries. These procedures offer the accused an opportunity to explain his or her viewpoint, to understand what offended the target, to participate in forging a fair resolution, and to continue working without stigma. Alternate dispute resolution addresses concerns of the employers by fulfilling their mandate to take prompt remedial action, by preserving a productive and harmonious workforce, by keeping resolution costs low, and by minimizing negative publicity and rumors. Despite criticisms centered on the fact that some public concerns are not well served by mediation, other public interests are furthered. For instance, this process can be instrumental in securing a safe workplace, in providing a prompt resolution, and in maintaining the confidence of private matters. Because many employers are now entering into mandatory arbitration agreements with employees, alternative dispute resolution is undergoing significant growth. This growth may be an arena in which psychologists may expand their practices.

APPENDIX A
Complex Case Involving Male on Female Sexual Harassment Allegations

In this appendix, we present a psychological evaluation report illustrating how a case may be approached. The report is adapted from a real case and, in accordance with the APA ethics code, is disguised by changing all of the names and many of the facts that might have identified the case. Some of the facts were altered to create better examples, although many of the most dramatic and vivid details are based on real events that were retained if they were sufficiently anonymous.

April 20, 2003

Nancy Robertson
Robertson and Merrill, P.A.
PO Box 251
Albuquerque, NM 87103

Re: Eloisa Chavez

Dear Ms. Robertson:

As requested, this is my report of my forensic psychological examination of Eloisa Chavez. This examination and report were prepared in anticipation of the current litigation and should not be used for any other purpose. Thank you for your cooperation during this evaluation.

In my office, we have administered an extensive battery of tests to the party, reviewed any legal documents provided to me, and spoken to any collateral sources of information, who were also informed of the nonconfidential nature of our discussion. After considering the party interviews, party psychometric testing, collateral records, and collateral interviews, I have attempted to generate legally relevant hypotheses and to provide helpful information to the court. Most of all, I have viewed my role in this matter as expert to the court, attempting to assist the trier of fact.

As you requested, I conducted a psychological evaluation with your client Eloisa Chavez. I met with her initially on December 16, 2002. At that time, she came to my office and completed the Minnesota Multiphasic Personality Inventory—2 (MMPI–2) and the Personality Assessment Inventory (PAI). In addition, she completed a brief battery of cognitive testing with my testing assistant, Mary Reiser, MS. Ms. Reiser administered the Wechsler Adult Intelligence Scale—III, the Wide Range Achievement Test—3, the Rey Complex Figure Test, and the Test Of Memory Malingering. Ms. Chavez returned to my office on the next day, December 17, 2002. At that time I conducted a 5.5-hour clinical interview with her. I also conducted a 1-hour follow-up telephone interview with her on April 15, 2003. I have also conducted telephone collateral interviews with her husband, Victor Chavez, and her therapist, Susan Porter. I have reviewed her records from her therapist, Susan Porter, MA, her psychiatrist, Guillermo Narvais, MD, the Palo Duro Assault Recovery Services, and the Alamogordo Counseling Center. I have also reviewed the Alamogordo Department of Public Safety reports related to a number of domestic violence incidents.

The purpose of this evaluation is to assess Ms. Chavez's condition relative to the complaint that she has filed against Mega-Shop. In her complaint, Ms. Chavez alleges that she was severely sexually harassed in the context of her employment. In this case, she alleges that two of her supervisors at the Mega-Shop store in Alamogordo, New Mexico, coerced her into having sexual relations with them. It appears that in addition to the claimed quid pro quo harassment, she claims that she was functioning in a generally sexually charged hostile work environment. She left her employment with Mega-Shop on April 7, 2001.

I was hired by the plaintiff's counsel, Ms. Robertson. At the beginning of my first session with Ms. Chavez, I provided her with a written informed-consent form. I explained that the information she provided to me in the form of interview and test data would be shared with retaining counsel and would quite likely be conveyed to the defendant's counsel in the form of a written report or sworn testimony. I also informed her that I might be asked to testify about the contents of the evaluation in open court if the case comes to trial. Ms. Chavez asked no questions and signed the informed-consent document.

HISTORY

Eloisa Chavez was born in El Paso, Texas, on July 15, 1971. Her father, Sergio Mendez, works as a mechanic in an automotive garage in El Paso. Her mother is Maria (née Villanueva) Mendez. Eloisa Chavez is the second of eight children born of that union. She has an older sister, a younger sister, and five younger brothers. Her parents divorced when she was eight years old. She reports that her father had a drinking problem and was physically abusive to her mother. The abuse was very serious, resulting in her father being arrested and incarcerated and her mother divorcing him. Despite this history, because her mother was very likely disabled by her own mental illness, Eloisa Chavez was raised by her father. Over time, apparently, the situation with her father improved and she lived with him in El Paso and also stayed with her paternal uncle.

Ms. Chavez became pregnant at age 16 and had a baby, whom her mother eventually claimed as her own. Since that time, Ms. Chavez's residence, housemates, and living situation changed quite often. She had relationships with a number of men. The longest of those relationships was with Julio Chavez. This was apparently an abusive and repressive relationship in which he controlled many of her activities, friends, and even her work. In 1998, she married Victor Chavez (no relation to Julio), a Mexican national. She reported that she has a total of five children from these relationships.

She reports that she experienced one prior rape assault perpetrated by a neighbor boy when she was 16 years old. She reports that she experienced symptoms of posttraumatic stress disorder (PTSD) for several years after the events. These symptoms included nightmares and intrusive recollections tied in with some sexual activity and with the house in which the assault occurred. These symptoms were generally resolved and no longer substantially impairing her functioning by the time of the incidents integral to this case, although she still had occasional nightmares about this assault.

She worked at a series of jobs in fast food restaurants, clothing manufacture, and beauty salons, following training as a cosmetologist. She worked for a small appliance manufacturing company and even sold vacuums door-to-door. Her job with Mega-Shop, which began on November 25, 1999, was her first long-term, full-time employment.

She reports that she started working at Mega-Shop on November 25, 1999. Eloisa Chavez was initially hired as a seafood clerk in the grocery section of the store. Her initial supervisor was Alfred Pacheco, the seafood manager. She reports that his boss was Max Garcia, the meat and seafood manager. When she was first hired, because she had never worked in any place like that before, she was scared and nervous. The produce department, adjacent to the seafood department, was a location in which a number of men worked. She was one of the few women in this workplace. Over the first few months that she worked for Mega-Shop, she reports that she had a number of negative experiences in the workplace. It seemed to her as if the men she worked with were always talking to her and about her. The men in produce started saying she was a topless dancer. She confronted the person who was spreading this rumor, and he told her that he said that just to make her popular. She told him that she did not want to be popular, that she just wanted to work. Because this rumor spread around the produce department, a number of the produce workers joked with her about it. They asked her if her breasts were real. They talked constantly about her breasts and asked if they could touch her, if they could see her breasts, or if she would participate in a wet T-shirt contest. According to her description, there was great deal of rowdy horseplay in the workplace. The male coworkers would throw things and ask her to pick them up so she would be forced to bend over to expose her chest to them. They put cucumbers between their legs and asked, "How would you like this?" Another worker would grab her buttocks and her breasts. Alfred Pacheco would pick her up (she is of small stature) and move her out of the way and would playfully hit her on the head with a knife sharpener. On occasion, she was locked in the freezer. One day, in the back of the store, one man grabbed her and kissed her.

By the end of the first week, she wanted to quit because she did not like the way things were on the job. However, because she was making $8 an hour, more than she had earned in any previous job and enough to support her children, and she decided to stay.

Eloisa Chavez complained about these incidents to Alfred Pacheco and told him to "tell the guys to stop," but she reports that Alfred did nothing. When she complained to his boss, Max Garcia, he started telling the men working in produce to get out of the seafood department and leave her alone. He told Ms. Chavez that he had had a talk with the produce manager, Sergio, and told him to tell them to stop. But some of her coworkers said others said that she was a "crybaby" because she complained.

Jimmy Pierce was the comanager of the store. Eloisa Chavez told him what was happening in the seafood section about a week after it all started and told him that she did not like these men to talk to her "so nasty." Pierce said that he would take care of it. However, she reported that what he actually started doing was to go to see her every day. This was known to almost everyone in the store. She noticed that after a while he was talking to her "really nice" and would talk to her about topics outside of work, as if she reminded him of somebody else. At first it was okay with her because the men in the produce department started backing off and it was "kind of neat" because they would let her alone for a while and were not "so nasty" with her. Next, Martin Winfield, the store manager, started coming to her section and asking personal questions such as why she was working there, whether she had a husband, and about her five kids.

She reported that after a while, if Martin was not there, it was Jimmy. Over time, both Jimmy and Martin would hug her. Jimmy would insist that she hug him really tight, as if he wanted to feel her breasts. She would tell Jimmy that no one would hug him like that. He told her not to turn her face away from his. She became very nervous. They would hug her in front of other workers and even customers. She was bothered and felt really small and felt that the other ladies and employees talked about her because they stopped talking when she came into the employees' lounge.

One day, she was having a lot of trouble with her husband, Victor, and had to leave work suddenly because she was concerned that Victor would kidnap the children and go to Mexico. Jimmy took care of her work that day, and she appreciated that because she knew she could keep her job and would not have to take Victor back because she could support herself. Her financial and living situations were very precarious given that she had very little emotional or financial support from outside.

After this incident, Jimmy transferred her from seafood to the packaged meats section. He told her he liked that better because he could touch her without having to lean over the counter. He started to touch her body more often. Throughout this time, her living situation was again unstable, and because of conflict with her husband, Victor, she moved in with her mother until she was able to move to her own mobile home. By this time, she had told Jimmy about her precarious financial situation, and he was bothering her a great deal. He would not leave her alone, even when others were around. She reports that he kept telling her he wanted her to leave the store with him to go someplace to have sex because of all the things that he did for her and for other members of her family. She recalls that he said he was taking care of her and giving her raises. By this time, she was making $9.10 per hour. In October 2000, he started pressuring her to have sex with him. She started to hate going to work because she was worried about what Jimmy was going to do. By this time, the men in the store were calling her "a little whore."

In October 2000, Roberto Orona replaced Max Garcia as meat manager. At first, he was really nice to her. But, as time went on, he would try to kiss her, follow her around, and push himself against her. On one occasion, she was bending over a box to retrieve some products, and he came behind her and rubbed up against her. She could feel his erect penis through her clothing. During this same time, he reports that he was always complaining to his supervisors about how she did her work, and she thought he was trying to get her fired.

At about this time, Ms. Chavez reports that she had sex with Jimmy Pierce for the first time. On one occasion, he came by when she was at work and said, "Let's go." Eloisa Chavez told him that she had to "clock out," but he told her not to. He gave her the keys to his car and told her to hide on the floor. She did, and a little while later, he came out and drove the car to a nearby motel. On the way, he stopped at a liquor store and asked her what she wanted to drink. She requested some beer. They took the beer to the motel. Once at the motel, after a brief conversation, he undressed her and had sex with her. Eventually, she called her husband,

and he picked her up from a nearby location. She was really afraid to talk to Victor about what had happened because he had told her he would kill her if she ever had sex with another man.

After that, on more than six occasions, Jimmy Pierce told her to meet him at a specific time at a motel. She did not refuse but did not go, and then he would be really mad at her for not following through. She went back to the motel a second time with him only because he told her that he would fire her if she did not come and that the only way she was going to get out of Roberto Orona's department was to sleep with him. He promised her that if she slept with him one more time he would move her. This time, he took her to a motel and had sex with her. She recalls that on that occasion the sex "hurt really bad." On a later occasion, he took her from work to his own home, but they did not have sex because she was "on her period." After that, he was really nice to her, and although he did not get her out of Roberto's department, he would fix the write-ups for not showing up at work that she would get from Roberto.

At one point, Martin, the store manager, started teasing her as if he knew she was having an affair with Jimmy. She enlisted the aid of a friend to explain to Martin what was happening at work. She and her friend met with Martin, but he acted "real cold" and angry. Eloisa Chavez thought that maybe he was angry because her friend was smart, could talk really well, and could tell Jimmy or Martin what was going on, what the men in the produce section were doing, and what Roberto Orona was doing. However, Martin did not seem to care.

Eloisa Chavez reports that Roberto Orona continued to say things to her and touch her on a regular basis. When she was working as a stocker, he would rub himself on her and moan and push her against the cabinet. He would kiss her, grab her breasts, rub himself on her, and follow her to the bathroom and break room. Roberto's sexual behavior toward her became so blatant that Roberto and Jimmy would occasionally argue over her. The day after she tried to talk with him, Martin was angry with her, but she wanted to tell him about what was going on with Roberto Orona and other men in the produce department. She just could not get the confidence up to talk with him by herself.

On February 6, 2001, Mercedes, a friend and coworker, asked her to go out for a drink after work. When she got there, it turned out that Roberto Orona and a number of other people from work were there. Roberto became quite drunk in the course of the evening and insisted on dancing with Eloisa Chavez, pushing himself against her. Eventually Eloisa Chavez felt like she was "set up" to be forced to ride home with Roberto, and she got into his car. He took her out to the desert and forcefully had anal and oral sex with her. She was afraid that he might have a gun in the car and that she was going to die. After he was done with her, he drove all over the town while telling her not to tell anyone what had happened. He eventually took her back to the bar where they had been earlier in the evening. She got out of Roberto's car, went back inside the bar, and went to the bathroom and washed her hands and face. She felt so dirty because she could not get his smell off of her. Eventually, she was able to get her keys back and went home. She stood in the shower for what seemed like the whole night and kept washing and felt so stupid because she felt as if it was her fault. It was over a month before she could report this event to the police.

The day after the events with Roberto, Eloisa went to work and told Nina, the assistant store manager what had happened. Roberto did not show up for work that day and did not show up for work the next day either. When he did come to work, he avoided her. However, about that same time, Jimmy started coming over to where she worked, and she told him that she had to talk to him and told him that something had happened. Nina apparently had already told him something about it. Later, she wrote a letter to the district manager. In this letter, she mentioned only the in-store sexual harassment that Roberto Orona had been doing and all the other sexual harassment by other employees. She did not talk about what happened with Roberto in the desert or any of the other things that supervisors such as Jimmy and Martin had been doing. The district manager told her that he would take care of it. She went back to work, and Jimmy thanked her for not telling on him about the sex that they had in the motels and the other sexual harassment.

About a week later, the district manager asked her to come talk with him. He started yelling at her and told her he had already investigated and wanted to know if she was having an affair with Jimmy, Martin, or Sergio. She told him that she had not had affairs with these people, that the only person that she was afraid of was Roberto, and that she would quit if he came back. She felt really bad because the district manager was clearly upset and angry.

On Easter Sunday, she went to the police department to report what Roberto Orona had done to her. She told the people at work that this was what was going on and that she wanted to be protected from Roberto. It was unclear whether Roberto would continue to work at the store. Because she was fearful of returning to work where Roberto might be, she quit her job on April 7, 2001. Since that time she has not returned to work.

HISTORY OF BATTERING

Throughout the time of Eloisa Chavez's employment at Mega-Shop, the situation with her husband, Victor Chavez, was very unstable and at times quite terrifying. From her description, he is a domineering and jealous man who tries to control his wife's every action and often battered her as a way of intimidating her and keeping her afraid. She reports that he would question her intensively after she came home from work and was upset that she worked on a job where there were a lot of other men.

Eloisa Chavez reports, and police records confirm, that she was the victim of considerable domestic violence at the hands of Victor Chavez. Although she recalls battering incidents before she was employed at the Mega-Shop, the violence increased over the course of her employment at Mega-Shop. Not long after she started working there, Victor Chavez was arrested on two occasions for battering Eloisa Chavez. After a third battering incident, he fled to Mexico to avoid arrest. However, after he went to Mexico, he called Eloisa Chavez and promised her that he would not hit her again. Eloisa Chavez agreed to allow him to return to the mobile home she had gotten for herself and the children, and Victor did not batter her again for a long time. However, at the time of the evaluation, she felt like she occasionally needed to leave the house when he had been drinking to avoid putting herself into situations in which he would hit her. She was very fearful about telling Victor about the alleged sexual assault by Roberto Orona. However, aside from threatening to track down and shoot Roberto, Victor has been verbally abusive but has not been physically aggressive toward her in relation to the incident. In fact, he alternated between telling her to be strong and put up with what was going on at work and accusing her of "asking for it."

EMOTIONAL REACTIONS TO THE HARASSMENT

Eloisa Chavez's emotional reactions to these events occurred in a number of areas. People often quite naturally remember the time before a traumatic event as being more idyllic than it actually was, and unverifiable self-reports should be understood in that light. In this matter, Ms. Chavez reported that in spite of her difficult home and family situation she had always had good sleep habits. However, not long after she began working at Mega-Shop, she developed occasional sleep problems. These occurred in the form of early awakening. She would wake up early in the morning and not be able to return to sleep. This left her feeling tired and sleepy later in the day. As weeks passed in her job in the seafood and produce sections, she began to have frequent stomach discomfort. This would start when she went to work in the morning, and she frequently felt severe stomach pain by the end of the day. She started developing headaches. These too got worse as the days and weeks went on.

She found that her relationship with Victor, which was already problematic, became more distant. She felt like she could not tell him what was going on at work because he would blame her for it and beat her up.

The first time she went to the motel with Jimmy Pierce in November 2000 marked a significant deterioration in her condition. Her sleep problems got worse, and she started drinking heavily. It is unclear whether this increase in drinking occurred primarily because of what happened with Jimmy or because of her increased general stress related to the battering relationship with Victor. She developed sleep onset insomnia and had frequent bad dreams that awakened her and prevented her from being able to return to sleep. She became fearful about people looking at her from outside her window. She kept having dreams and nightmares about being at MegaShop, being around Martin and Jimmy. At the time of the evaluation she had these dreams about three times a week.

She reports that her dreams and sleep problems got worse after she told the district manager. She would stay up all night, sit in her bed, look out the window, look in on her kids, and be really scared. Her fears became worse because Roberto would call her on the phone and talk to her little boy and tell him that he was going to kill them. Her family became afraid, and her little boy now draws pictures of dead people. Her oldest girl at one point took a bottle of aspirin and required hospitalization.

Eloisa Chavez has felt *beat up* all of the time. Her stomach has been hurting, her head aches, and she cannot remember normal things. She often forgets things her son tells her. She has felt as if she cannot concentrate or remember things now. She does not think she is crazy, but sometimes her head is "just so weird."

As noted previously, during the interval of her employment at MegaShop, her drinking increased. Prior to this time, she drank only about once a month, but during her employment she began to drink a six-pack a day and then as many as 18 beers a day. Eventually the drinking got to be too much, and she had to stop. She stopped drinking for two months in the spring of 2001 but has come back to drinking and will now have about 4 beers at one sitting about three times a week.

Also, after the first time she had sex with Jimmy, she felt as if going to work was almost unbearable. She felt that it ruined things for her at work. She did not want to be there anymore and did not care about what she was doing. She hated being there every single day of the week. During the days she was off work, Wednesdays and Thursdays, she slept. She found that on Thursday night she would "just drink and drink and drink" and wake up at 3 a.m. and go to work. There were times when she would go in very early in the mornings so she could get in and out of work more quickly, while many of the men who were bothering her were not at work.

This whole experience left her feeling that the bosses at work "messed up her life." She has not felt like a good mother anymore, and she is trying really hard, simply because she has not wanted her children to go through pain. These days, she feels as if she cannot make it. She has had fantasies about killing Jimmy, Martin, Roberto, and the men in the produce department. She knows that these are just fantasies, and she has talked to her physician about them and has no plan to act on them.

She feels as if she is doing somewhat better now. She thinks about her kids every day, tries to forget about what happened on the job, pretends it was just a dream, and acts like it did not happen to her. Her relationship with Victor is okay. What she did with Jimmy and what happened with Roberto hurt him very much, and he feels that it was his fault because he told her not to quit, to put up with it, and be strong. She has become very distrustful of other people.

She feels that her sex life with Victor has also been poisoned. She hates it because he does not understand, but she does not like to have sex. She feels that it is disgusting and does not like to do it. She feels as if her problems with sex are not Victor's fault and that she needs to have sex with him because "maybe he needs to have sex sometimes." She recalls that before all of this happened, she felt normal, and they would have sex about twice a month. She started having sexual difficulty after the thing with Jimmy and felt like she would get Victor dirty if she were to have sex with him.

She has also been a victim of occasional domestic violence from her husband; specifically when Victor gets really mad, he holds her tight and shakes her. She called the police about three months before the evaluation. The violence with Victor got worse after all this came up. In addition, sometimes she thinks about suicide and wishes she were dead. She prays and asks God to take her, but is too scared to hurt herself. She thinks about her kids and does not want to hurt them.

The salient issue in this case is whether each of Eloisa Chavez's impairments would not have occurred but for what she has alleged in her lawsuit. If the answer with regard to each impairment is that the impairment might reasonably be expected to occur as a consequence from another source of distress, then that impairment should not necessarily be considered to have been caused by the events claimed in the suit or attributed by her in her narrative.

PSYCHOLOGICAL TESTING

Psychological testing was conducted to provide an additional source of information about the person being evaluated. These data allow for comparisons between different aspects of the person's functioning and for the person to be compared with other people. Many of the measures used in the evaluation of Eloisa Chavez are sensitive to the impact of response set. That is, the tests allow the examiner to learn if the individual is overreporting or underreporting her distress. The standardization of the measures used in this evaluation included individuals whose cultural and linguistic background differ in some respects from Eloisa Chavez's Hispanic roots and first language of Spanish. These differences were taken into account in interpreting her test results.

The Wechsler Adult Intelligence Scale—III given to Ms. Chavez indicates that she is currently functioning at a Full Scale IQ of 82 with a Verbal IQ of 81 and a Performance IQ of 86. These place her at the 12th, 10th, and 18th percentiles, respectively, compared with the general population. Her Verbal Comprehension abilities are very poor and rank at the 4th percentile. Her Working Memory is somewhat better, almost at the average level, and her Processing Speed and Perceptual Organization are consistent with her below average IQs. Her reading, spelling, and math skills are equivalent to her low IQ and roughly equivalent to a sixth- or seventh-grade level. This pattern suggests that although Spanish is her first language, it has not affected her verbal skills significantly; they are comparable to her performance skills, which are less affected by cultural and linguistic factors. Her scores from neuropsychological screening instruments were within acceptable parameters. Likewise, her work on a test sensitive to malingering was well within normal parameters.

One self-report personality measure (the PAI) completed by Eloisa Chavez produced a rather elevated profile with primary elevations on the Paranoia scale. In the context of this case, this result may be interpreted in two ways. If it is interpreted in a way most favorable to the plaintiff, the pattern would be seen as one in which Eloisa Chavez was experiencing significant distress and wished emphatically to make that point through the testing. From this perspective, although this pattern shows some degree of overreporting, overall the pattern is one of a woman who experiences significant emotional disruption and alienation from other people. People with this pattern experience dysphoria, anger, and anhedonia. Depression is a common part of their lives, and they also feel very angry with others. Persons scoring similarly tend to be overly hostile and resentful toward other people, yet they are very sensitive, perhaps overly sensitive, and feel emotion more intensely than other people. Their feelings are easily hurt. People with these kinds of problems often find it hard to concentrate on their jobs and may lack self-confidence. People with this pattern often have impaired judgment. People with this pattern may be rather hypersensitive to criticism. In their interpersonal relationships, they tend to be shy and introverted and may feel lonely even when they are with other people. Specifically, for Eloisa

Chavez, the degree of her suspiciousness in this situation arises from her sense of being persecuted by others, which is not to say that psychological tests can prove that anyone was indeed persecuted.

Interpretation of the data is complex in this context. If the data are seen from the defendant's perspective, emphasis may fall on specific issues. First, Eloisa Chavez has been the frequent victim of battering in her marital relationship. This is a case in which the threat to her health and well-being has been real, and hypervigilance has been an adaptive response. Second, she is involved in litigation. In that context, she is feeling as if many private aspects of her life are under scrutiny by strangers. This too is a realistic response to her current circumstances and distrust may be appropriate. Both of these factors suggest that at least some of her elevations on scales reflecting suspiciousness are due to factors having little to do with the alleged sexual harassment at Mega-Shop.

Third, it could be that Eloisa Chavez was paranoid before she was employed by Mega-Shop. If her paranoid thinking was severe before she started work, it may be the case that her perception of other's behavior in the workplace was distorted by pervasive suspiciousness and attribution of hostile motives to what were, in reality, benign actions. If testimony adduced in the course of this litigation does not provide corroboration of what Eloisa Chavez contends was a pervasively sexualized environment, then misperception on her part could account for her allegations.

Fourth, her history of being a target of battering could account for the elevations on measures of depression and anxiety. Such reactions are common to battered women, and the fact that the battering occurred at a time close to the evaluation would suggest that she may be reporting reactions related more to ongoing life events than to events that occurred in the workplace months before.

However, if it is shown that she was exposed to a work environment as hostile as she reports, it could also be expected that she would experience increases in her sense of alienation from others. If it was the case that virtually every man in her workplace interacted with her as a sexual object and no man in her workplace proved to be protective of her, suspiciousness and distrust would naturally follow. The depressive and anxiety reactions would also flow from the stress of having to return on a daily basis to a stressful workplace.

Scores from this measure also indicate that she is a person who would be likely to respond to stressful circumstances by engaging in substance abuse. This is verified by her history, although nothing about her alcohol abuse pattern marks it as reactive to job stresses as opposed to the other stresses under which she lived during that time.

On the other self-report measure (the MMPI–2), there was also some evidence of overreporting. As with the PAI, these patterns bear two interpretations. Such elevations may reflect an attempt by a person involved in litigation to make her emotional reactions to the alleged on-the-job stresses appear more severe than they really are. Alternatively, patterns of this type are usually associated with serious distress and impairment of functioning. People with this kind of pattern suffer from significant thinking and concentration problems along with distress and ruminative worry. They are also more likely to be more withdrawn and isolated and to feel estranged from people around them. They may have severe specific anxiety as noted previously and experience a great deal of emotional constriction and loss of affective range in their current lives.

TREATMENT HISTORY

Records are available for Ms. Chavez's treatment with Guillermo Narvais, Susan Porter, Palo Duro Sexual Assault Recovery Services, and Alamogordo Counseling Center. This treatment occurred primarily between April of 2002 and the end of 2002, which would have been after she left her employment with Mega-Shop. The records indicate that Ms. Chavez initially presented with symptoms of serious PTSD, and in therapy she reported intrusive recollections, nightmares, and a high degree of anxiety concerning Roberto Orona. She had reported concerns to her therapist that she had seen him at a number of places around town and thought that he might harm her. This was seen in the context of her report of the rape by Roberto Orona.

She continued to get treatment from Susan Porter throughout spring, summer, and fall of that year. Although she had other issues that arose in the context of her treatment, such as problems with her daughter, most of the treatment focused on how she was coping with acute and chronic symptoms of trauma related to the rape incident. The stress from her daughter appears to have originated in the disrupted living situation of the family over the preceding several years and the stress of the domestic violence witnessed by the Chavez children. It is unlikely that the on-the-job stresses experienced by Eloisa Chavez would have translated directly into her daughter's behavioral problems. Her daughter's problems would have added to Eloisa Chavez's depression and anxiety.

Her therapists observed a pattern of reactions very similar to that of people who have PTSD in that her complaints were exacerbated whenever she was engaged in a process that reminded her of what was going on at the time of the assault. For example, when she became aware that the district attorney was not going to prosecute Roberto Orona, she became very upset almost to the point of becoming homicidal toward Roberto Orona.

This reaction is also similar to that of people who experience paranoid reactions.

Her treatment records also document an increase in the use of alcohol to the point that she became a problem drinker over the course of 2002. Although her treaters attempted to help her manage this alcohol problem, she reported to me that she was only able to manage it herself in late 2002 by abstaining from alcohol for several months. Since that time, she has returned to drinking but not at the level of her most severe drinking during 2002. Dr. Narvais had prescribed various medications for her, including several new antidepressants. She was still taking one of those antidepressants at the time I saw her in December 2002.

INFORMATION FROM COLLATERAL SOURCES

My interview with Victor Chavez was characterized by his frequent angry outbursts. He is angry at Eloisa Chavez, the defendants, the defendants' lawyers, and just about everyone else. He was able to describe changes that occurred in his wife since the time that she became employed at Mega-Shop. He said, "She used to be so happy. Sure, we would fight sometimes. But most of the time, she was happy." After she started at Mega-Shop, she would come home, fix dinner, go to their bedroom, and close the door. Their sex life declined, and he began to get angry with her for not wanting to have sex with him. She started drinking more, and he became worried about her drinking and whether she could care for the children. On one occasion, he had to take the children over to Eloisa Chavez's mother's house because she was upset and drinking and he had to go to work. Ever since she told him about the boss forcing her to have sex with him, he has been so angry that he has trouble feeling close to her. He was jealous before. Now, he can hardly stand to have her out of his sight for fear that she will have sex with someone.

SUMMARY AND CONCLUSIONS

A review of all of the information in this case indicates that Eloisa Chavez is a woman who had a very chaotic and disturbed childhood. She was a victim of sexual assault as a teenager. She had a series of very destructive relationships with men, many of which involved her being abused physically and emotionally. These were situations in which she had very little power in the relationship and, in some cases, felt like a prisoner to her husband's will.

She is also a woman with street smarts but limited intelligence and is naive about much of what goes on in the workplace. She has a limited social support system and, many times, has been faced with crises in fundamental areas of her life, such as obtaining child care, finding a residence, and having a functioning automobile. These are all considerations of alternative explanations for her difficulties.

She did not have a substantial work history at the time she was hired by Mega-Shop. However, once in this situation, if her report is accurate, she was exposed to a highly sexually charged work atmosphere. She reports that off-color jokes, sexual remarks, sexual gestures, obscene suggestions, and sexual innuendo were a significant component of her daily work environment. She also reports that she was subject to inappropriate touching, a great deal of inappropriate verbal behavior, and sexual advances from a number of men working in the store. This culminated in a sexual relationship with one of her bosses, Jimmy Pierce. He treated her differently from other female employees in the store by touching her sexually and allowing her special privileges. She recalls having sexual intercourse with him on two separate occasions. She was also subject to what she describes as a rape by another Mega-Shop supervisor, Roberto Orona.

THE DATA FROM THE PERSPECTIVE OF THE DEFENSE

Eloisa Chavez has had a difficult life in which she has experienced prior sexual assault and is the victim of ongoing domestic violence. She is a person of relatively meager intellectual resources, and much of her life has been characterized by poor planning, impulsive action, and bad choices, especially in regard to men. Because of this background, she developed a perspective in which she viewed others, especially men, as malevolent creatures who only desired to exploit her sexually or to otherwise abuse her. She carried this perspective into her work at Mega-Shop and quickly found that her daily contact with men in the workplace aroused her distrust, suspiciousness, and fears of threat to such an extent that she began to misperceive her coworker's actions. What they meant as good-natured joking, she saw as sexual innuendo. What amounted to incidental physical contact, unavoidable in the cramped confines of some work places, she interpreted as sexual touching. This pattern of suspiciousness and concern compounded until Eloisa Chavez felt it necessary to fabricate stories about sexual contact with one boss and even a rape by another. Although she now reports that she rebuffed her supervisors' and coworkers' sexual advances, it is unclear how consistently she indicated at the time of occurrence that each of the events was unwelcome. She admits that she omitted some of these events when she complained about her job situation when interviewed by the district manager.

The problem with this interpretation of the facts from this case is that there is, at this time, no evidence that Eloisa Chavez demonstrated suspiciousness or guardedness before her employment. If anything, she is a passive and rather gullible woman who was naive to many aspects of the workplace. She reported a pervasive pattern of sexualized behavior in a number of different places from a number of different people. This is consistent with research, which indicates that a permissive organizational climate may effectively give license to potential sexual harassers for inappropriate behavior. Also, her report of sexual intercourse with two of her bosses, if a fabrication, is so complex and developed as to be delusional. At this point in the case, there is no evidence that she has ever experienced a disorder sufficient to produce such serious symptoms.

CONCLUSIONS

After a review of all the data in this case, I offer five observations relevant to the legal issues.

1. Ms. Chavez came to this work situation with a history of trauma from a number of sources. She was a victim of prior sexual assault and was an ongoing victim of domestic violence. These situations relate to the evaluation of her case in three ways. First, the prior history of abuse and the repressive and abusive home environment that she endured explain why she did not object more strenuously or effectively about the hostile work environment she experienced in the seafood and produce sections of Mega-Shop. The research indicates that some people who have experienced prior victimization have more difficulty mobilizing effective resistance to subsequent victimization. Although Ms. Chavez attempted to resist Jimmy Pierce's efforts to get her to a motel room or his house, the fact that she acquiesced to pressure for several such sexual encounters may be a product of her prior history of sexual and violent victimization. Second, her history would have tended to exacerbate her reaction to on-the-job sexual events, if those events, in fact, took place. The research indicates that a prior history of sexual victimization may worsen outcomes for those who are subsequently abused. Third, the domestic violence and prior experiences could account for many of the symptoms that she currently exhibits. The fact that domestic violence occurred in her home before, during, and after her employment by Mega-Shop raises the probability that these events are the source of some or all of her emotional distress.

2. Ms. Chavez says that she experienced three kinds of trauma related to her employment at Mega-Shop. First, if her report is accurate, she was subjected to unwanted and uninvited sexual verbal behavior and sexual

touching from her coworkers and supervisors. This was almost constant and followed her from workplace to workplace within the Mega-Shop environment. Second, she reports that she was subject to coerced sexual intercourse by her manager and supervisor, Jimmy Pierce. Third, Ms. Chavez claims that she was the victim of a sexual assault by Roberto Orona. Although she acknowledges that this sexual incident occurred off of the Mega-Shop premises, Roberto Orona was her supervisor. Also, when she requested that she not be returned to the same work location where her alleged rapist worked, according to her, she was not provided with reasonable protection from him.

3. It is reasonably predictable that her reactions to these three different kinds of experiences would differ in course and severity. For the situation in the seafood and produce section, her account of worsening anxiety symptoms, increasing social isolation, worsening somatic symptoms, and impairments in functioning as a mother and wife corresponds with common reactions seen in women who endure stress over time. Her desire not to go to work and her impairments of work performance are also consistent with what is known about reactions to difficult environments. For the alleged coerced sexual activity with Jimmy Pierce, her responses reflect a higher level of anxiety and depressive reactions along with panic about how her sexual activities with her supervisor might affect her relationship with her volatile and abusive husband. Following the alleged rape, she exhibited a classic posttraumatic reaction with intrusive, avoidant, and hyperarousal symptoms.

4. Similar to what is known about women in domestic violence situations, her decision to leave her job at Mega-Shop can be seen as an adaptive psychological response to what she believed was an overwhelmingly toxic work environment. If this case is evaluated as a whole, the remarkable fact is that Ms. Chavez endured working at Mega-Shop as long as she did. In comparison to a reasonably prudent person in her situation, one might conclude that a more *reasonable* person in the same circumstances would have quit the job within a few weeks of the initiation of the sexual speech and touching. However, that same literature regarding victims of domestic violence sheds light on two considerations: the person's past experience and the person's estimates regarding viable alternatives to the current situation. Her past abuse history coupled with exigent financial circumstances and her naiveté about available options were part of the problem. From her perspective, her work environment offered no effective complaint mechanism for solving the problem. Whenever she went up the chain of command to have someone make her coworkers stop their behavior toward her, the person she went to often responded by engaging in sexualized behavior toward her. This created a situation in which she saw resignation as her only option to put an end to what she felt was the pervasive and increasingly

dangerous harassment at Mega-Shop. It was not unrealistic for her to see her only eventual escape from these circumstances as resignation, especially considering her precarious financial situation and her anticipation of the violence that she might experience at home if she resigned.

5. More likely than not, as a matter of reasonable psychological probability, Eloisa Chavez developed functional impairments as a result of the three kinds of events she endured at Mega-Shop. She developed the impairments related to a posttraumatic reaction to the sexual incident with Roberto Orona. Her symptomatic impairments in response to this trauma were functionally and measurably different from what had been her trauma-related impairments from the prior sexual assault and the ongoing domestic violence. In addition, it is my opinion that she has become hypervigilant to the point of diagnosable paranoia in reaction to the hostile work environment and sexual coercion. She has persisting fearfulness and anxiety that were not present before going to work for Mega-Shop. She is almost constantly on the alert for bad things happening to her and is afraid much of the time. These reactions have, at times, been extreme, and she has received ongoing treatment from Susan Porter in Alamogordo for these problems. These reactions may arise from her ongoing domestic violence situation or may be exacerbated by the abuse she receives at home. She has also been prescribed antidepressant medications to help her deal with her suicidal ideation and depression. The damage to her self-concept and her self-blame for what happened to her have been substantial contributors to her suicidal behavior. Again, her reactions to the situation with her husband could account for impaired self-concept and self-blame. In addition, the fear she has of her husband could also contribute to her suicidal behavior.

These problems are ongoing, and it appears that she is in need of continuing treatment for symptoms that she has experienced for at least a year. At this writing, it is my opinion that she will need an additional two to three years of individual psychotherapy to return to her level of functioning before the onset of these workplace traumas and distresses. These sessions should occur on a once weekly basis with a therapist skilled in dealing with later trauma in individuals who have suffered childhood trauma. This combination of traumas may make the treatment process very difficult, as the development of trust and a stable lifestyle lacks a firm foundation in social support or past mastery of anxious circumstances.

Given her history of an unstable lifestyle and domestic violence, it is reasonable to provide any financial recovery in the form of a structured settlement or under the protection of an administrator. The court should consider that her makeup is likely to render her vulnerable to duress by others and, therefore, the court should act in ways, where possible, to ensure that any compensation that she receives is actually available for her benefit.

I hope this report meets the legal requirements at this time. As very little discovery has been done in this case, please be aware that I may revise this report based on later information. If I may be of further assistance to you, please feel free to call or write.

Sincerely yours,

APPENDIX B
Allegations of Male on Male Sexual Harassment and Retaliation

In this appendix, we present a second psychological evaluation report illustrating how a case may be approached. The report is adapted from a real case and, in accordance with the APA ethics code, is disguised by changing all of the names and many of the facts that might have identified the case. Some of the facts were altered to create better examples, although many of the most dramatic and vivid details are based on real events that were retained if they were sufficiently anonymous.

February 20, 2003

Maria Martinez
414 Copper, NE
Albuquerque, NM 87103

Re: Dan Swenson

Dear Ms. Martinez:

In your role as defense counsel, you asked me to conduct a psychological evaluation of Dan Swenson as part of the matter of *Swenson v. Charles McGinnis and New Mexico Film Hall of Fame*. I met with Mr. Swenson on February 13, 17, and 19, 2003. On the first occasion, I met with him for a two-hour clinical interview, and also on that date, he completed the Minnesota Multiphasic Personality Inventory—2 and the Personality Assessment Inventory. On February 17, he met with my testing assistant, Bob Williams, MA, who administered the Wechsler Adult Intelligence Scale—III, the Rey Complex Figure Test, Trials A and B, the Wide Range Achievement Test, and the Test of Memory Malingering. I met with him for the third time on February 19, 2003, and conducted a 2.5-hour clinical interview. Mr. Swenson has reviewed the notes from both interviews and has made corrections. The corrected notes are part of the basis for this evaluation.

These corrections are limited to the history as he reported it. Neither he nor anyone else has been given the opportunity to make changes to my impressions, opinions, or recommendations.

In addition to the interviews of the plaintiff, I have had an opportunity to review a number of documents in this case. These include the complaint for retaliation filed on November 21, 2002, by Mr. Swenson's counsel, the defendants' answers to that complaint, the plaintiff's medical records, the plaintiff's performance appraisals, the defendants' responses to charges of discrimination, the Notice of Contemplated Action/Suspension, Mr. Swenson's response to the Notice of Contemplated Action/Suspension, the Notice of Final Action/Suspension, the Notice of Contemplated Action/Termination, Mr. Swenson's response to the Notice of Contemplated Action/Termination, and the Notice of Final Action/Termination. I have also reviewed Mr. Swenson's and Mr. McGinnis's testimony from a Human Rights Commission hearing that took place in July 2002.

In my initial visit with Mr. Swenson, I reviewed a written informed-consent form with him, and he provided consent to proceed. This form had previously been provided to Mr. Swenson's counsel and then to him, so he had had an opportunity to review it before the meeting. Nevertheless, I explained that I was retained by the defendants' counsel in this case and that he could expect that I would share the results of the evaluation with them. He was informed that I did not know if a report would be generated by the evaluation. If one were generated, he and his counsel would be provided with a copy.

As a matter of usual practice, I conduct collateral interviews with the plaintiff's friends and family. I provided Mr. Swenson with a form to complete to give me permission to complete these telephone interviews and to provide the names and phone numbers of those people. As of the completion of this report, Mr. Swenson has not completed the form or provided those names. Thus, no collateral interviews have been conducted. Although conducting collateral interviews is likely to have been helpful, I ultimately felt that I had adequate information to form opinions even in their absence. Should they become available later or should the defense allow me to conduct collateral interviews of their witnesses, my report may later be revised or supplemented as a result.

Pursuant to Civil Rule 35, the purpose of this examination is to assess Mr. Swenson's psychological condition relative to his charges of retaliation against the supervisors and the organization of the New Mexico Film Hall of Fame. I begin by reviewing Mr. Swenson's account of his personal history and continue with his account of his litigation-related experiences. I then discuss the psychological test data and conclude with a summary.

PERSONAL HISTORY

Mr. Swenson was born on January 27, 1959, in Albuquerque, New Mexico, to Joe and Elaine Swenson. His father died some five years ago and had worked as an electrician most of his adult life. Mr. Swenson says his father was a strict disciplinarian, having been a Marine during World War II. Although Mr. Swenson first characterized his father as benevolent, on later questioning he revealed that his father was verbally abusive and yelled at the children in the family. He was an alcoholic and forced the children to leave the house frequently because they were making too much noise. His mother, Elaine Swenson, is 81 years old and had a stroke about five years ago. Dan Swenson lives with her and is her primary caretaker. She needs assistance in a number of daily activities and cannot be left alone for any protracted period.

Dan Swenson is the second youngest of five children and reports that none of his siblings have a history of mental health or substance abuse problems. He reports the he did not experience any physical or sexual abuse as a child or young adult. He reports that he was "a halfway decent student" and was involved in track and field through his junior high school years. He also played some junior high school football.

He attended Midland High School, was a wrestler during his junior year, and attended Latin Club. He reports no disciplinary problems in school. He graduated from Midland High School in 1978. He went to work for the first time as a laborer in a nursery following his graduation from high school. He quit that job in the fall and began at the University of New Mexico (UNM) in the winter of 1979 as a full-time student. He received his bachelor's degree in film in 1984.

Through his college years, he worked part time at a number of jobs, including at a gas station as a work/study student, as a cashier at a local drugstore, at a pizza place, and as a security guard. He attended Central New Mexico University in Claunch "just for a change" for a year with no serious intentions of continuing his education. In the fall of 1985, he returned to UNM and started to work on his teaching certification and to take upper division film courses. After taking courses in the College of Education, he discerned that he hated the program because it seemed more like babysitting than teaching and he was "not into that." In the winter of 1986, he started taking film courses part time and working at a local Protestant church as a maintenance man, where he worked for four and a half years. He next worked for a tutoring organization, tutoring undergraduate students in history, geography, and anthropology. Throughout this time, he was attending graduate courses part time. He was eventually accepted into the graduate program in American Studies, focusing on American Western Film. He completed his master's thesis, but it was never approved, and he reports that he has never completed his master's degree. He reports that he did not make the corrections that he needed to make because he started working full-time at the State Film Archives in Santa Fe in 1992.

RELATIONSHIP HISTORY

Dan Swenson reports that he has never been married, although he was once engaged when he was in college completing his bachelor's degree. He and a woman had gone out for about a year, and she thought they would get married after his bachelor's degree, but he wanted to continue his education. She was disappointed and started dating someone else. When he was a graduate student, he dated another woman for close to a year, but she went to Texas to be a nurse, and they could not pull it together in the context of a long-distance relationship.

He contends that his relationship with Danina Cohen, a coworker, was "never a boyfriend or girlfriend," although he holds her in the highest regard and considers her a good friend. On further questioning, Dan Swenson admitted that he had romantic interests in her, but they are just best friends. They were never dating, and it was never serious in a romantic or intimate sense. When questioned about medical records mentioning his marriage proposal to her, Dan Swenson downplayed the incident and said that he only said to her, "Why don't we get married or live together?" and he admits that those words may constitute a marriage proposal. There was never any physical relationship, and the relationship was one that was destined to fail because they were "never meant to be a couple."

Subsequently, he had a relationship with a woman named Maureen, which continued until August 2002. It turns out that she was married at the time to another man, and she told him that she was going to get a divorce, but she never did. He was also dating another woman up until last Christmas, but it was "too difficult, because they were too different."

He admits that he has had a problem with women. He says, "I feel like I don't much care for the idea of commitment, that is, marriage or living with someone."

WORK HISTORY WITH THE STATE FILM ARCHIVES

In 1992, he was employed by the State Film Archives as an archivist. He assisted researchers and did cataloging and indexing of collections. He was in charge of the film and photograph collections. He was charged with developing a specialty of silent films made in New Mexico during the first quarter of the 20th century. He worked there until 1996. In that year, he left that job, in part because Dominic Romano, his mentor, had left the organization. More than anything, he was tired of the commute and did not want to move to Santa Fe. He had occasional difficulty getting along with some of his supervisors and coworkers in that position. He and a woman named Cindy had arguments "over procedural things," and he would sometimes confront her because he did not think she was carrying her load in assisting the researchers. He left the organization on good terms with her.

When Dominic Romano left his position as head of the State Film Archives, it seemed as though "there was no direction in that place anymore." Following his departure from the State Film Archives, he did some contract work for a company called Wayneco and maintained their video collection. He was trained as a database specialist, making changes to the company database. He did that for about a year, full-time. He left that job because he was in a contract position, and there was no opportunity for advancement and growth. His supervisors did not express any dissatisfaction with his work.

Mr. Swenson worked for the Zoning Board of the City of Albuquerque in 1997 and 1998 as a zoning coordinator, a position in which he assisted people in making zoning variance applications. He did that job for only about eight months because he found it was very demanding. He had to make a number of decisions in reference to liquor establishments wanting to locate near schools and churches and did not feel competent making those decisions. In the course of working for that organization, he says he was never reprimanded for working too slowly or not getting the job done nor was he criticized for any aspects of his performance on the job or for conflicts with supervisors.

He did some contract work for Rubaco as a database specialist, organizing training schedules and putting data together. He worked for them for about a year and left that position when he was hired at the New Mexico Film Hall of Fame (NMFHF) in November 1999.

WORK AT THE FILM HALL OF FAME

Mr. Swenson was hired as the senior film archivist. In that position, he helped run the library and assisted researchers; he sometimes did tours and even, occasionally, swept the floors where the collections were housed. He worked with volunteers and did collection development with the film collections and with New Mexico film memorabilia. Mr. Swenson reports that he was comfortable with his job in part because he felt as if the NMFHF was an important place. Although the job was stressful and difficult, he enjoyed working there and enjoyed being an archivist.

His supervisor was Charles McGinnis. From Mr. Swenson's recollection, he got along with Mr. McGinnis pretty well when he was first hired. But within a few days after he started the job, he recalls that Mr. McGinnis threatened to let him go. It was Dan Swenson's contention that Charles McGinnis wanted to hire another fellow who used to work for him at the University of New Mexico. Instead, Dan Swenson was hired and felt that he was already in a bad position relative to Charles McGinnis and that their relationship was strained.

Dan Swenson reports that from the beginning of his work at the NMFHF, Charles McGinnis was abusive and vulgar in the workplace and commonly used the "F word." After the first three months of being told daily that he could be replaced, Dan Swenson felt that he had to stay on top of things and that although he met every deadline that was given to him, he was already being criticized for failure to meet deadlines. He took a complaint about Charles McGinnis's treatment of him to their boss, and it seemed as if Charles McGinnis turned over a new leaf for quite a while; that is, he was less abusive and allowed Dan Swenson to do his work. However, he reported that following a particular incident things "went downhill" again.

An incident occurred on April 15, 2001, in which Dan Swenson and Danina Cohen were talking in the NMFHF's library about a half hour before the workday ended. Danina Cohen worked at the theater at the Hall of Fame and was "only a friend." Dan Swenson recalls that Ms. Cohen was consoling him in relation to the medical problems that his mother had encountered. He reports that Charles McGinnis came by and was abusive to him. Charles McGinnis reported that the lights were off and the door locked when he entered the room and that he saw Dan Swenson and Ms. Cohen locked in an embrace. Charles McGinnis said he was embarrassed, so he just coughed and left.

The next day, there was a meeting between Dan Swenson and Charles McGinnis in the latter's office. McGinnis recalls a businesslike conversation in which he told Dan Swenson it was inappropriate for him to be in a locked, darkened room with another employee during working hours and that Dan Swenson was expected to pursue Hall of Fame business and not his personal affairs during business hours. From Dan Swenson's recollection, he told Charles McGinnis that he and Danina Cohen were just talking about his mother's stroke and explained it was the end of the workday and that it was a legitimate discussion. Dan Swenson contends that Charles McGinnis was abusive to him and told him "get a piece of ass on your own time." Dan Swenson recalls that he told Charles McGinnis that he had no right to talk to him like that and Charles McGinnis responded, "I am the boss here, and you are just an employee. Just do what you are told." Dan

Swenson threatened to put in his resignation, and Charles McGinnis told him to give him his keys right now if he wanted to resign. Dan Swenson, in fact, wrote a letter of resignation. During the 48 hours he had to rescind his resignation, he thought about it. The next day he felt that he did not do anything wrong and there was no reason to leave, so he rescinded his resignation.

On July 13, 2001, Dan Swenson filed a sexual harassment complaint with the Human Rights Commission on the basis of this incident with Charles McGinnis. When asked what about this incident constituted sexual harassment, Mr. Swenson said, "by his comment." When asked what it was about the comment, he said, "because it was demeaning" to Dan Swenson and to Danina Cohen. He thought it was inappropriate and illegal for Charles McGinnis to use that kind of language. Dan Swenson reports that it was his understanding that the Human Rights Commission complaint failed because there was insufficient evidence to support a sexual harassment complaint and because the incident occurred between two men.

Following his filing of the Human Rights Commission complaint, Dan Swenson felt as if he was harassed on a daily basis because of filing that complaint. Dan Swenson felt that Charles McGinnis's complaints about him were overblown. "He said I cannot file a paperclip. As far as Charles was concerned, I was insubordinate; I destroyed the team environment; I could not keep deadlines; my work was inefficient. I was accused of stealing some files from him. Anything and everything." This examiner asked Dan Swenson whether there were any aspects of his work that he felt he was not performing up to standards. He reports that he felt as if he was doing everything the same after he filed the complaint as he did before, but after he filed the complaint he could not do anything right.

Dan Swenson felt that whenever he tried to present anything about his work, it was "shot down" or taken away from him. He had an idea of developing a database of New Mexico silent films and was told that he did not have time to pursue that activity. At one point, he was sitting on a committee for developing a long-term plan for preserving New Mexico's ephemeral cultural resources, but he was told by Charles McGinnis not to be involved in the project and the NMFHF was pulled out of it. Dan Swenson believed that this latter action was part of McGinnis's retaliation against him.

Eventually, from Dan Swenson's perspective, he was fired entirely under false pretexts in the spring of 2002. Before he was fired, he had been suspended several times on the basis of what Dan Swenson called "trumped up charges."

REVIEW OF VOCATIONAL RECORDS

Vocational records indicate that Dan Swenson had two performance appraisals in the course of his work with the NMFHF. His first, for the period November 1999 through November 2000, before the NMFHF moved into its new facility, reflected performance that "meets expectations" in all areas except "emotional control." In that regard, his supervisor noted, "needs improvement in controlling his emotions." On the form, Dan Swenson noted, "Even though I am constantly faced with hostility from others, I manage to keep my emotions in check. I have engaged in no negative behaviours even when I must contend with the active opposition of others on a daily basis."

His second personnel appraisal was not issued until a year later for the period May through November 2001. It gave him "less than acceptable scores" for teamwork, productivity, and self-control. In the last area, he was seen as needing improvement. In a memo accompanying this appraisal, dated December 26, 2001, Charles McGinnis noted that Dan Swenson's performance had noticeably declined since the last evaluation and that this decline was marked by the fact that Dan Swenson was put on paid administrative leave on one occasion and suspended without pay on another. The memo noted that Dan Swenson

> tends to overreact to criticism. He often will personalize conflict and become obsessed with it. He does not talk to people he has conflicts with and seems incapable of resolving conflicts. He has turned his workplace into a tense and uncomfortable place for his supervisors, coworkers, and outside contractors. His behaviour generally lacks professionalism and discretion.

On the basis of these and many other problems, Dan Swenson was given a Notice of Final Action/Dismissal on April 10, 2002.

Whenever Dan Swenson received documentation, he answered in writing comprehensively, denying the problems were true. He invariably noted that McGinnis's criticism of him was retaliatory. The tone of his responses was always defensive and angry. In the interview, Dan Swenson was asked if he felt any of the criticisms by Charles McGinnis were correct. He said, "This criticism was totally unjustified. Not a single statement is correct." He felt that Charles McGinnis set him up to fail in getting things in on time and often changed deadlines just to make Dan Swenson look bad.

The records indicate that in July 2002, Dan Swenson filed a second Human Rights Commission complaint against Mr. McGinnis, this time for reprisal. In this case, following a hearing on the matter, he was given a "right to sue" letter by the Commission.

REPORTED EMOTIONAL REACTIONS

Dan Swenson reports that before his work at the NMFHF, he never had any kind of psychiatric treatment or medication for depression, sleep, or nerves and was only hospitalized for a broken wrist in 1994. He was never arrested for any reason and has never contemplated suicide.

From Dan Swenson's perspective, he had a number of emotional reactions to what happened on the job at the NMFHF. He felt as if he was being "put through the mill" every day and "put through a lot of stress." His coworkers would tell him all the time that "Charles had it in for" him. He felt depressed, anxious, and nervous. He said, "Every day I would turn in a quality product, and I knew it was never going to be good enough. I felt like I was being set up because I knew beforehand that anything I did would be unfairly criticized." He was aware that Charles McGinnis knew how to eliminate people from the workplace and had specific strategies to "get all he could from someone and then stomp on them and get rid of them."

When asked about symptoms of depression, Dan Swenson reports that he was not sleeping very well and did not care to go out and do things with his family. He found that he had a sleep problem related to thinking about what was going on all of the time. He would go to bed thinking about it and wake up thinking about it. He had some difficulty getting to sleep and would sometimes stay up an extra two or three hours thinking about what was happening on the job. He experienced no early awakening in this context.

He reports that he changed his leisure activities as a result of the on-the-job events. Before this, he enjoyed cooking, reading, fishing, and exercising. After difficulties started with Charles McGinnis, he did not feel like doing those things. He did not have the energy for leisure activities. He stopped going fishing. On weekends, he did not feel good enough to do very much. However, when he tried doing things, he found that he actually did enjoy them. His energy level seemed okay, but he feels as if he lost his self-confidence. He worried a lot and felt that he could get fired any minute. Dan Swenson reports that he had some difficulty with concentration, but he felt it was important for him not to let his work suffer because he was told to keep up his level of production. Although it was hard for him to concentrate, he tried to stay functional at a professional level. Dan Swenson felt he was "walking on eggshells" and "always anxious," worried about what kind of criticism he was going to get. He reports no increase in irritability or muscle tension. He reports no symptoms consistent with panic attacks.

Dan Swenson reports the following alcohol use history. He drank for the first time when he was a senior in high school. He drank heavily in high school and would go to "keggers" and drink "a lot of beer" on weekends.

Before he graduated, he went through a very conservative Christian conversion by the Campus Christians. He became a "counselor for Jesus." He was a part of Campus Christians from about 19 to 29 years old. However, he began to believe at that point that certain experiences were good in moderation and that it was okay to drink alcohol occasionally and have occasional relationships with girls.

He started drinking socially and often went with his friend to a local bar. He would also go to buffet restaurants for drinks and dancing. In the period before he went to work for the NMFHF, he recalls that at times, on weekends, he would have more to drink than he should have had. He never felt as if his drinking was out of control because he was never drinking very much during the week. He reports that he never drank on Sundays and would never go to work on Mondays drunk, although he might have a couple of glasses of wine or meet somebody after work for a beer. Dan Swenson does not believe that he has had a problem with drinking.

When asked about his gambling activities, he says that once in a while in the years before he went to work for the NMFHF, he "would throw a few dollars into a slot machine." When asked if he thought his gambling was ever out of control, he said that there were times, both before and after his employment with the NMFHF, when maybe it would have been a better idea not to gamble. He reports, however, that he never gambled money that he needed for other obligations and never felt that spending more than $50 was overdoing it or a waste of money. One time he lost over $100 at the casino when he and his friend were "trying to impress some girls."

MEDICAL RECORDS

Medical records indicate that Dan Swenson met with James Dominguez, PhD, for the first time on June 6, 2001. This would have been after the "library incident," but before he filed his first Human Rights Commission complaint. In the initial assessment, Dr. Dominguez quotes Dan Swenson saying, "I feel like I am drowning. I have lost control over everything in my life and I feel overwhelmed." He also noted "women scare me." At the time, Dan Swenson was in a depressed and anxious mood and noted that he had a problem with his appetite, his sleep, and feeling nervous all the time. He reported no changes in daily functioning. At the time of the interview, Dr. Dominguez noted, "Father was an alcoholic. He died three and one half years ago and was physically and verbally abusive to Dan and the whole family." In reporting Mr. Swenson's problems, Dr. Dominguez's noted: "Over the last year, he gambles every weekend and sometimes during the week, losing as much as $300 per time. He is concerned that he has been sabotaging his financial status. Dan is overwhelmed by his feelings and responsibilities at this time. His responsibility to care for his mother has worn him out, and he has been jilted by the woman he was dating. He spends too much time alone and gambles too much. He feels stuck in life. He carries a diagnosis of 309.28, Adjustment Disorder with Mixed Anxiety and Depressed Mood. I will defer Axis II diagnosis. On Axis IV, Dan reports problems with his family and friends, occupational problems with his supervisor, and problems with his mother and girlfriend." Specific goals of treatment included reduction of depression and anxiety and finding healthier outlets to reduce these needs and to reduce isolation, when possible and appropriate.

Subsequent therapy sessions indicated that on June 13, 2001, Dan Swenson's affect was better; he was walking for exercise more and had a better outlook on life. In that session, Dr. Dominguez noted that Dan Swenson told him: "My boss is making my life miserable! He is turning up the heat and threatening me with termination. I am drinking just to not think about missing Danina. I want to continue working on my job problems, my mom, and my life."

Subsequent session notes indicate that Dr. Dominguez was treating Dan Swenson for a number of life circumstance problems, including those related to his mother, to problems in his emotional relationships with women, particularly with Danina Cohen, and to problems related to his job. On one occasion, the notes reflect that he dated another woman named Maureen as a means of making Danina Cohen jealous. At the end of 2001, Dan Swenson was drinking more, and by August 2001, he reported continuing problems with his supervisor. In addition, by mid-August 2001, Dan Swenson was again losing large amounts of money at the casino and was seeing Danina Cohen again. Dr. Dominguez completed a note to Ronald Martin, Dan Swenson's lawyer, on November 2, 2002. In that note, Dr. Dominguez focused on Dan Swenson's reactions to work situations and his relationship with Charles McGinnis. From Dr. Dominguez's perspective, his work with Dan Swenson was undermined by Dan's encounters with Charles McGinnis, which Dan perceived as negative. A review of these records indicates that Dan Swenson continued to work with Dr. Dominguez until April 2002, when Dan Swenson was discharged from his employment at the NMFHF.

Several observations concerning Dan Swenson's treatment with Dr. Dominguez are merited. From a perspective most favorable to the plaintiff in this case, two features are important. First, Dan Swenson showed an increase in a number of psychiatric symptoms once he began to be criticized and disciplined by Charles McGinnis. Second, his increased drinking and gambling problems may have been another symptom of his stress as opposed to being seen as evidence of problems generated by a lack of impulse control. It may be that he came into his employment with the NMFHF with a tendency to behave impulsively when under stress. Dan Swenson denies he has a gambling problem.

From a perspective most favorable to the defendants in this case, several things should be noted. First, Dr. Dominguez was not provided with information concerning Dan Swenson's performance on the job other than Dan Swenson's perspective. Therefore, he would have no basis for determining if Dan Swenson's perceptions concerning Charles McGinnis's actions were accurate. Second, the records note that Dan Swenson had life problems in a number of areas besides what was going on in his job. These include (a) a relatively isolated lifestyle in which he had only one significant friend, (b) problems in relation to his obligations toward his mother and his need to care for her, and (c) problems in his relationships with women. These are evident in interventions in relation to Danina Cohen and other women with whom Dan Swenson interacted. Dr. Dominguez did not sort out the relative contribution of these problems to Dan Swenson's ongoing reported distress, so he cannot be a source of information about the individual impact of the events that took place on the job.

PSYCHOLOGICAL TESTING

The psychological testing on Dan Swenson included both an intellectual assessment and a personality assessment. The intellectual assessment included the Wechsler Adult Intelligence Scale—III. That scale yielded a Full Scale IQ of 124, a Verbal IQ of 133, and a Performance IQ of 110. These place him, respectively, at the 95th, 99th, and 75th percentile of the population within his age group. A closer look at his component scores indicates that his verbal skills are even higher than those measured by his Verbal IQ. His purely verbal skills would be equivalent to an IQ of 145, equivalent to the 99th percentile. His performance skills, as broken down as a primary skill area, are roughly equivalent to his Performance IQ. His attention and concentration are at a level significantly below that measured by his Verbal scores. This may reflect impairment of attention and concentration. His motor speed in timed tasks was lower than expected. There was no evidence in the intellectual assessment that Dan Swenson attempted to do worse on these measures than he was actually capable of doing.

Dan Swenson completed the Minnesota Multiphasic Personality Inventory—2. On that measure, he produced a pattern that indicates underreporting, although the profile was valid. That is, he tended to report fewer problems than the average person. As a result, he had a profile that was entirely below the clinical limits and appeared to be unusually well adjusted as compared with the general population and especially as compared with the typical personal injury plaintiff.

He produced a similarly defensive pattern with the Personality Assessment Inventory. The computer readout notes that Dan Swenson scores similarly to people who present themselves to others as having few of the common problems that most people would report and is reluctant to recognize even trivial faults of his own. In the context of this defensiveness, his profile showed no evidence of any serious pathology.

SUMMARY AND CONCLUSIONS

Results from this evaluation shed light on two main issues. The first is how Dan Swenson's psychological functioning affected his on-the-job performance. The second relates to how the criticism and discipline Dan Swenson received from Charles McGinnis may have affected him. These are discussed in sequence.

I first offer observations that are intended to clarify the nature of Dan Swenson's job-related problems. The first is that Dan Swenson shows a pattern of behavior that suggests that he has difficulty relating to others. He has only one close friend and has never been able to develop or maintain a long-term relationship with a woman. Based on the medical records and his statements regarding his relationships, he appears to have difficulty reading social cues and often interprets the behavior of others in accord with his preconceptions rather than on the basis of their actual intent. This problem has been reflected in his romantic relationships in which he has misinterpreted the other's desire to intensify the relationship. This problem may also have entered into his perception that each and every action of Charles McGinnis was unfair and an attempt to make his life miserable.

The second observation is that Dan Swenson sees all of his problems arising from the bad intentions and actions of Charles McGinnis. In the course of my interview with Dan Swenson, he was asked whether he had any problem in the performance of his work duties. He reported that he felt he performed all of his work to the highest standards and that all of Dan McGinnis's criticisms were unfair. I find these assertions noteworthy in that most people will admit that their performance on the job is, at times, less than adequate. Most people make mistakes on the job. People like some aspects of their work better and perform more effectively in those aspects than they do in the ones that they do not like. Dan Swenson admitted no such human frailty. He may have thought that such concessions would harm his legal case because a psychologist hired by the defendants was evaluating him. Alternatively, his defensiveness suggests that he might, in fact, be out of touch with the appraisal of his own work. That is, he may not be able to accurately assess how effective he is in his job, thus criticisms from others feel especially burdensome and inappropriate. In the alternative, he is aware of his failings but becomes defensive when others criticize him. In his review of Dan Swenson's performance, Charles McGinnis noted that Dan Swenson did not accept criticism from supervisors.

The following observations are offered to place into context Dan Swenson's claims of emotional distress related to his treatment at the NMFHF. The first observation is that in addition to his failure to admit normal human failings in his testing, Dan Swenson frankly mischaracterized some aspects of his history in his interview with me. He characterized his family history as relatively benign, but on further questioning and on the basis of the records from Dr. Dominguez, the data indicated that he was actually raised in an abusive and alcoholic home where he was the recipient of significant verbal abuse by his father. This suggests that he tends to present his history in an unduly positive light. Second, when questioned about his relationship with Danina Cohen, his initial characterization was that they were "just friends." However, on questioning based on information from Dr. Dominguez's records, Dan Swenson admitted that this was, in fact, an emotional and romantic relationship and that he wanted to marry Danina Cohen but was rebuffed in his proposals. The medical records reflect that this was a highly emotional relationship and one that caused him great emotional distress that he now significantly downplays. He also downplays the demands placed on him by his mother and her care and the emotional cost of those demands. In short, Dan Swenson is likely to underreport non-job-related sources of emotional distress. This may have affected how Dr. Dominguez evaluated and treated him

The second observation is that Dan Swenson had many events going on in his life at the time the job actions were occurring at the NMFHF. His mother was seriously ill, and he was her primary caregiver. His love for Danina Cohen was not reciprocated. He was drinking too much and losing too much money gambling. In addition, he had complaints of being treated badly by his supervisor. All of these problems could have given rise to the distress noted by Dr. Dominguez in his treatment of Dan Swenson. The relative contribution of these other life events to Dan Swenson's overall distress is difficult to sort out. It may be the case that he developed emotional reactions to the negative job events and this distress was added to that from already existing family stressors. It is also the case that if Dan Swenson did experience emotional distress as a result of job-related activities, this distress would have occurred even if he had been criticized and reprimanded for his actual failings. In other words, being reprimanded for one's actions and being the recipient of frequent criticism are stressful even when that criticism is valid. Whether those reprimands were appropriate and nonretaliatory is an issue to be decided by the finder of fact in this case.

The third observation is that Dan Swenson evinces and reports in response to the test questions little objective evidence of emotional distress at the time of this evaluation. Although his test data were affected by his tendency to underreport his emotional distress, his scores on psychological tests were well below the clinical range, generally indicating a self-report of being psychologically healthier and happier than the average person. On the cognitive testing, he does show some degree of impairment of attention and concentration and a reduced motor speed, which may have been attributable to depression and anxiety. These may reflect continuing emotional distress from the on-the-job events. In the alternative, these are general symptoms and may have antedated on-the-job events because he had many nonwork life stressors before he was hired at the NMFHF. The currently low levels of impairments and symptoms suggest that leaving that workplace substantially reduced any difficulties he had related to on-the-job problems. The reduction of symptoms on leaving a workplace in which a worker was the recipient of frequent criticism and discipline would be expected to occur whether the criticism was justified or retaliatory.

Respectfully submitted,

REFERENCES

Abbey, A. (1987). Misperceptions of friendly behavior as sexual interest: A survey of naturally occurring incidents. *Psychology of Women Quarterly, 11*, 173–194.

Abbey, A., & Melby, C. (1986). The effects of nonverbal cues on gender differences in perceptions of sexual intent. *Sex Roles, 15*, 283–298.

Abell, N. L., & Jackson, M. N. (1996). Sexual harassment investigations—Cues, clues, and how-to's. *The Labor Lawyer, 12*, 17–56.

Alexander v. Gardner-Denver Co., 415 U.S. 36 (1974).

Amaro, H., Russo, N. F., & Johnson, J. (1987). Family and work predictors of psychological well-being among Hispanic women professionals. *Psychology of Women Quarterly, 11*, 505–521.

American Psychiatric Association. (1994). *Diagnostic and statistical manual of mental disorders* (4th ed.). Washington, DC: Author.

American Psychiatric Association. (2000). *Diagnostic and statistical manual of mental disorders* (4th ed., text rev.). Washington, DC: Author.

American Psychological Association. (1992). Ethical principles of psychologists and code of conduct. *American Psychologist, 47*, 1597–1611.

American Psychological Association. (2002). Ethical principles of psychologists and code of conduct. *American Psychologist, 57*, 1060–1073.

American Psychological Association, Committee on Legal Issues. (1996). Strategies for private practitioners coping with subpoenas or compelled testimony for client records and/or test data. *Professional Psychology: Research and Practice, 27*, 245–251.

Americans With Disabilities Act of 1990, 42 U.S.C.A. § 12101 *et seq.* (West 1993).

Andrews v. City of Philadelphia, 895 F.2d 1469, 1481 (3d Cir. 1990).

Antikainen, R., Hintikka, J., Lehtonen, J., Koponen, H., & Arstila, A. (1995). A prospective three-year follow-up study of borderline personality disorder inpatients. *Acta Psychiatrica Scandinavica, 92*, 327–335.

Appelbaum, P. S. (1985). Tarasoff and the clinician: Problems in fulfilling the duty to protect. *American Journal of Psychiatry, 142*, 425–429.

Aquino, K., Tripp, T. M., & Bies, R. J. (2001). How employees respond to personal offense: The effects of blame attribution, victim status, and offender status on revenge and reconciliation in the workplace. *Journal of Applied Psychology, 86*, 52–59.

Arata, C. M. (2000). From child victim to adult victim: A model for predicting sexual revictimization. *Child Maltreatment: Journal of the American Professional Society on the Abuse of Children, 5*, 28–38.

Armstrong-Stassen, M. (2001). Reactions of older employees to organizational downsizing: The role of gender, job level, and time. *Journals of Gerontology Series B Psychological Sciences & Social Sciences, 4*, 234–243.

Avina, C., & O'Donohue, W. (2002). Sexual harassment and PTSD: Is sexual harassment diagnosable trauma? *Journal of Traumatic Stress, 15*, 69–75.

Babitsky, S., & Mangraviti, J. J., Jr. (2002). *Writing and defending your expert report: The step-by-step guide with models*. Falmouth, MA: SEAK, Inc.

Bailey v. Runyon, 220 F.3d 879, 880–81 (8th Cir. 2000).

Baird, C. L., Bensko, N. L., Bell, P. A., Viney, W., & Woody, W. D. (1995). Gender influence on perceptions of hostile environment sexual harassment. *Psychological Reports, 77*, 79–82.

Baker, D. D., Terpstra, D. E., & Cutler, B. D. (1990). Perceptions of sexual harassment: A re-examination of gender differences. *Journal of Psychology, 124*, 409–416.

Baker, D. D., Terpstra, D. E., & Larntz, K. (1990). The influence of individual characteristics and severity of harassing behavior on reactions to sexual harassment. *Sex Roles, 22*, 305–325.

Baki v. B. F. Diamond Constr. Co., 71 F.R.D. 179 (D. Md. 1976).

Barak, A., Fisher, W. A., & Houston, S. (1992). Individual difference correlates of the experience of sexual harassment among female university students. *Journal of Applied Social Psychology, 22*, 17–37.

Barak, A., Pitterman, Y., & Yitzhaki, R. (1995). An empirical test of the role of power differential in originating sexual harassment. *Basic & Applied Social Psychology, 17*, 497–517.

Bargh, J. A., & Raymond, P. (1995). The naive misuse of power: Nonconscious sources of sexual harassment. *Journal of Social Issues, 51*, 85–96.

Bargh, J. A., Raymond, P., Pryor, J. B., & Strack, F. (1995). Attractiveness of the underling: An automatic power–sex association and its consequences for sexual harassment and aggression. *Journal of Personality and Social Psychology, 68*, 768–781.

Barling, J., Rogers, A. G., & Kelloway, E. K. (2001). Behind closed doors: In-home workers' experience of sexual harassment and workplace violence. *Journal of Occupational Health Psychology, 6*, 255–269.

Barnes v. Costle, 561 F.2d 983 (1977).

Barnes v. Train, 13 Fair Empl. Prac. Cas. 123 (D.D.C. 1974), *aff'd sub nom* Barnes v. Costle, 561 F.2d 983 (D.C. Cir. 1977).

Barsade, S., & Wiesenfeld, B. (1997). *Attitudes in the American workplace III*. New Haven, CT: Yale University School of Management.

Bastian, L. D., Lancaster, A. R., & Reyst, H. E. (1996, December). *Department of Defense 1995 sexual harassment survey* (DMDC Report No. 96-014). Washington, DC: U.S. Government Printing Office.

Becerra v. Dalton, 94 F.3d 145 (4th Cir. 1996), *cert. denied*, 117 S. Ct. 1987 (1997).

Beehr, T. A., & Bhagat, R. S. (Eds.). (1985). *Human stress and cognition in organizations*. New York: Wiley.

Beehr, T. A., & Schuler, R. S. (1982). Current and future perspectives on stress in organizations. In G. R. Ferris & K. M. Rowland (Eds.), *Personnel management: New perspectives*. Boston: Allyn & Bacon.

Begany, J. J., & Milburn, M. A. (2002). Psychological predictors of sexual harassment, authoritarianism, hostile sexism, and rape myths. *Psychology of Men & Masculinity, 3*, 119–126.

Beitchman, J. H., Zucker, K. J., Hood, J. E., daCosta, G. A., Akman, D., & Cassavia, E. (1992). A review of the long-term effects of child sexual abuse. *Child Abuse & Neglect, 16*, 101–118.

Berdahl, J. L., Magley, V. J., & Waldo, C. R. (1996). The sexual harassment of men? Exploring the concept with theory and data. *Psychology of Women Quarterly, 20*, 527–547.

Berg, M., & Bengt, A. (1996). An occupational study of employees with VDU-associated symptoms: The importance of stress. *Stress Medicine, 12*, 51–54.

Bergman, M. E., & Drasgow, F. (2003). Race as a moderator in a model of sexual harassment: An empirical test. *Journal of Occupational Health Psychology, 8*, 131–145.

Bergman, M. E., Langhout, R. D., Palmieri, P. A., Cortina, L. M., & Fitzgerald, L. F. (2002). The (un)reasonableness of reporting antecedents and consequences of reporting sexual harassment. *Journal of Applied Psychology, 87*, 230–242.

Bingham, S. G., & Scherer, L. L. (1993). Factors associated with responses to sexual harassment and satisfaction with outcome. *Sex Roles, 29*, 239–269.

Birt, C. M., & Dion, K. L. (1987). Relative deprivation theory and responses to discrimination in a gay male and lesbian sample. *British Journal of Social Psychology, 26*, 139–145.

Bisom-Rapp, S. (2001). An ounce of prevention is a poor substitute for a pound of cure: Confronting the developing jurisprudence of education and prevention in employment discrimination law. *Berkeley Journal of Employment and Labor Law, 22*, 1–47.

Blake, D. D., Weathers, F. W., & Nagy, L. M. (1990). A clinician rating scale for assessing current and lifetime PTSD: The CAPS 1. *Behavior Therapist, 13*, 187–188.

Blakely, G. L., Blakely, E. H., & Moorman, R. H. (1995). The relationship between gender, personal experience, and perceptions of sexual harassment in the workplace. *Employee Responsibilities & Rights Journal*, 8(4), 263–274.

Blakely v. Continental Airlines, 164 N.J. 38, 751 A. 2d 538 (N.J. 2000).

Blazer, D. G., Hughes, D., George, L. K., Swartz, M., & Boyer, R. (1991). Generalized anxiety disorder. In L. N. Robins & D. A. Regier (Eds.), *Psychiatric disorders in America: The Epidemiologic Catchment Area study* (pp. 180–203). New York: Free Press.

Bloom, L. (1997). Gretel fights back: Representing sexual harassment plaintiffs who were sexually abused as children. *Berkeley Women's Law Journal*, 1–19.

Blumenthal, J. A. (1998). The reasonable woman standard: A meta-analytic review of gender differences in perceptions of sexual harassment. *Law & Human Behavior, 22*(1), 33–58.

Boney-McCoy, S., & Finkelhor, D. (1995). Prior victimization: A risk factor for child sexual abuse and for PTSD-related symptomatology among sexually abused youth. *Child Abuse & Neglect, 19*, 1401–1421.

Bottomly v. Leucadia National, 163 F.R.D. 617, 620-22 (D. Utah 1995).

Breitenbecher, K. H. (1999). The association between the perception of threat in a dating situation and sexual victimization. *Violence & Victims, 14*(2), 135–146.

Briere, J. (1995). *Trauma Symptom Inventory professional manual*. Odessa, FL: Psychological Assessment Resources.

Briere, J. (1997). *Psychological assessment of posttraumatic states*. Washington, DC: American Psychological Association.

Briere, J., Evans, J., Runtz, M., & Wall, T. (1988). Symptomology in men who were molested as children: A comparison study. *American Journal of Orthopsychiatry, 58*, 457–461.

Briere, J., & Runtz, M. (1987). Post sexual abuse trauma: Data and implications for clinical practice. *Journal of Interpersonal Violence, 2*, 367–379.

Briere, J., & Runtz, M. (1988). Symptomatology associated with childhood sexual victimization in a nonclinical adult sample. *Child Abuse & Neglect, 12*, 51–59.

Briere, J., & Zaidi, L. Y. (1989). Sexual abuse histories and sequelae in female psychiatric emergency room patients. *American Journal of Psychiatry, 146*, 1602–1606.

Brock, D. (1993). *The real Anita Hill: The untold story*. New York: Free Press.

Broderick v. Ruder, 685 F. Supp. 1269 (D.C. Cir. 1988).

Brodsky, S. L. (1991). *Testifying in court: Guidelines and maxims for the expert witness*. Washington, DC: American Psychological Association.

Brodsky, S. L. (1999). *The expert expert witness: More maxims and guidelines for testifying in court*. Washington, DC: American Psychological Association.

Brogan, D. J., Frank, E., Elon, L., Sivanesan, P., & O'Hanlan, K. A. (1999). Harassment of lesbians as medical students and physicians. *Journal of the American Medical Association, 282*, 1290–1292.

Brown, G. R., & Anderson, B. (1991). Psychiatric morbidity in adult inpatients with childhood histories of sexual and physical abuse. *American Journal of Psychiatry, 148*, 55–61.

Brown, J., Campbell, E. A., & Fife-Shaw, C. (1995). Adverse impacts experienced by police officers following exposure to sex discrimination and sexual harassment. *Stress Medicine, 11*(4), 221–224.

Brown, T. J., & Allgeier, E. R. (1995). Managers' perceptions of workplace romances: An interview study. *Journal of Business & Psychology, 10*(2), 169–176.

Brownmiller, S., & Alexander, D. (1992, January/February). From Carmita Wood to Anita Hill. *Ms.*, 70–71.

Buehrer, S. (1998). A clash of the titans: Judicial deference to arbitration and the public policy exception in the context of sexual harassment. *American University Journal of Gender and the Law, 6*, 265–297.

Bureau of National Affairs. (1988). *Corporate affairs: Nepotism, office romance, and sexual harassment*. Washington, DC: Author.

Burgess, D., & Borgida, E. (1997a). Refining sex-role spillover theory: The role of gender subtypes and harasser attributions. *Social Cognition, 15*, 291–311.

Burgess, D., & Borgida, E. (1997b). Sexual harassment: An experimental test of sex-role spillover theory. *Personality & Social Psychology Bulletin, 23*(1), 63–75.

Burian, B. K., Yanico, B. J., & Martinez, C. R. (1998). Group gender composition effects on judgments of sexual harassment. *Psychology of Women Quarterly, 22*, 465–480.

Burlington Industries, Inc. v. Ellerth, 524 U.S., S. Ct. 2257, 141 L.Ed.2d 662, 77 Fair Empl. Prac. Cas. 1 (1998).

Burns, S. E., (1995). Issues in workplace sexual harassment law and related social science research. *Journal of Social Issues, 51*, 193–207.

Bursik, K. (1992). Perceptions of sexual harassment in an academic context. *Sex Roles, 27*, 401–412.

Bushell v. Dean, 803 S.W.2d 711, 712 (Tex. 1991) (op. on reh'g).

Carey v. Piphus, 435 U.S. 247 (1978).

Casteneda v. Partida, 430 U.S. 482 (1977).

Chapman, N. J., Ingersoll-Dayton, B., & Neal, M. B. (1994). Balancing the multiple roles of work and caregiving for children, adults, and elders. In G. P. Keita & J. J. Hurrell, Jr. (Eds.), *Job stress in a changing workforce: Investigating gender, diversity, and family issues* (pp. 283–300). Washington, DC: American Psychological Association.

Charney, D. A., & Russell, R. C. (1994). An overview of sexual harassment. *American Journal of Psychiatry, 151*, 10–17.

Cherry, N. (1984). Women and work stress: Evidence from the 1946 birth cohort. *Ergonomics, 27*, 519–526.

Chu, J. A., & Dill, D. L. (1990). Dissociative symptoms in relation to childhood physical and sexual abuse. *American Journal of Psychiatry, 147*, 887–892.

Civil Rights Act of 1871, 42 U.S.C. § 1983.

Civil Rights Act of 1964, 42 U.S.C. § 2000e *et seq., as amended* (1964).

Civil Rights Act of 1991, § 102, subd. (B)(3), 42 U.S.C. § 1981a (1991).

Clark County School District v. Shirley A. Breeden, 121 S. Ct. 1508 (April 23, 2001).

Clark v. World Airways, 24 E.P.D. 18, 287 (1980).

Classen, C., Field, N. P., Koopman, C., Nevill-Manning, K., & Spiegel, D. (2001). Interpersonal problems and their relationship to sexual revictimization among women sexually abused in childhood. *Journal of Interpersonal Violence, 16*, 495–509.

Cobb, S., & Kasl, S. V. (1977). *Termination: The consequences of job loss*. Cincinnati, OH: U.S. Department of Health, Education, and Welfare.

Cochran, C. C., Frazier, P.A., & Olson, A.M. (1997). Predictors of responses to unwanted sexual attention. *Psychology of Women Quarterly, 21*(2), 207–226.

Cody v. Marriott Corp., 103 FRD 421, 44 Fair Empl. Prac. Cas. 1228 (D. Mass. 1984).

Coles, F. (1986). Forced to quit: Sexual harassment complaints and agency response. *Sex Roles, 14*, 81–95.

Committee on Ethical Guidelines for Forensic Psychologists. (1991). Specialty guidelines for forensic psychologists. *Law & Human Behavior, 15*, 655–665.

Connell, M. C., & Koocher, G. (2003). HIPAA and forensic practice. *American Psychology–Law Newsletter, 23*(2), 16–19.

Conte, J. R., & Schuerman, J. R. (1987). Factors associated with an increased impact of child sexual abuse. *Child Abuse & Neglect, 11*(2), 201–211.

Conway, T. L., Vickers, R. R., Ward, H. W., & Rahe, R. H. (1981). Occupational stress and variation in cigarette, coffee, and alcohol consumption. *Journal of Health & Social Behavior, 22*(2), 155–165.

Cook, D. J., Liutkus, J. F., Risdon, C. L., Griffith, L. E., Guyatt, G. H., & Walter, S. D. (1996). Residents' experiences of abuse, discrimination and sexual harassment during residency training. *Canadian Medical Association Journal, 154*, 1657–1665.

Cooke, G. (1996). The role of the mental health professional in harassment/discrimination cases: A moderate perspective. *American Journal of Forensic Psychology, 14*(2), 37–48.

Corne v. Bausch & Lomb Inc., 390 F. Supp. 161 (D. Ariz. 1975).

Cortina, L. M., Magley, V. J., Williams, J. H., & Langhout, R. D. (2001). Incivility in the workplace: Incidence and impact. *Journal of Occupational Health Psychology, 6*(1), 64–80.

Crocker, D., & Kalemba, V. (1999). The incidence and impact of women's experiences of sexual harassment in Canadian workplaces. *Canadian Review of Sociology & Anthropology, 36*, 541–558.

Crosby, F. J. (1987). *Spouse, parent, worker: On gender and multiple roles*. New Haven, CT: Yale University Press.

Crull, P. (1982). Stress effects of sexual harassment on the job: Implications for counseling. *American Journal of Orthopsychiatry, 52*, 539–544.

Curcio, A. A. (1988). Rule 412 laid bare: A procedural rule that cannot adequately protect sexual harassment plaintiffs from embarrassing exposure. *University of Cincinnati Law Review, 67*, 125–183.

Curry, M. A., Hassouneh-Phillips, D., & Johnston-Silverberg, A. (2001). Abuse of women with disabilities: An ecological model and review. *Violence Against Women, 7*, 60–69.

Daley, T. T. (1996). Pretrial preparations can improve a physician's value as an expert witness. *Canadian Medical Association Journal, 154*, 573.

Dansky, B. S., Brady, K. T., Saladin, M. E., Killeen, T., Becker, S., & Roitzsch, J. (1996). Victimization and PTSD in individuals with substance use disorders: Gender and racial differences. *American Journal of Drug and Alcohol Abuse, 22*(1), 75–93.

Dansky, B. S., & Kilpatrick, D. G. (1997). Effects of sexual harassment. In W. O' Donohue (Ed.), *Sexual harassment: Theory, research, and treatment* (pp. 152–174). Boston: Allyn & Bacon.

Dansky, B. S., Roitzsch, J. C., Brady, K. T., & Saladin, M. E. (1997). Posttraumatic stress disorder and substance abuse: Use of research in a clinical setting. *Journal of Traumatic Stress, 10*, 141–148.

Daubert v. Merrell Dow Pharmaceuticals, Inc., 509 U.S. 579, 113 S. Ct. 2786 (1993).

Davidson, J. R. T., & Fairbank, J. A. (1993). The epidemiology of Posttraumatic Stress Disorder. In J. R. T. Davidson & E. B. Foa (Eds.), *Posttraumatic stress disorder:* DSM–IV *and beyond* (pp. 147–169). Washington, DC: American Psychiatric Press.

Day, N. E., & Schoenrade, P. (2000). The relationship among reported disclosure of sexual orientation, anti-discrimination policies, top management support and work attitudes of gay and lesbian employees. *Personnel Review, 29*, 346–363.

DeCintio v. Westchester County Medical Center, 807 F.2d 304 (2d Cir. 1986), *cert. denied*, 484 U.S. 825 (1987).

DeCoster, S., Estes, S. B., & Mueller, C. W. (1999). Routine activities and sexual harassment in the workplace. *Work and Occupations, 26*(1), 21–49.

Dekker, I., & Barling, J. (1998). Personal and organizational predictors of workplace sexual harassment of women by men. *Journal of Occupational Health Psychology, 3*(1), 7–18.

Delahunty v. Cahoon, 66 Wn. App. 829, 832 P.2d 1378 (1992).

Dhaliwal, G. K., Gauzas, L., Antonowicz, D. H., & Ross, R. R. (1996). Adult male survivors of childhood sexual abuse: Prevalence, sexual abuse characteristics, and long-term effects. *Clinical Psychology Review, 16*, 619–639.

Diener, E., Emmons, R. A., Larsen, R. J., & Griffin, S. (1985). The Satisfaction With Life scale. *Journal of Personality Assessment, 49*, 71–75.

Dormann, C., & Zapf, D. (1999). Social support, social stressors at work, and depressive symptoms: Testing for main and moderating effects with structural equations in a three-wave longitudinal study. *Journal of Applied Psychology, 84*, 874–884.

Dougherty, T. W., Turban, D. B., Olson, D. E., Dwyer, P. D., & LaPreze, M. W. (1996). Factors affecting perceptions of workplace sexual harassment. *Journal of Organizational Behavior, 17*, 489–501.

Dozier, J. B., & Miceli, M. P. (1985). Potential predictors of whistle-blowing: A prosocial behavior perspective. *Academy of Management Review, 10*, 823–836.

Driscoll, R. J., Worthington, K. A., & Hurrell, J. J., Jr. (1995). Workplace assault: An emerging job stressor. *Consulting Psychology Journal: Practice & Research, 47*(4), 205–212.

DuBois, C. L. Z., Knapp, D. E., Faley, R. H., & Kustis, G. A. (1998). An empirical examination of same- and other-gender sexual harassment in the workplace. *Sex Roles, 39*, 731–749.

Duffield v. Robertson Stephens & Co., 144 F.3d 1182 (9th Cir.), *cert. denied*, 119 S. Ct. 465 (1998).

Dunbar, E. (2001). Counseling practices to ameliorate the effects of discrimination and hate events: Toward a systematic approach to assessment and intervention. *Counseling Psychologist, 29*, 279–307.

Duncan, J. (1995). *Medication compliance in schizophrenic patients*. Unpublished doctoral dissertation, University of North Texas, Denton.

Eaton, W. W., Dryman, A., & Weissman, M. (1991). Panic and phobia. In L. N. Robins & D. A. Regier (Eds.), *Psychiatric disorders in America: The epidemiologic catchment area study* (pp. 155–179). New York: Free Press.

Edwards, J. R., & Harrison, R.V. (1993). Job demands and worker health: A reexamination of the relationship between person-environment fit and strain. *Journal of Applied Psychology, 78*, 628–648.

EEOC v. Mitsubishi, 990 F. Supp. 1059 (C.D. Ill. 1998).

Eisenman, R. (1995). Dubious value of the "reasonable woman" standard in understanding sexual harassment. *Psychological Reports, 77*, 1145–1146.

Ellis, S., Barak, A., & Pinto, A. (1991). Moderating effects of personal cognitions on experienced and perceived sexual harassment of women at the workplace. *Journal of Applied Social Psychology, 21*, 1320–1337.

Ellison v. Brady, 924 F. 2d 872, 877-878 (CA9 1991).

Elliston, F. A. (1982). Civil disobedience and whistle-blowing: A comparative appraisal of two forms of dissent. *Journal of Business Ethics, 1*, 23–28.

Evans, N. J., & Broido, E. M. (2002). The experiences of lesbian and bisexual women in college residence halls Implications for addressing homophobia and heterosexism. *Journal of Lesbian Studies*, 6(3/4), 29–42.

Fain, T. C., & Anderton, D. L. (1987). Sexual harassment: Organizational context and diffuse status. *Sex Roles, 17*, 291–311.

Faragher v. City of Boca Raton, 524 U.S., 118 S. Ct. 2275, 141 L.Ed.2d. 663, 77 Fair Empl. Prac. Cas. 14 (1998).

Federal Arbitration Act. Title IX, U.S. Code § 1–14 (1990).

Federal Rules of Civil Procedure. (2001). Retrieved March 23, 2004, from http://www.house.gov/judiciary/civil2001.pdf

Federal Rules of Evidence. (2000). Washington, DC: Lexis-Nexis Group.

Feldman-Schorrig, S.P. (1994). Special issues in sexual harassment cases. In J. J. McDonald, Jr., & F. B. Kulick (Eds.), *Mental and emotional injuries in employment litigation* (pp. 332–390). Washington, DC: Bureau of National Affairs.

Feldman-Schorrig, S. (1995). Need for expansion of forensic psychiatrists' role in sexual harassment cases. *Bulletin of the American Academy of Psychiatry & Law, 23*, 513–522.

Feldman-Schorrig, S. (1996). Factitious sexual harassment. *Bulletin of the American Academy of Psychiatry & Law, 24,* 387–392.

Feldman-Schorrig, S. P., & McDonald, J. J., Jr. (1992). The role of forensic psychiatry in the defense of sexual harassment cases. *Journal of Psychiatry & Law, 20*(1), 5–33.

Fennig, S., Bromet, E. J., Jandorf, L., Schwartz, J. E., Lavelle, J., & Ram, R. (1994). Eliciting psychotic symptoms using a semi-structured diagnostic interview: The importance of collateral sources of information in a first-admission sample. *Journal of Nervous & Mental Disease, 182*(1), 20–26.

Feuerstein, M., Sult, S., & Houle, M. (1985). Environmental stressors and chronic low back pain: Life events, family and work environment. *Pain, 22,* 295–307.

Finkelhor, D. (1984). *Child sexual abuse: New theory and research.* New York: Free Press.

Finkelhor, D., Hotaling, G., Lewis, I. A., & Smith, C. (1990). Sexual abuse in a national survey of adult men and women: Prevalence, characteristics, and risk factors. *Child Abuse & Neglect, 14,* 19–28.

Finley, M. H., & Lee, A. T. (1981). The terminated executive: It's like dying. *Personnel & Guidance Journal, 59,* 382–384.

Fitzgerald, L. F. (1993). Sexual harassment: Violence against women in the workplace. *American Psychologist, 10,* 1070–1076.

Fitzgerald, L. F. (2003). Sexual harassment and social justice: Reflections on the distance yet to go. *American Psychologist, 58,* 915–924.

Fitzgerald, L. F., Buchanan-Biddle, N. T., Collinsworth, L. L., Magley, V. J., & Ramos, A. M. (1999). Junk logic: The abuse defense in sexual harassment litigation. *Psychology, Public Policy, and Law, 5,* 730–759.

Fitzgerald, L. F., Drasgow, F., Hulin, C. L., Gelfand, M. J., & Magley, V. J. (1997). Antecedents and consequences of sexual harassment in organizations: A test of an integrated model. *Journal of Applied Psychology, 82,* 578–589.

Fitzgerald, L. F., Drasgow, F., & Magley, V. J. (1999). Sexual harassment in the armed forces: A test of an integrated model. *Military Psychology, 11,* 329–349.

Fitzgerald, L. F., Gelfand, M. J., & Drasgow, F. (1995). Measuring sexual harassment: Theoretical and psychometric advances. *Basic & Applied Social Psychology, 17,* 425–445.

Fitzgerald, L. F., Magley, V. J., Drasgow, F., & Waldo, C. R. (1999). Measuring sexual harassment in the military: The Sexual Experiences Questionnaire (SEQ-DoD). *Military Psychology, 11,* 243–264.

Fitzgerald, L. F., Shullman, S. L., Bailey, N., Richards, M., Swecker, J., Gold, Y., Ormerod, M., & Weitzman, L. (1988). The incidence and dimensions of sexual harassment in academia and the workplace. *Journal of Vocational Behavior, 32,* 152–175.

Fitzgerald, L. F., Swan, S., & Fischer, K. (1995). Why didn't she just report him? The psychological and legal implications of women's responses to sexual harassment. *Journal of Social Issues, 51*(1), 117–138.

FitzGibbon, S. A. (2000). Arbitration, mediation, and sexual harassment. *Psychology, Public Policy, and Law, 5*, 693–729.

Fontana, A., & Rosenheck, R. (1998). Duty-related and sexual stress in the etiology of PTSD among women veterans who seek treatment. *Psychiatric Services, 49*, 658–662.

Foote, W. E., & Goodman-Delahunty, J. (1999). Same-sex harassment: Implications of the *Oncale* decision for forensic evaluation of plaintiffs. *Behavioral Sciences & the Law, 17*(1), 123–139.

Ford, C. A., & Donis, F. J. (1996). The relationship between age and gender in workers' attitudes toward sexual harassment. *The Journal of Psychology, 130*, 627–633.

Ford, J. D., & Kidd, P. (1998). Early childhood trauma and disorders of extreme stress as predictors of treatment outcome with chronic Posttraumatic Stress Disorder. *Journal of Traumatic Stress, 11*, 743–761.

Franke, K. M. (1997). What's wrong with sexual harassment? *Stanford Law Review, 49*, 691–772.

Frankenhaeuser, M. (1991). A biopsychosocial approach to work life issues. In J. V. Johnson & G. Johansson (Eds.), *The psychosocial work environment* (pp. 49–60). Amityville, NY: Baywood.

Frederick, R. (1997). *The Validity Indicator Profile manual*. Minneapolis, MN: National Computer Systems.

French, J. R. P., Caplan, R. D., & Harrison, R.V. (1982). *Mechanisms of job stress and strain*. New York: Wiley.

Fritz, G. S., Stoll, K., & Wagner, N. N. (1981). A comparison of males and females who were sexually molested as children. *Journal of Sex & Marital Therapy, 7*(1), 54–59.

Fromuth, M. E., & Burkhart, B. R. (1987). Childhood sexual victimization among college men: Definitional and methodological issues. *Violence & Victims, 2*(4), 241–253.

Fromuth, M. E., & Burkhart, B. R. (1989). Long-term psychological correlates of childhood sexual abuse in two samples of college men. *Child Abuse & Neglect, 13*, 533–542.

Frye v. United States, 293 F.1013 (DC Ct. App., 1923).

Fuller, R. K., Lee, K. K., & Gordis, E. (1988). Validity of self-report in alcoholism research: Results of a Veterans Administration cooperative study. *Alcoholism: Clinical & Experimental Research, 12*(2), 201–205.

Gadlin, H. (1991). Careful maneuvers: Mediating sexual harassment. *Negotiation Journal, 7*(2), 139–153.

Gazeley, B. J. (1997). Venus, mars and the law: On mediation of sexual harassment cases. *Willamette Law Review, 33*, 605–623.

Gebers v. Commercial Data Center, Inc., 1995 U.S. App. LEXIS 614 (6th Cir. 1995).

General Electric Co. v. Joiner, 522 U.S. 136 (1997).

George, W. H., & Martinez, L. J. (2002). Victim blaming in rape: Effects of victim and perpetrator race, type of rape, and participant racism. *Psychology of Women Quarterly*, *26*(2), 110–119.

George v. Frank, 761 F. Supp. 256 (S.D.N.Y. 1991).

Gervasio, A. H., & Ruckdeschel, K. (1992). College students' judgments of verbal sexual harassment. *Journal of Applied Social Psychology*, *22*, 190–211.

Gier v. Educational Service Unit No. 16, 845 F. Supp. 1342, 1351– 52 (D. Neb. 1994).

Gillmer v. Interstate/Johnson Lane Corp., 500 U.S. 20 (1991).

Ginexi, E. M., Howe, G. W., & Caplan, R. D. (2000). Depression and control beliefs in relation to reemployment: What are the directions of effect? *Journal of Occupational Health Psychology*, *5*, 323–336.

Gladsjo, J. A., Tucker, J. A., Hawkins, J. L., & Vuchinich, R. E. (1992). Adequacy of recall of drinking patterns and event occurrences associated with natural recovery from alcohol problems. *Addictive Behaviors*, *17*, 347–358.

Glassman, J. B. (1998). Preventing and managing board complaints: The downside risk of custody evaluation. *Professional Psychology: Research and Practice*, *29*, 121–124.

Glomb, T. M., Munson, L. J., Hulin, C. L., Bergman, M. E., & Drasgow, F. (1999). Structural equation models of sexual harassment: Longitudinal explorations and cross-sectional generalizations. *Journal of Applied Psychology*, *84*, 14–28.

Gold, S. N., Lucenko, B. A., Elhai, J. D., Swingle, J. M., & Sellers, A. H. (1999). A comparison of psychological/psychiatric symptomatology of women and men sexually abused as children. *Child Abuse & Neglect*, *23*, 683–692.

Goldenhar, L. M., Swanson, N. G., Hurrell, J. J., Jr., Ruder, A., & Deddens, J. (1998). Stressors and adverse outcomes for female construction workers. *Journal of Occupational Health Psychology*, *3*(1), 19–32.

Goodman, J., & Croyle, R. T. (1989). Social framework testimony in employment discrimination cases. *Behavioral Sciences & the Law*, *7*, 227–241.

Goodman-Delahunty, J. (1999). Pragmatic support for the reasonable victim standard in hostile workplace sexual harassment cases. *Psychology, Public Policy, and Law*, *5*, 519–555.

Goodman-Delahunty, J. (2000). Psychological impairment under the Americans with Disabilities Act: Legal guidelines. *Professional Psychology: Research and Practice*, *31*, 197–205.

Goodman-Delahunty, J., & Foote, W. E. (1995). Compensation for pain, suffering, and other psychological injuries: The impact of Daubert on employment discrimination claims. *Behavioral Sciences & the Law*, *13*(2), 183–206.

Goodman-Delahunty, J., Shanahan, C., & Charlson, J. (2003). *Consequences of sexual harassment.* Manuscript submitted for publication.

Gore v. Turner, 563 F.2d 159 (5th Cir. 1977).

Green, R. (2000). *The MMPI–2: An interpretive manual*. Boston: Allyn & Bacon.

Greenberg, S. (2004, April). *Psychological consultation in personal injury cases*. Paper presented by the American Academy of Forensic Psychology in New Orleans, LA.

Greenberger, D. B., Miceli, M. P., & Cohen, D. J. (1987). Oppositionists and group norms: The reciprocal influence of whistle-blowers and co-workers. *Journal of Business Ethics, 6*, 527–542.

Greenburg, S., & Shuman, D. W. (1997). The role of ethical norms in the admissibility of expert testimony. *Judges Journal, 4*, 37.

Greene, B. L. (1995). Recent research findings on the diagnosis of Posttraumatic Stress Disorder. In R. I. Simon (Ed.), *Posttraumatic stress disorder in litigation* (pp. 13–29). Washington, DC: American Psychiatric Press.

Griggs v. Duke Power Co., 401 U.S. 324 (1971).

Gruber, J. E. (1997). An epidemiology of sexual harassment: Evidence from North America and Europe. In W. O'Donohue (Ed.), *Sexual harassment: Theory, research, and treatment* (pp. 84–98). Needham Heights, MA: Allyn & Bacon.

Gruber, J. E. (1998). The impact of male work environments and organizational policies on women's experiences of sexual harassment. *Gender & Society, 12*, 301–320.

Gruber, J. E., & Bjorn, L. (1982). Blue-collar blues: The sexual harassment of women autoworkers. *Work and Occupations, 9*, 271–298.

Gruber, J. E., & Smith, M. D. (1995). Women's responses to sexual harassment: A multivariate analysis. *Basic and Applied Social Psychology, 17*, 543–562.

Gupta, N., & Beehr, T. A. (1979). Job stress and employee behaviors. *Organizational Behavior & Human Decision Processes, 23*, 373–387.

Gutek, B. A. (1985). *Sex and the workplace*. San Francisco: Jossey-Bass.

Gutek, B. A. (1995). How subjective is sexual harassment? An examination of rater effects. *Basic and Applied Social Psychology, 17*, 447–467.

Gutek, B. A., Cohen, A. G., & Konrad, A. M. (1990). Predicting social–sexual behavior at work: A contact hypothesis. *Academy of Management Journal, 33*, 560–577.

Gutek, B. A., Cohen, A. G., & Tsui, A. (1996). Reactions to perceived sex discrimination. *Human Relations, 49*, 791–813.

Gutek, B. A., & Done, R. S. (2001). Sexual harassment. In R. K. Unger (Ed.), *Handbook of the psychology of women and gender* (pp. 367–387). New York: Wiley.

Gutek, B. A., & Koss, M. P. (1993). Changed women and changed organizations: Consequences of and coping with sexual harassment. *Journal of Vocational Behavior, 42*, 28–48.

Gutek, B. A., & Morasch, B. (1982). Sex ratios, sex-role spillover, and sexual harassment of women at work. *Journal of Social Issues, 38*, 55–74.

Gutek, B. A., & O'Connor, M. A. (1995). The empirical basis for the reasonable woman standard. *Journal of Social Issues, 51*(1), 151–166.

Gutek, B. A., O'Connor, M. A., Melancon, R., Stockdale, M. S., Geer, T. M., & Done, R. S. (1999). The utility of the reasonable woman legal standard in hostile environment sexual harassment cases: A multimethod, multistudy examination. *Psychology, Public Policy, and Law, 5*, 596–629.

Gutheil, T. G. (1998). *The psychiatrist as expert witness*. Washington, DC: American Psychiatric Press.

Gutierres, S. E., Saenz, D. S., & Green, B. L. (1994). Job stress and health outcomes among White and Hispanic employees: A test of the person-environment fit model. In G. P. Keita & J. J. Hurrell, Jr. (Eds.), *Job stress in a changing workforce: Investigating gender, diversity, and family issues* (pp. 107–125). Washington, DC: American Psychological Association.

Gutierrez v. California Acrylic Industries, No. BC055641 (Cal. Super. Ct., May 26, 1993).

Hall, C. A. (1998). White counselors' attributions and diagnosis as a function of victim race and attribution about rape. *Dissertation Abstracts International, 58* (08), 4449B.

Hall v. Gus Construction Co., 842 F.2d 1010 (8th Cir. 1988).

Hamilton, M. J. (1989). A comparison of psychological symptoms of treated and nontreated incestuous male perpetrators. *Dissertation Abstracts International, 50* (02), 748B–749B.

Harkavy, J. (1999). Privatizing workplace justice: The advent of mediation in resolving sexual harassment disputes. *Wake Forest Law Review, 34*, 135–169.

Harned, M. S., Ormerod, A. J., Palmieri, P. A., Collinsworth, L. L., & Reed, M. (2002). Sexual assault and other types of sexual harassment by workplace personnel: A comparison of antecedents and consequences. *Journal of Occupational Health Psychology, 7*, 174–188.

Harris v. Forklift Systems, Inc., 510 U.S. 17, 114 S. Ct. 367, 126 L.Ed.2d 295 (1993).

Hay, M. S., & Elig, T. W. (1999). The 1995 Department of Defense sexual harassment survey: Overview and methodology. *Military Psychology, 11*, 233–242.

Health Insurance Portability and Accountability Act of 1996, 45 C.F.R. §§ 160, 164.

Heilbrun, K. (1990). Response style, situation, third party information, and competency to stand trial. *Law & Human Behavior, 14*, 193–196.

Heilbrun, K. (1992). The role of psychological testing in forensic assessment. *Law & Human Behavior, 16*, 257–272.

Heilbrun, K. (2001). *Principles of forensic mental health assessment*. New York: Kluwer Academic/Plenum Publishers.

Heilbrun, K., Rosenfeld, B., Warren, J. I., & Collins, S. (1994). The use of third-party information in forensic assessments: A two state comparison. *Bulletin of the American Academy of Psychiatry & Law, 22*, 399–406.

Hellkamp, D. T., & Lewis, J. E. (1995). The consulting psychologist as an expert witness in sexual harassment and retaliation cases. *Consulting Psychology Journal: Practice & Research, 47*(3), 150–159.

Hemmasi, M., Graf, L. A., & Russ, G. S. (1994). Gender-related jokes in the workplace: Sexual humor or sexual harassment? *Journal of Applied Social Psychology, 24*, 1114–1128.

Hendrix, W. H., Rueb, J. D., & Steel, R. P. (1998). Sexual harassment and gender differences. *Journal of Social Behavior and Personality, 13*(2), 235–252.

Henry, J., & Meltzoff, J. (1998). Perceptions of sexual harassment as a function of target's response type and observer's sex. *Sex Roles, 39*, 253–271.

Henson v. Dundee, 682 F.2d 897 (1982).

Herek, G. M. (1989). Hate crimes against lesbians and gay men: Issues for research and policy. *American Psychologist, 44*, 948–955.

Herek, G. M., Gillis, J. R., Cogan, J. C., & Glunt, E. K. (1997). Hate crime victimization among lesbian, gay, and bisexual adults: Prevalence, psychological correlates, and methodological issues. *Journal of Interpersonal Violence, 12*, 195–215.

Hersch, P. D., & Alexander, R. W. (1990). MMPI profile patterns of emotional disability claimants. *Journal of Clinical Psychology, 46*, 795–799.

Hesson-McInnis, M. S., & Fitzgerald, L. F. (1997). Sexual harassment: A preliminary test of an integrative model. *Journal of Applied Social Psychology, 27*, 877–901.

Hill, A. F., & Jordan, E. C. (1995). *The legacy of the Hill–Thomas hearings: Race, gender and power in America.* New York: Oxford University Press.

Hirschfeld, A. H., & Behan, R. C. (1966). The accident process: III. Disability: Acceptable and unacceptable. *Journal of the American Medical Association, 197*(2), 85–89.

Hoffman, L., Clinebell, S., & Kilpatrick, J. (1997). Office romances: The new battleground over employees' rights to privacy and the employers' right to intervene. *Employee Responsibilities & Rights Journal, 10*, 263–275.

House, J. S., & Wells, J. A. (1978). Occupational stress, social support, and health. In A. McLean, G. Black, & M. Colligan (Eds.), *Reducing occupational stress: Proceedings of a conference.* (DHEW Publication No. 78-140, pp. 8–29). Washington, DC: Department of Health, Education, and Welfare.

Humphrey, J. A., & White, J. W. (2000). Women's vulnerability to sexual assault from adolescence to young adulthood. *Journal of Adolescent Health, 27*, 419–424.

Hurley v. Atlantic City Police Dept., 933 F. Supp. 1114 (W.D. Va. 1996).

Irvine, M. (1993). Mediation: Is it appropriate for sexual harassment grievances? *Ohio State Journal on Dispute Resolution, 9*, 27–53.

Isley v. Capuchin Province, 877 F. Supp. 1055 (E.D. Mich. 1995).

Jacobson, A., & Herald, C. (1990). The relevance of childhood sexual abuse to adult psychiatric inpatient care. *Hospital and Community Psychiatry, 41*(2), 154–158.

Jacobson, D. (1987). Models of stress and meanings of unemployment: Reactions to job loss among technical professionals. *Social Science Medicine, 41*(1), 13–21.

Jaffee v. Redmond, 518 U.S. 1 (1996).

Jaschik-Herman, M. L., & Fisk, A. (1995). Women's perceptions and labeling of sexual harassment in academia before and after the Hill–Thomas hearings. *Sex Roles, 33*, 439–446.

Jayakody, R., Danziger, S., & Kessler, R. C. (1998). Early-onset psychiatric disorders and male socioeconomic status. *Social Science Research, 27*, 371–387.

Jensen v. Eveleth Taconite Co., 130 F.3d 1287, 1294-95 (8th Cir. 1997).

Jensvold, M. F. (1993). Workplace sexual harassment: The use, misuse, and abuse of psychiatry. *Psychiatric Annals, 23*, 438–445.

Johnson v. County of Los Angeles Fire Department, 865 F. Supp. 1430, 1434-35 (C.D. Cal. 1994).

Johnson, D. A., & Pany, K. (1981). Expose or cover-up: Will an employee blow the whistle? *Management Accounting, 59*, 32–36.

Johnson, J. D., Benson, C., Teasdale, A., Simmons, S., & Reed, W. (1997). Perceptual ambiguity, gender, and target intoxication: Assessing the effects of factors that moderate perceptions of sexual harassment. *Journal of Applied Social Psychology, 27*, 1209–1221.

Johnston, J. H., Driskell, J. E., & Salas, E. (1997). Vigilant and hypervigilant decision making. *Journal of Applied Psychology 82*, 614–622.

Jones v. Clinton, 72 F.3d 1354 (8th Cir. 1996).

Jones, G. E. (1999). Hierarchical workplace romance: An experimental examination of team member perceptions. *Journal of Organizational Behavior, 20*, 1057–1072.

Jones, L. P. (1991). Unemployment: The effect on social networks, depression, and reemployment opportunities. *Journal of Social Service Research, 15*(1/2), 1–22.

Jones, T. S., & Remland, M. S. (1992). Sources of variability in perceptions of and responses to sexual harassment. *Sex Roles, 27*, 121–142.

Kalichman, S. C. (1993). *Mandated reporting of suspected child abuse: Ethics, law, and policy*. Washington, DC: American Psychological Association.

Kanter, R. M. (1977). *Men and women of the corporation*. New York: Basic Books.

Karasek, R. A. (1979). Job demands, job decision latitude and mental strain: Implications for job redesign. *Administrative Science Quarterly, 24*, 285–306.

Karasek, R. A., & Theorell, T. (1990). *Healthy work: Stress, productivity and the reconstruction of working life*. New York: Basic Books.

Karcher v. Emerson Electric, 94 F.3d 502, 509 (8th Cir. 1996).

Karl, K. A., & Sutton, C. L. (2000). An examination of the perceived fairness of workplace romance policies. *Journal of Business & Psychology, 14*, 429–442.

Kasl, S. V. (1979). Mortality and the business cycle: Some questions about research strategies when utilizing macro-social and ecological data. *American Journal of Public Health, 69*, 784–788.

Kasl, S. V., & Cobb, S. (1970). Blood pressure changes in men undergoing job loss: a preliminary report. *Psychosomatic Medicine, 32*, 19–38.

Kasl, S. V., & Cobb, S. (1979). Some mental health consequences of plant closing and job loss. In L. A. Ferman & J. P. Gordus (Eds.), *Mental health and the economy* (pp. 255–299). Kalamazoo, MI: W. E. Upjohn Institute.

Katz, R. C., Hannon, R., & Whitten, L. (1996). Effects of gender and situation on the perception of sexual harassment. *Sex Roles, 31*, 35–42.

Keane, T. M. (1995). Guidelines for the forensic psychological assessment of post-traumatic stress disorder claimants. In R. I. Simon (Ed.), *Posttraumatic stress disorder in litigation* (pp. 99–115). Washington, DC: American Psychiatric Press.

Keenan, J. P. (1990). Upper-level managers and whistleblowing: Determinants of perceptions of company encouragement and information about where to blow the whistle. *Journal of Business and Psychology, 5*, 223–235.

Kendall-Tackett, K. A., & Simon, A. F. (1992). A comparison of the abuse experiences of male and female adults molested as children. *Journal of Family Violence, 7*(1), 57–62.

Kendall-Tackett, K. A., Williams, L. M., & Finkelhor, D. (1993). Impact of sexual abuse on children: A review and synthesis of recent empirical studies. *Psychological Bulletin, 113*, 164–180.

Kestenbaum v. Pennzoil Co., 108 NM 20, 766 P.2d 280, 283 (N.M. 1988).

Kidder, L. H., Lafleur, R. A., & Wells, C. V. (1995). Recalling harassment, reconstructing experience. *Journal of Social Issues, 51*(1), 53–67.

Kilpatrick, D. G., & Resnick, H. S. (1993). Posttraumatic Stress Disorder associated with exposure to criminal victimization in clinical and community populations. In J. R. T. Davidson & E. B. Foa (Eds.), *Post traumatic stress disorder:* DSM–IV *and beyond* (pp. 113–146). Washington, DC: American Psychiatric Press.

King v. Palmer, 778 F.2d 878 (D.C. Cir. 1985).

Kite, M. E., & Whitely, B. E., Jr. (1998). Do heterosexual women and men differ in their attitudes towards homosexuality? A conceptual and methodological analysis. In G. M. Herek (Ed.), *Psychological perspectives on lesbian and gay issues: Vol. 4. Stigma and social orientation: Understanding prejudice against lesbians, gay men, and bisexuals* (pp. 39–61). Thousand Oaks, CA: Sage.

Knapp, D. E., Faley, R. H., Ekeberg, S. E., & DuBois, C. L. Z. (1997). Determinants of target responses to sexual harassment: A conceptual framework. *Academy of Management Review, 22*, 687–729.

Kohn, M. L., & Schooler, C. (1973). Occupational experience and psychological functioning: An assessment of reciprocal effects. *American Sociological Review, 38*(1), 97–118.

Kolstad v. American Dental Association, 119 S. Ct. 2118 (1999).

Koss, M. P., Goodman, L. A., Browne, A., Fitzgerald, L. F., Keita, G. P., & Russo, N. F. (1994). *No safe haven: Male violence against women at home, at work, and in the community*. Washington, DC: American Psychological Association.

Kovera, M. B., & McAuliff, B. D. (2000). The effects of peer review and evidence quality on judge evaluations of psychological science: Are judges effective gatekeepers? *Journal of Applied Psychology, 85*, 574–586.

Kovera, M. B., McAuliff, B. D., & Hebert, K. S. (1999). Reasoning about scientific evidence: Effects of juror gender and evidence quality on juror decisions in a hostile work environment case. *Journal of Applied Psychology, 84*, 362–375.

Kovera, M. B., Russano, M. B., & McAuliff, B. D. (2002). Assessment of the commonsense psychology underlying Daubert: Legal decision makers' abilities to evaluate expert evidence in hostile work environment cases. *Psychology, Public Policy, and Law, 8*, 180–200.

Krieger, L. H. (2001). Employer liability for sexual harassment: Normative, descriptive, and doctrinal interactions. *University of Arkansas, Little Rock Law Review, 24*, 164.

Kumho Tire Co. v. Carmichael, 526 U.S. 137 (1999).

Lancaster, A. R. (1999). Department of Defense sexual harassment research: Historical perspectives and new initiatives. *Military Psychology, 11*, 219–232.

Landsbergis, P. A., Schnall, P. L., Schwartz, J. E., Warren, K., & Pickering, T. G. (1995). Job strain, hypertension, and cardiovascular disease: Empirical evidence, methodological issues, and recommendations for future research. In S. L. E. Sauter & L. R. E. Murphy (Eds.), *Organizational risk factors for job stress* (pp. 97–112). Washington, DC: American Psychological Association.

Leeser, J., & O'Donohue, W. (1997). The definition of sexual harassment: Normative issues. In W. O'Donohue (Ed.), *Sexual harassment: Theory, research, and treatment*. Boston: Allyn & Bacon.

Lees-Haley, P. R., Lees-Haley, C. E., Price, J. R., & Williams, C. W. (1994). A sexual harassment–emotional distress rating scale. *American Journal of Forensic Psychology, 12*(3), 39–54.

Leitenberg, H., Greenwald, E., & Cado, S. (1992). A retrospective study of long-term methods of coping with having been sexually abused during childhood. *Child Abuse & Neglect, 16*, 399–407.

Lengnick-Hall, M. L. (1995). Sexual harassment research: A methodological critique. *Personnel Psychology, 48*, 841–864.

Lester, D., Banta, B., Barton, J., Elian, N., Mackiewicz, L., & Winkelried, J. (1986). Judgments about sexual harassment: Effects of the power of the harasser. *Perceptual and Motor Skills, 63*, 990.

Levine, M., & Doueck, H. J. (1995). *The impact of mandated reporting on the therapeutic process*. Thousand Oaks, CA: Sage.

Liem, R., & Rayman, P. (1982). Health and social costs of unemployment: Research and policy considerations. *American Psychologist, 37*, 1116–1123.

Lindemann, B., & Kadue, D. D. (1999). *Sexual harassment in employment law*. Washington, DC: Bureau of National Affairs.

Lipsett v. Univ. of Puerto Rico, 864 F.2d 881 (1st Cir. 1988), 745 F. Supp. 793 (1990).

Little, L., & Hamby, S. L. (1999). Gender differences in sexual abuse outcomes and recovery experiences: A survey of therapist-survivors. *Professional Psychology: Research and Practice, 30,* 378–385.

Livingston, J. A. (1982). Responses to sexual harassment on the job: Legal, organizational, and individual actions. *Journal of Social Issues, 38*(4), 5–22.

Long, B. L. (1994). Psychiatric diagnoses in sexual harassment cases. *Bulletin of the American Academy of Psychiatry & Law, 22,* 195–203.

Loredo, C., Reid, A., & Deaux, K. (1995). Judgments and definitions of sexual harassment by high school students. *Sex Roles, 32,* 29–45.

Loy, P. H., & Stewart, L. P. (1984). The extent and effects of sexual harassment on working women. *Sociological Focus, 17*(1), 31–43.

MacKinnon, C. A. (1979). *Sexual harassment of working women: A case of sex discrimination.* New Haven, CT: Yale University Press.

MacNamara, D. E. J. (1991). The victimization of whistle-blowers in the public and private sectors. In R. J. Kelly & D. E. J. MacNamara (Eds.), *Perspectives on deviance: Dominance, degradation and denigration* (pp. 121–134). New York: Anderson Publishing.

Magley, V. J. (2002). Coping with sexual harassment: Reconceptualizing women's resistance. *Journal of Personality and Social Psychology, 83,* 930–946.

Magley, V. J., Waldo, C. R., Drasgow, F., & Fitzgerald, L. F. (1999). The impact of sexual harassment on military personnel: Is it the same for men and women? *Military Psychology, 11,* 283–302.

Maker, A. H., Kemmelmeier, M., & Peterson, C. (2001). Child sexual abuse, peer sexual abuse, and sexual assault in adulthood: A multi-risk model of revictimization. *Journal of Traumatic Stress, 14,* 351–368.

Malamut, A. B., & Offerman, L. R. (2001). Coping with sexual harassment: Personal, environmental, and cognitive determinants. *Journal of Applied Psychology, 86,* 1152–1166.

Malmuth, N. (1981). Rape proclivity among males. *Journal of Social Issues, 37*(4), 138–157.

Malovich, N. J., & Stake, J. E. (1990). Sexual harassment on campus: Individual differences in attitudes and beliefs. *Psychology of Women Quarterly, 14*(1), 63–81.

Manning v. Wire Rope Corp., 63 Fair Empl. Prac. Cas. 1156 (Mo. Cir. Ct. 1993).

Marcus, E. H. (1993). Human reactions to life events: From joy to death. *American Journal of Forensic Psychiatry, 12,* 67.

Marks, M. A., & Nelson, E. S. (1993). Sexual harassment on campus: Effects of professor gender on perception of sexually harassing behaviors. *Sex Roles, 28,* 207–217.

Martin, L. (2000). Personality characteristics that increase vulnerability to sexual harassment among U. S. Army soldiers. *Military Medicine, 10,* 709–713.

Martindale, M. (1990). *Sexual harassment in the military: 1988.* Arlington, VA: Defense Manpower Data Center.

Matarazzo, J. D. (1987). Validity of psychological assessment: From the clinic to the courtroom. *Clinical Neuropsychologist, 1*, 307–314.

Mayer, J., & Abramson, J. (1995). *Strange justice: The selling of Clarence Thomas*. New York: Penguin Books.

Mazer, D. B., & Percival, E. F. (1989). Ideology or experience? The relationships among perceptions, attitudes, and experiences of sexual harassment in university students. *Sex Roles, 20*, 135–147.

McDonald, J. J., Jr. (2000). *Mental and emotional injuries in employment litigation: 2000 supplement*. Washington, DC: Bureau of National Affairs.

McDonald, J. J., Jr., & Feldman-Schorrig, S. P. (1994). The relevance of childhood sexual abuse in sexual harassment cases. *Employee Relations Law Journal, 20*, 221–236.

McDonald, J. J., Jr., & Kulick, F. B. (2001). *Mental and emotional injuries in employment litigation* (2nd ed.). Washington, DC: Bureau of National Affairs.

McDonald, J. J., Jr., & Lees-Haley, P. R. (1995). Avoiding "junk science" in sexual harassment litigation. *Employee Relations Law Journal, 21*(2), 51–71.

McDonald, J. J., Jr., & Lees-Haley, P. R. (1996). Personality disorders in the workplace: How they may contribute to claims of employment law violations. *Employee Relations Law Journal, 22*, 57–81.

McLain, D. L. (1995). Responses to health and safety risk in the work environment. *Academy of Management Journal, 38*, 1726–1743.

McMillen, C., Zuravin, S., & Rideout, G. (1995). Perceived benefit from child sexual abuse. *Journal of Consulting and Clinical Psychology, 63*, 1037–1043.

McNair, L. D., & Neville, H. A. (1996). African American women survivors of sexual assault: The intersection of race and class. *Women & Therapy, 19*(3/4), 107–118.

Melton, G. B., Petrila, J., Poythress, N. G., & Slobogin, C. (1997). *Psychological evaluations for the courts: A handbook for mental health professionals and lawyers* (2nd ed.). New York: Guilford Press.

Meritor Savings Bank, FSB v. Vinson, 477 U.S. 57, 106 S. Ct. 2399, 91 L.Ed.2d 49 (1986).

Messman-Moore, T. L., & Long, P. J. (2000). Child sexual abuse and revictimization in the form of adult sexual abuse, adult physical abuse, and adult psychological maltreatment. *Journal of Interpersonal Violence, 15*, 489–502.

Meyer, I. H. (1995). Minority stress and mental health in gay men. *Journal of Health & Social Behavior, 36*, 38–56.

Miceli, M.P., Dozier, J. B., & Near, J. P. (1991). Blowing the whistle on data fudging—A controlled field experiment. *Journal of Applied Psychology, 21*, 271–295.

Miceli, M. P., & Near, J. P. (1984). The relationships among beliefs, organizational position, and whistle-blowing status: A discriminant analysis. *Academy of Management Journal, 27*, 687–705.

Miceli, M. P., & Near, J. P. (1985). Characteristics of organizational climate and perceived wrongdoing associated with whistle-blowing decisions. *Personnel Psychology, 38,* 525–544.

Miceli, M. P., & Near, J. P. (1988). Individual and situational correlates of whistle-blowing. *Personnel Psychology, 41,* 267–281.

Miceli, M. P., & Near, J. P. (1989). The incidence of wrongdoing, whistle-blowing, and retaliation: Results of a naturally occurring field experiment. *Employee Responsibilities & Rights Journal, 2*(2), 91–108.

Miceli, M. P., & Near, J. P. (1992). *Blowing the whistle: The organizational and legal implications for companies and employees.* New York: Lexington Books.

Miceli, M. P., Near, J. P., & Schwenk, C. R. (1991). Who blows the whistle and why? *Industrial and Labor Relations Review, 45,* 113–130.

Miceli, M. P., Rehg, M., Near, J. P., & Ryan, K. C. (1999). Can laws protect whistle-blowers? Results of a naturally occurring field experiment. *Work and Occupations, 26*(1), 129–151.

Miceli, M. P., Roach, B. L., & Near, J. P. (1988). The motivations of anonymous whistle-blowers: The case of federal employees. *Public Personnel Management, 17,* 281–296.

Millon, T. (1994). *Millon Clinical Multiaxial Inventory—III manual.* Minneapolis, MN: Interpretive Scoring Systems.

Millon, T. (1996). *Personality and psychopathology: Building a clinical science: Selected papers of Theodore Millon.* New York: Wiley.

Moffett v. Gene B. Glick Co., Inc., 621 F. Supp. 244 (N.D. Ind. 1985).

Monahan, J. (1993). Limiting therapist exposure to Tarasoff liability: Guidelines for risk containment. *American Psychologist, 48,* 242–250.

Monroe, S. M., Bromet, E. J., Connell, M. M., & Steiner, S. C. (1986). Social support, life events, and depressive symptoms: A 1-year prospective study. *Journal of Consulting and Clinical Psychology, 54,* 424–431.

Morgan, P. A. (1999). Risking relationships: Understanding the litigation choices of sexually harassed women. *Law & Society Review, 33*(1), 67–92.

Morrey, L. C. (1991). *Personality Assessment Inventory professional manual.* Odessa, FL: Psychological Assessment Resources.

Mosher, D. L., & Sirkin, M. (1984). Measuring a macho personality constellation. *Journal of Research in Personality, 18,* 150–163.

Mulder, R. T., Beautrais, A. L., Joyce, P. R., & Fergusson, D. M. (1998). Relationship between dissociation, childhood sexual abuse, childhood physical abuse, and mental illness in a general population sample. *American Journal of Psychiatry, 155,* 806–811.

Munson, L. J., Hulin, C., & Drasgow, F. (2000). Longitudinal analysis of dispositional influences and sexual harassment: Effects on job and psychological outcomes. *Personnel Psychology, 53*(1), 21–46.

National Institute for Occupational Safety and Health. (2000). *Stress at work.* Washington, DC: U.S. Department of Health and Human Services.

National Organization on Male Sexual Victimization, Men Stopping Rape, Oakland Men's Project, Men Against Pornography, Sexual Exploitation Education Project, Men Overcoming Sexual Assault, Stop Prisoner Rape, Men Overcoming Violence, Community United Against Violence, Emerge: A Men's Counseling Service on Domestic Violence, Men Stopping Violence, Men's Rape Prevention Project, New York City Gay & Lesbian Anti-Violence Project, & National Coalition Against Sexual Assault. (1997). Brief for Amicus Curiae in support of appellees, *Oncale v. Sundowner Offshore Services, Inc.*, 83 F.3d 118 (5th. Cir. 1996). New York: Counsel Press.

Near, J. P., & Miceli, M. P. (1986). Retaliation against whistle-blowers: Predictors and effects. *Journal of Applied Psychology, 71*, 137–145.

Near, J. P., & Miceli, M. P. (1987). Whistle-blowers in organizations: Dissidents or reformers? *Research in Organizational Behavior*, 9, 321–368.

Newhill, C. E. (1990). The role of culture in the development of paranoid symptomatology. *American Journal of Orthopsychiatry, 60*, 176–185.

Newman, J. E., & Beehr, T. A. (1979). Personal and organizational strategies for handling job stress: A review of research and opinion. *Personnel Psychology, 32*(1), 1–43.

Niebuhr, R. E. (1997). Sexual harassment in the military. In W. O' Donohue (Ed.), *Sexual harassment: Theory, research, and treatment* (pp. 250–262). Needham Heights, MA: Allyn & Bacon.

Nieva, V., & Gutek, B. A. (1981). *Women and work: A psychological perspective*. New York: Praeger.

Northwestern National Life Insurance Company. (1991). *Employee burnout: America's newest epidemic*. Minneapolis, MN: Author.

Northwestern National Life Insurance Company. (1992). *Employee burnout: Causes and cures*. Minneapolis, MN: Author.

O'Connell, C. E., & Korabik, K. (2000). Sexual harassment: The relationship of personal vulnerability, work context, perpetrator status, and type of harassment to outcomes. *Journal of Vocational Behavior, 56*, 299–329.

Offerman, L. R., & Malamut, A. B. (2002). The impact of target perceptions of organizational leadership and climate on harassment reporting and outcomes. *Journal of Applied Psychology, 87*, 885–893.

O'Hare, E. A., & O'Donohue, W. (1998). Sexual harassment: Identifying risk factors. *Archives of Sexual Behavior, 27*, 561–580.

Oncale v. Sundowner Offshore Services, Inc., 83 F.3d 118 (5th. Cir. 1996).

Oncale v. Sundowner Offshore Services, Inc., 523 U.S., 118 S. Ct. 998, 140 L.Ed.2d 201 (1998).

Otto, R. K. (1994). On the ability of mental health professionals to "predict dangerousness": A commentary on interpretations of the "dangerousness" literature. *Law & Psychology Review, 18*, 43–68.

Paetzold, R. L., & Willborn, S. L. (1994). *The statistics of discrimination: Using statistical evidence in discrimination cases*. Colorado Springs, CO: Shepard's/McGraw-Hill.

Paolucci, E. O., Genuis, M. L., & Violato, C. (2001). A meta-analysis of the published research on the effects of child sexual abuse. *The Journal of Psychology*, *135*(1), 17–36.

Paris, J., Zweig-Frank, H., & Guzder, J. (1994). Risk factors for borderline personality in male outpatients. *Journal of Nervous & Mental Disease*, *182*, 375–380.

Parmerlee, M. A., Near, J. P., & Jensen, T. C. (1982). Correlates of whistle-blower's perceptions of organizational retaliation. *Administrative Science Quarterly*, *27*, 17–24.

Patterson v. PHP Healthcare Corp., 90 F.3d 927 (5th Cir. 1996), *cert. denied*, 117 S. Ct. 767, 136 L.Ed.2d 713 (1997).

Perrucci, R., Anderson, R. M., Schendel, D. E., & Trachtman, L. E. (1980). Whistle-blowing professionals' resistance to organizational authority. *Social Problems*, *28*, 149–164.

Pfohl, B., Blum, N., Zimmerman, M., & Stangl, D. (1989). *Structured Interview for DSM–III–R Personality (SIDP–R)*. Iowa City: University of Iowa.

Pfohl, B., Stangl, D., & Zimmerman, M. (1982). *Structured Interview for DSM–III Personality (SIDP)*. Iowa City: University of Iowa.

Pierce, C. A. (1998). Factors associated with participating in a romantic relationship in a work environment. *Journal of Applied Social Psychology*, *28*, 1712–1730.

Pierce, C. A., Aguinis, H., & Adams, S. K. R. (2000). Effects of a dissolved workplace romance and rater characteristics on responses to a sexual harassment accusation. *Academy of Management Journal*, *43*, 869–880.

Piltch, C. A., Walsh, D. C., Mangione, T. W., & Jennings, S. E. (1994). Gender, work, and mental distress in an industrial labor force: An expansion of Karasek's job strain model. In G. P. Keita & J. J. Hurrell, Jr. (Eds.), *Job stress in a changing workforce: Investigating gender, diversity, and family issues* (pp. 39–54). Washington, DC: American Psychological Association.

Piotrkowski, C. S. (1998). Gender harassment, job satisfaction, and distress among employed White and minority women. *Journal of Occupational Health Psychology*, *3*(1), 33–43.

Pleck, J. H. (1985). *Working wives, working husbands*. Beverly Hills, CA: Sage.

Polusny, M. A., & Follette, V. M. (1995). Long-term correlates of child sexual abuse: Theory and review of the empirical literature. *Applied & Preventive Psychology*, *4*(3), 143–166.

Pope, K. S., Butcher, J. N., & Seelen, J. (1997). *The MMPI, MMPI–2, & MMPI–A in Court*. Washington, DC: American Psychological Association.

Popovich, P. M., Jolton, J. A., Mastrangelo, P. M., Everton, W. J., Somers, J. M., & Gehlauf, D. N. (1995). Sexual harassment scripts: A means to understanding a phenomenon. *Sex Roles*, *32*, 315–335.

Powell, G. N. (1986). Effects of sex role identity and sex on definitions of sexual harassment. *Sex Roles, 14,* 9–19.

Powell, G. N. (2000). Workplace romance in the public sector: Sex differences in reactions to the Clinton–Lewinsky affair. *Psychological Reports, 87,* 1043–1049.

Pribor, E. F., & Dinwiddie, S. H. (1992). Psychiatric correlates of incest in childhood. *American Journal of Psychiatry, 149,* 52–56.

Price-Waterhouse v. Hopkins, 490 U.S. 228 (1989).

Princeton Survey Research Associates. (1997). *Labor Day survey: State of workers.* Princeton, NJ: Author.

Prunty v. Arkansas Freightways, Inc., 16 F.3d 649, 654–55 (5th Cir. 1994).

Pryor, J. B. (1985). The layperson's understanding of sexual harassment. *Sex Roles, 13,* 273–286.

Pryor, J. B. (1987). Sexual harassment proclivities of men. *Sex Roles, 17,* 269–290.

Pryor, J. B. (1995). The phenomenology of sexual harassment: Why does sexual behavior bother people in the workplace? *Consulting Psychology Journal: Practice & Research, 47*(3), 160–168.

Pryor, J. B., DeSouza, E. R., Fitness, J., Hutz, C., Kumpf, M., Lubbert, K., et al. (1997). Gender differences in the interpretation of social-sexual behavior: A cross-cultural perspective on sexual harassment. *Journal of Cross-Cultural Psychology, 28,* 509–534.

Pryor, J. B., Giedd, J. L., & Williams, K. B. (1995). A social psychological model for predicting sexual harassment. *Journal of Social Issues, 51*(1), 69–84.

Pryor, J. B., LaVite, C. M., & Stoller, L. M. (1993). A social psychological analysis of sexual harassment: The person/situation interaction. *Journal of Vocational Behavior, 42,* 68–83.

Pryor, J. B., & Stoller, L. M. (1994). Sexual cognition processes in men high in the likelihood to sexually harass. *Personality & Social Psychology Bulletin, 20,* 163–169.

Pryor, J. B., & Whalen, N. J. (1997). A typology of sexual harassment: Characteristics of harassers and the social circumstances under which sexual harassment occurs. In W. O'Donohue (Ed.), *Sexual harassment: Theory, research, and treatment* (pp. 129–151). Needham Heights, MA: Allyn & Bacon.

Rabidue v. Osceola Refining Co., 805 F.2d 611 (6th Cir. 1986), *cert. denied,* 481 U.S. 1041 (1987).

Ragins, B. R., & Scandura, T. A. (1995). Antecedents and work-related correlates of reported sexual harassment: An empirical investigation of competing hypotheses. *Sex Roles, 32,* 429–455.

Ramsey v. American Filter Co., 772 F.2d 1303 (7th Cir. 1985).

Reifman, A., Biernat, M., & Lang, E. L. (1991). Stress, social support, and health in married professional women with small children. *Psychology of Women Quarterly, 15,* 431–445.

Reilly, M. E., Lott, B., Caldwell, D., & DeLuca, L. (1992). Tolerance for sexual harassment related to self-reported sexual victimization. *Gender & Society, 6*(1), 122–138.

Reilly, T., Carpenter, S., Dull, V., & Bartlett, K. (1982). The factorial survey: An approach to defining sexual harassment on campus. *Journal of Social Issues, 38*(4), 99–109.

Repetti, R. L. (1993). Short-term effects of occupational stressors on daily mood and health complaints. *Health Psychology, 12*, 125–131.

Resnick, H. S., Kilpatrick, D. G., Dansky, B. S., Saunders, B. E., & Best, C. L. (1993). Prevalence of civilian trauma and posttraumatic stress disorder in a representative national sample of women. *Journal of Consulting and Clinical Psychology, 61*, 984–991.

Richman, J., Rospenda, K., Nawyn, S. Flaherty, J., Fendrich, M., Drum, M., & Johnson, T. (1999). Sexual harassment and generalized workplace abuse among university employees: Prevalence and mental health correlates. *American Journal of Public Health, 89*, 358–363.

Richman, J. A., Shinsako, S. S., Rospenda, K. M., Flaherty, J. A., & Freels, S. (2002) Workplace harassment/abuse and alcohol-related outcomes the mediating role of psychological distress. *Journal of Studies on Alcohol, 63*, 412–419.

Rind, B., Bauserman, R., & Tromovitch, P. (1998). A meta-analytic examination of assumed properties of child sexual abuse using college samples. *Psychological Bulletin, 124*, 22–53.

Roberts, R. J. (2003, October 2). *When mediation goes awry: Reflections on the internal complexities of being human*. Retrieved from http://www.mediate.com/articles/robertsJ1.cfm.

Robins, L. N., Helzer, J. E., Cottler, L. B., & Golding, E. (1989). *NIMH Diagnostic Interview Schedule* (Version III, Rev.). St. Louis, MO: Washington University.

Robins, L. N., & Regier, D. A. (1991). *Psychiatric disorders in America: The Epidemiologic Catchment Area study*. New York: Free Press.

Robinson v. Jacksonville Shipyards, Inc., 760 F. Supp. 1486 (M.D. Fla. 1991).

Roe v. Wade, 410 U.S. 113 (1973).

Roesler, T. A., & McKenzie, N. (1994). Effects of childhood trauma on psychological functioning in adults sexually abused as children. *Journal of Nervous & Mental Disease,182*(3), 145–150.

Rogers, R. (1987). Ethical dilemmas in forensic evaluations. *Behavioral Sciences & the Law, 5*, 149–160.

Rogers, R. (1988). *Clinical assessment of malingering and deception*. New York: Guilford Press.

Rogers, R. (1992). *Structured Interview of Reported Symptoms (SIRS)*. Odessa, FL: Psychological Assessment Resources.

Rogers, R. (1995). *Diagnostic and structured interviewing: A handbook for psychologists*. Odessa, FL: Psychological Assessment Resources.

Rogers, R. (1997a). *Clinical assessment of malingering and deception* (2nd ed.). New York: Guilford Press.

Rogers, R. (1997b). Structured interviews and dissimulation. In R. Rogers (Ed.), *Clinical assessment of malingering and deception* (pp. 301–327). New York: Guilford Press.

Rohsenow, D.J., Corbett, R., & Devine, D. (1988). Molested as children: A hidden contribution to substance abuse. *Journal of Substance Abuse Treatment, 5*, 13–18.

Rosell, E., Miller, K., & Barber, K. (1995). Firefighting women and sexual harassment. *Public Personnel Management, 24*, 339–350.

Rosen, G. M. (1995a). The Aleutian Enterprise sinking and posttraumatic stress disorder: Misdiagnosis in clinical and forensic settings. *Professional Psychology: Research and Practice, 26*, 82–87.

Rosen, G. M. (1995b). The misdiagnosis in clinical and forensic settings. *Professional Psychology: Research and Practice, 26*, 82–87.

Rosen, L. N., & Martin, L. (1998). Childhood maltreatment history as a risk factor for sexual harassment among U.S. Army soldiers. *Violence & Victims, 13*, 269–286.

Rosman, J. P., & McDonald, J. J., Jr. (1999). Forensic aspects of sexual harassment. *Forensic Psychiatry, 22*(1), 129–145.

Rospenda, K. M., Richman, J. A., & Nawyn, S. J. (1998). Doing power: The confluence of gender, race, and class in contra-power sexual harassment. *Gender & Society, 12*, 40–60.

Rotundo, M., Nguyen, D. H., & Sackett, P. R. (2001). A meta-analytic review of gender differences in perceptions of sexual harassment. *Journal of Applied Psychology, 86*, 914–922.

Rudman, L. A., & Borgida, E. (1995). The afterglow of construct accessibility: The behavioral consequences of priming men to view women as sexual objects. *Journal of Experimental Social Psychology, 31*, 493–517.

Runtz, M. G., & Schallow, J. R. (1997). Social support and coping strategies as mediators of adult adjustment following childhood maltreatment. *Child Abuse & Neglect, 21*, 211–226.

Safran, C. (1976, November). What men do to women on the job: A shocking look at sexual harrassment. *Redbook*, 149, 217–223.

Salisbury, J., Ginorio, A. B., Remick, H., & Stringer, D. M. (1986). Counseling victims of sexual harassment. *Psychotherapy, 23*, 316–324.

Sandberg, D., Lynn, S., & Green, J. (1994). Sexual abuse and re-victimization: Mastery, dysfunctional learning, and dissociation. In S. Lynn & J. Rhue (Eds.), *Clinical and theoretical perspectives* (pp. 242–267). New York: Guilford Press.

Sandberg, D. A., Matorin, A. I., & Lynn, S. J. (1999). Dissociation, posttraumatic symptomatology, and sexual re-victimization: A prospective examination of mediator and moderator effects. *Journal of Traumatic Stress, 12*(1), 127–138.

Saperstein, A., Triolo, B., & Heinzen, T. E. (1995). Ideology or experience: A study of sexual harassment. *Sex Roles, 32,* 835–842.

Saunders, B. E., Arata, C. M., & Kilpatrick, D. G. (1990). Development of a Crime-Related Post-Traumatic Stress Disorder scale for women within the Symptom Checklist—90—Revised. *Journal of Traumatic Stress, 3,* 439–448.

Saunders, B. E., Villeponteaux, L. A., Lipovsky, J. A., Kilpatrick, D. G., & Veronen, L. J. (1992). Child sexual assault as a risk factor for mental disorders among women: A community survey. *Journal of Interpersonal Violence, 7,* 189–204.

Sbraga, T. P., & O'Donohue, W. (2000). Sexual harassment. *Annual Review of Sex Research, 11,* 258–285.

Schlagenhauf v. Holder, 379 U.S. 104 (1964).

Schlossberg, N. K., & Leibowitz, Z. (1980). Organizational support systems as buffers to job loss. *Journal of Vocational Behavior, 17,* 204–217.

Schneider, B. E. (1991). Put up and shut up: Workplace sexual assaults. *Gender & Society, 5,* 533–548.

Schneider, K. T., Swan, S., & Fitzgerald, L. F. (1997). Job-related and psychological effects of sexual harassment in the workplace: Empirical evidence from two organizations. *Journal of Applied Psychology, 82,* 401–415.

Schwarzer, R., Hahn, A., & Fuchs, R. (1994). Unemployment, social resources, and mental and physical health: A three-wave study on men and women in a stressful life transition. In G. P. Keita & J. J. Hurrell, Jr. (Eds.), *Job stress in a changing workforce: Investigating gender, diversity, and family issues* (pp. 75–87). Washington, DC: American Psychological Association.

Seymour, R. T. (1999). Is there a disconnect between EEO law and the workplace? Proceedings of the 1999 Annual Meeting, Association of American Law Schools Section on Employment Discrimination Law. *Employee Rights and Employment Policy Journal, 3.* Retrieved April 2, 2004, from http://www.kentlaw.edu/ilw/erepj/v3n1/Scherer.html

Shaffer, M. A., Joplin, J. R. W., Bell, M. P., Lau, T., & Oguz, C. (2000). Disruptions to women's social identity: A comparative study of workplace stress experienced by women in three geographic regions. *Journal of Occupational Health Psychology, 54,* 441–456.

Sheffey, S., & Tindale, S. R. (1992). Perceptions of sexual harassment in the workplace. *Journal of Applied Social Psychology, 22,* 1502–1520.

Shuman, D. (1993). The use of empathy in forensic examinations. *Ethics & Behavior, 3,* 289–302.

Shuman, D. W. (2000a). *Psychiatric and psychological evidence* (2nd ed.). St. Paul, MN: West Publishing.

Shuman, D. W. (2000b). The role of apology in tort law. *Judicature, 83*(4), 180–190.

Shuman, D. W., & Foote, W. E. (1999). Jaffee v. Redmond's impact: Life after the Supreme Court's recognition of a psychotherapist–patient privilege. *Professional Psychology: Research & Practice, 30,* 479–487.

Shuman, D. W., & Greenberg, S. A. (2003). The expert witness, the adversary system, and the voice of reason: Reconciling impartiality and advocacy. *Professional Psychology: Research & Practice, 34*, 219–224.

Shuman, D. W., Greenberg, S., Heilbrun, K., & Foote, W. E. (1998). Special perspective—an immodest proposal: Should treating mental health professionals be barred from testifying about their patients? *Behavioral Sciences & the Law, 16*, 509–523.

Siegrist, J. (1996). Adverse health effects of high-effort/low-reward conditions. *Journal of Occupational Health Psychology, 1*, 27–41.

Silk, K. R., Lee, S., Hill, E. M., & Lohr, N. E. (1995). Borderline Personality Disorder symptoms and severity of sexual abuse. *American Journal of Psychiatry, 152*, 1059–1064.

Simon, R. I. (1995). *Posttraumatic stress disorder in litigation*. Washington, DC: American Psychiatric Press.

Snider v. Consolidation Coal Co., 973 F.2d 555 (7th Cir. 1992), *cert. denied*, 506 U.S. 1054 (4th Cir. 1993).

Society for Human Resource Management. (1998). *Workplace romance survey* (Item No. 62.17014). Alexandria, VA: SHRM Public Affairs Department.

Socks-Brunot v. Hirschvogel Inc., 184 F.R.D. 113, 118–119 (S.D. Ohio 1999).

Spratlen, L. P. (1997). The psychiatric advanced practice nurse's role as sexual harassment ombudsman. *Perspectives in Psychiatric Care, 33*(4), 5–13.

Sprecher, S., Sullivan, Q., & Hatfield, E. (1994). Mate selection preferences: Gender differences examined in a national sample. *Journal of Personality and Social Psychology, 66*, 1074–1080.

Spitzer, R. L., & Endicott, J. (1978). *Schedule for Affective Disorders and Schizophrenia (SADS)*. New York: Biometric Research.

Spitzer, R. L., Williams, J. B. W., Gibbon, M., & First, M. B. (1990). *Structured Clinical Interview for DSM–III–R—Non-Patient edition (SCID–NP, Version 1.0)*. Washington, DC: American Psychiatric Press.

Stein, J. A., Golding, J. M., Siegel, J. M., Burnam, M. A., & Sorenson, S. B. (1988). Long-term psychological sequelae of child sexual abuse: The Los Angeles epidemiologic catchment area study. In G. E. Wyatt & G. J. Powell (Eds.), *Lasting effects of child sexual abuse* (pp. 135–154). Newbury Park, CA: Sage.

Stein, M. B., Walker, J. R., Anderson, G., Hazen, A. L., Ross, C.A., Eldridge, G., & Forde, D. R. (1996). Childhood physical and sexual abuse in patients with anxiety disorders and in a community sample. *American Journal of Psychiatry, 153*, 275–277.

Stockdale, M. S. (1993). The role of sexual misperceptions of women's friendliness in an emerging theory of sexual harassment. *Journal of Vocational Behavior, 42*, 84–101.

Stockdale, M. S. (1998). The direct and moderating influences of sexual-harassment pervasiveness, coping strategies, and gender on work-related outcomes. *Psychology of Women Quarterly, 22*, 521–535.

Stockdale, M. S. (2004a). The sexual harassment of men: Articulating the approach–rejection distinction in sexual harassment motives. In J. E. Gruber & P. Morgan (Eds.), *In the company of men: Rediscovering the links between sexual harassment and male domination*. Boston: Northeastern University Press.

Stockdale, M. S. (2004b). What we know and what we need to learn about sexual harassment. In M. E. Stockdale (Ed.), *Sexual harassment in the workplace: Perspectives, frontiers, and response strategies* (pp. 3–25). Thousand Oaks, CA: Sage.

Stockdale, M. S., Bisom-Rapp, S., O'Connor, M., & Gutek, B. A. (2004). Coming to terms with zero tolerance sexual harassment policies. *Journal of Forensic Psychology Practice, 4*(1).

Stockdale, M. S., O'Connor, M., Gutek, B. A., & Geer, T. M. (2002). The relationship between prior sexual abuse and reactions to sexual harassment: Literature review and empirical study. *Psychology, Public Policy, and Law, 8*, 3–63.

Stockdale, M. S., & Vaux, A. (1993). What sexual harassment experiences lead respondents to acknowledge being sexually harassed? A secondary analysis of a university survey. *Journal of Vocational Behavior, 43*, 221–234.

Stockdale, M. S., Vaux, A., & Cashin, J. (1995). Acknowledging sexual harassment: A test of alternative models. *Basic & Applied Social Psychology, 17*, 469–496.

Stockdale, M. S., Visio, M., & Batra, L. (1999). The sexual harassment of men: Evidence for a broader theory of sexual harassment and sexual discrimination. *Psychology, Public Policy, and Law, 5*, 630–664.

Stone, M. H. (1990). *The fate of borderline patients, successful outcome and psychiatric practice*. New York: Guilford Press.

Storzbach, D., Campbell, K. A., Binder, L. M., McCauley, L., Anger, W. K., Rohlman, D. S., et al. (2000). Psychological differences between veterans with and without Gulf War unexplained symptoms. *Psychosomatic Medicine, 62*, 726–735.

St. Paul Fire and Marine Insurance Company. (1992). *American workers under pressure technical report*. St. Paul, MN: Authors.

Streseman, K. N. (1995). Headshrinkers, manmunchers, moneygrubbers, nuts and sluts: Reexamining compelled mental examinations in sexual harassment actions under the Civil Rights Act of 1991. *Cornell Law Review, 80*, 1268–1330.

Studd, M. V., & Gattiker, U. E. (1991). The evolutionary psychology of sexual harassment in organizations. *Ethology and Sociobiology, 12*, 249–290.

Summers, R. J. (1996). The effect of harasser performance status and complainant tolerance on reactions to a complaint of sexual harassment. *Journal of Vocational Behavior, 49*, 53–67.

Summers, R. J., & Myklebust, K. (1992). The influence of a history of romance on judgments and responses to a complaint of sexual harassment. *Sex Roles, 27*, 345–357.

Tangri, S. S., Burt, M. R., & Johnson, L. B. (1982). Sexual harassment at work: Three explanatory models. *Journal of Social Issues, 38*, 33–54.

Tangri, S. S., & Hayes, S. M. (1997). Theories of sexual harassment. In W. O'Donohue (Ed.), *Sexual harassment: Theory, research, and treatment* (pp. 112–128). Boston: Allyn & Bacon.

Taris, T. W., Peeters, M. C. W., Le Blanc, P. M., Schreurs, P. J. G., & Schaufeli, W. B. (2001). From inequity to burnout: The role of job stress. *Journal of Occupational Health Psychology*, 6, 303–323.

Tata, J. (1993). The structure and phenomenon of sexual harassment: Impact of category of sexually harassing behavior, gender, and hierarchical level. *Journal of Applied Social Psychology*, *23*, 199–277.

Terpstra, D. E., & Baker, D. D. (1986). Psychological and demographic correlates of perception of sexual harassment. *Genetic, Social, & General Psychology Monographs*, *112*, 459–478.

Terpstra, D. E., & Baker, D. D. (1989). The identification and classification of reactions to sexual harassment. *Journal of Organizational Behavior*, *10*(1), 1–14.

Terpstra, D. E., & Baker, D. D. (1992). Outcomes of federal court decisions on sexual harassment. *Academy of Management Journal*, *35*, 181–190.

Thacker, R. A. (1996). A descriptive study of situational and individual influences upon individuals' responses to sexual harassment. *Human Relations*, *49*, 1105–1122.

Thacker, R. A., & Gohmann, S. F. (1996). Emotional and psychological consequences of sexual harassment: A descriptive study. *Journal of Psychology*, *130*, 429–446.

Theorell, T., & Karasek, R. A. (1996). Current issues relating to psychosocial job strain and cardiovascular disease research. *Journal of Occupational Health Psychology*, *1*, 9–26.

Thoits, P. (1983). Dimensions of life events that influence psychological distress: An evaluation and synthesis of the literature. In H. Kaplan (Ed.), *Psychosocial stress: Trends in theory and research* (pp. 33–103). New York: Academic Press.

Title VII of the Civil Rights Act of 1964, 78 Stat. 253, as amended, 42 U.S.C. § 2000e et seq. (1994 ed. and Supp. III).

Tombough, T. M. (1997). The Test of Memory Malingering (TOMM): Normative data from cognitively intact and cognitively impaired individuals. *Psychological Assessment*, 9, 260–268.

Treadway, B. M. (1990). Tarasoff in the therapeutic setting. *Hospital and Community Psychiatry*, *41*(1), 88–89.

Trocki, K. F., & Orioli, E. M. (1994). Gender differences in stress symptoms, stress-producing contexts, and coping strategies. In G. P. Keita & J. J. Hurrell, Jr. (Eds.), *Job stress in a changing workforce: Investigating gender, diversity, and family issues* (pp. 7–22). Washington, DC: American Psychological Association.

Turner v. Imperial Stores, 161 F.R.D. 89 (S.D. Cal. 1995).

TXO Production Corp. v. Alliance Resources Corp., 113 S. Ct. 2711 (1993).

Tyler, T. R., & Lind, E. A. (2001). Procedural justice. In J. Saunders & V. L. Hamilton (Eds.), *Handbook of law and social science*. New York: Plenum.

Tyler v. U.S. District Court, 561 P.2d 1260 (Colo. 1997).

Uomoto, J. M. (1986). Examination of psychological distress in ethnic minorities from a learned helplessness framework. *Professional Psychology: Research and Practice, 17*, 448–453.

Urquiza, A. J., & Capra, M. (1990). The impact of sexual abuse: Initial and long-term effects. In M. Hunter et al. (Eds.), *The sexually abused male: Prevalence, impact, and treatment* (Vol. 1, pp. 105–135). Lexington, MA: Lexington Books/ D. C. Heath.

U.S. v. Hall, 93 F.3d 1337 (7th Cir. 1996).

U.S. Equal Employment Opportunity Commission (1999). *Enforcement guidance: Vicarious employer liability for unlawful harassment by supervisors* (EEOC Notice No. 915.002). Washington, DC. U.S. Government Printing Office.

U.S. Merit Systems Protection Board. (1981). *Sexual harassment in the federal workplace: Is it a problem?* Washington, DC: U.S. Government Printing Office.

U.S. Merit Systems Protection Board. (1988). *Sexual harassment in the federal government: An update*. Washington, DC: U.S. Government Printing Office.

U.S. Merit Systems Protection Board. (1994). *Working for America: An update*. Washington, DC: U.S. Government Printing Office.

U.S. Merit Systems Protection Board. (1995). *Sexual harassment in the federal workplace: Trends, progress, continuing challenges*. Washington, DC: U.S. Government Printing Office.

Ustad, K. L. (1996). *Assessment of malingering on the SADS in a jail referral sample*. Unpublished doctoral dissertation, University of North Texas, Denton.

Utsey, S. O., Ponterotto, J. G., Reynolds, A. L., & Cancelli, A. A. (2000). Racial discrimination, coping, life satisfaction, and self-esteem among African Americans. *Journal of Counseling and Development, 78*, 72–80.

Vadie v. Mississippi State University, 218 F.3d 365 (5th Cir. 2000).

Vagg, P. R., & Spielberger, C. D. (1998). Occupational stress: Measuring job pressure and organizational support in the workplace. *Journal of Occupational Health Psychology, 3*, 294–305.

Vaux, A. (1993). Paradigmatic assumptions in sexual harassment research: Being guided without being misled. *Journal of Vocational Behavior, 42*, 116–135.

Veit, C. T., & Ware, J. E. (1983). The structure of psychological distress and well-being in general populations. *Journal of Consulting and Clinical Psychology, 51*, 730–742.

Viki, G. T., & Abrams, D. (2002). But she was unfaithful: Benevolent sexism and reactions to rape victims who violate traditional gender role expectations. *Sex Roles, 47*, 289–293.

Waldo, C. R., Berdahl, J. L., & Fitzgerald, L. F. (1998). Are men sexually harassed? If so, by whom? *Law & Human Behavior, 22*, 59–79.

Wang, J., & Patten, S. B. (2001). Perceived work stress and major depression in the Canadian employed population, 20–49 years old. *Journal of Occupational Health Psychology, 6*, 283–289.

Warr, P. (1982). Psychological aspects of employment and unemployment. *Psychological Medicine, 12,* 7–11.

Wayne, J. H. (2000). Disentangling the power bases of sexual harassment: Comparing gender, age, and position power. *Journal of Vocational Behavior, 57,* 301–325.

Weaver, T. L., & Clum, G. A. (1993). Early family environments and traumatic experiences associated with borderline personality disorder. *Journal of Consulting and Clinical Psychology, 61,* 1068–1075.

Webb v. Hyman, 861 F. Supp. 1094 (D.D.C. 1994).

Wechsler, D. (1997). *Wechsler Adult Intelligence Scale—Third edition administration and scoring manual.* San Antonio, TX: Psychological Corporation.

Weeks v. Baker & McKenzie, 63 Cal. App. 4th 1128, 1145 (1998).

Weissman, M. M., Bruce, M. L., Leaf, P. J., Florio, L. P., & Holzer, C. E. (1991). Affective disorders. In L. N. Robins & D. A. Regier (Eds.), *Psychiatric disorders in America: The Epidemiologic Catchment Area study* (pp. 53–80). New York: Free Press.

Wells, R. D., McCann, J., Adams, J., Voris, J., & Ensign, J. (1995). Emotional, behavioral, and physical symptoms reported by parents of sexually abused, non-abused, and allegedly abused prepubescent females. *Child Abuse & Neglect, 19,* 155–163.

Welsh, S. (1999). Gender and sexual harassment. *Annual Review of Sociology, 25,* 169–190.

West, C. M., Williams, L. M., & Siegel, J. A. (2000). Adult sexual re-victimization among Black women sexually abused in childhood: A prospective examination of serious consequences of abuse. *Child Maltreatment: Journal of the American Professional Society on the Abuse of Children, 5*(1), 49–57.

Widom, C. S., & Kuhns, J. B. (1996). Childhood victimization and subsequent risk for promiscuity, prostitution, and teenage pregnancy: A prospective study. *American Journal of Public Health,* 86, 1607–1612.

Wiener, R. L., Hackney, A., Kadela, K., Rauch, S., Seib, H., Warren, L. & Hurt, L. E. (2002). The fit and implementation of sexual harassment law to workplace evaluations. *Journal of Applied Psychology,* 87, 747–764.

Wiener, R. L., & Hurt, L. E. (1999). An interdisciplinary approach to understanding social sexual conduct at work. In R. Wiener & B. Gutek (Eds.), Advances in sexual harassment research, theory, and policy. *Psychology, Public Policy, and Law, 5,* 556–595.

Wiener, R. L., & Hurt, L. E. (2000). How do people evaluate social-sexual conduct: A psycholegal model. *Journal of Applied Psychology, 85,* 75–85.

Wiener, R. L., Hurt, L. E., Russell, B., Mannen, K., & Gasper, C. (1997). Perceptions of sexual harassment: The effects of gender, legal standard, and ambivalent sexism. *Law & Human Behavior, 24,* 71–93.

Wiener, R. L., Watts, B. A., Goldkamp, K. H., & Gasper, C. (1995). Social analytic investigation of hostile work environments: A test of the reasonable woman standard. *Law & Human Behavior, 19*, 263–281.

Williams, C. W., Brown, R. S., Lees-Haley, P. R., & Price, J. R. (1995). An attributional (causal dimensional) analysis of perceptions of sexual harassment. *Journal of Applied Social Psychology, 25*, 1169–1183.

Williams, C. W., Lees-Haley, P. R., & Djanogly, S. E. (1999). Clinical scrutiny of litigants' self-reports. *Professional Psychology: Research and Practice, 30*, 361–367.

Williams, D. R., & Williams-Morris, R. (2000). Racism and mental health: The African American experience. *Ethnicity and Health, 5*, 243–268.

Williams, J. H., Fitzgerald, L. F., & Drasgow, F. (1999). The effects of organizational practices on sexual harassment and individual outcomes in the military. *Military Psychology, 11*, 303–328.

Williams, K. B., & Cyr, R. R. (1992). Escalating commitment to a relationship: The sexual harassment trap. *Sex Roles, 27*, 47–72.

Williger, S. D. (1995). A trial lawyer's perspective on mental health professionals as expert witnesses. *Consulting Psychology Journal: Practice & Research, 47*(3), 141–149.

Willis, C. (1992) The effect of sex-role stereotype, victim and defendant race, and prior relationship on rape culpability attributions. *Sex Roles, 26*, 213–226.

Wilson, A. E., Calhoun, K. S., & Bernat, J. A. (1999). Risk recognition and trauma-related symptoms among sexually re-victimized women. *Journal of Consulting and Clinical Psychology, 67*, 705–710.

Wilson v. City of Chicago, 6 F.3d 1233 (7th Cir. 1993).

Wolfe, D.A., Sas, L., & Wekerle, C. (1994). Factors associated with the development of posttraumatic stress disorder among child victims of sexual abuse. *Child Abuse & Neglect, 18*, 37–50.

Wolfe, J., Sharkansky, E. J., Read, J. P., Dawson, R., Martin, J. A., & Ouimette, P. C. (1998). Sexual harassment and assault as predictors of PTSD symptomatology among U.S. female Persian Gulf War military personnel. *Journal of Interpersonal Violence, 13*, 40–57.

Woody, W. D., Viney, W., Bell, P. A., & Bensko, N. L. (1996). Sexual harassment: The "reasonable person" versus "reasonable woman" standards have not been resolved. *Psychological Reports, 78*, 329–330.

Wright v. Universal Maritime Service Corp., 525 U.S. 70 (1998).

Wulsin, L. R., Bursztajn, H., & Gutheil, T. G. (1983). Unexpected clinical features of the Tarasoff decision: The therapeutic alliance and the "duty to warn." *American Journal of Psychiatry, 140*, 601–603.

Wyatt, G. E., Guthrie, D., & Notgrass, C. M. (1992). Differential effects of women's sexual abuse and subsequent sexual revictimization. *Journal of Consulting and Clinical Psychology, 60*, 167–173.

Wyatt, G. E., & Riederle, M. (1995). The prevalence and context of sexual harassment among African American and White American women. *Journal of Interpersonal Violence, 10,* 309–321.

Zatzick, D.F., Marmar, C. R., Weiss, D. S., Browner, W. S., Metzler, T. J., Golding, J. M., et al. (1997). Posttraumatic stress disorder and functioning and quality of life outcomes in a nationally representative sample of male Vietnam veterans. *American Journal of Psychiatry, 154,* 1690–1695.

TABLE OF AUTHORITIES

Alexander v. Gardner-Denver Co., 159
Andrews v. City of Philadelphia, 56

Bailey v. Runyon, 67
Baki v. B. F. Diamond Constr. Co., 81
Barnes v. Costle, 53
Barnes v. Train, 53
Becerra v. Dalton, 54
Blakely v. Continental Airlines, 67
Bottomly v. Leucadia National, 67
Broderick v. Ruder, 54, 68
Burlington Industries, Inc. v. Ellerth, 8, 55, 56, 60, 151
Bushell v. Dean, 66

Carey v. Piphus, 63
Casteneda v. Partida, 57
Clark County School District v. Shirley A. Breeden, 121
Clark v. World Airways, 51
Cody v. Marriott Corp., 125
Corne v. Bausch & Lomb, Inc., 52

Daubert v. Merrell Dow Pharmaceuticals, Inc., 5, 69–70, 80, 87
DeCintio v. Westchester County Medical Center, 54
Delahunty v. Cahoon, 68
Duffield v. Robertson Stephens & Co., 152, 159

EEOC v. Mitsubishi, 65
Ellison v. Brady, 65, 111

Faragher v. City of Boca Raton, 8–9, 55–56, 58, 60, 66, 70
Frye v. United States, 69

Gebers v. Commercial Data Center, Inc., 50
General Electric Co. v. Joiner, 80
George v. Frank, 68
Gier v. Educational Service Unit No. 16, 70
Gillmer v. Interstate/Johnson Lane Corp., 159
Gore v. Turner, 62
Griggs v. Duke Power Co., 60

Hall, U.S. v., 68
Hall v. Gus Construction Co., 56
Harris v. Forklift Systems, Inc., 4, 47, 51, 57, 58, 59, 67, 76, 111
Hurley v. Atlantic City Police Dept., 66, 68, 104

Isely v. Capuchin Province, 69, 70

Jaffee v. Redmond, 74, 76, 102
Jensen v. Eveleth Taconite Co., 4
Johnson v. County of Los Angeles Fire Dept., 70

Karcher v. Emerson Electric, 68
Kestenbaum v. Pennzoil Co., 66–67
King v. Palmer, 54
Kolstad v. American Dental Assn., 64
Kumho Tire Co. v. Carmichael, 5, 80, 87

Lipsett v. Univ. of Puerto Rico, 69

Manning v. Wire Rope Corp., 69
Meritor Savings Bank, FSB v. Vinson, 4, 7, 52–53
Mitsubishi, EEOC v., 65
Moffett v. Gene B. Glick Co., Inc., 67, 69

Oncale v. Sundowner Offshore Services, Inc., 4, 8, 56–57, 59

Patterson v. PHP Healthcare Corp., 67
Plaintiff Jones's Appeal to the 8th Circuit Court, 8
Price-Waterhouse v. Hopkins, 66
Prunty v. Arkansas Freightways, Inc., 50

Rabidue v. Osceola Refining Co., 58, 65
Ramsey v. American Filter Co., 67
Robinson v. Jacksonville Shipyards, Inc., 66, 67, 70
Roe v. Wade, 73

Schlagenhauf v. Holder, 80
Snider v. Consolidated Coal Co., 66
Snider v. Consolidation Coal Co., 66, 70
Socks-Brunot v. Hirschvogel, Inc., 103

Turner v. Imperial Stores, 81
TXO Production Corp. v. Alliance Resources Corp., 63
Tyler v. U.S. District Court, 125

U.S. v. Hall, 68

Vadie v. Mississippi State Univ., 63

Webb v. Hyman, 62, 70
Weeks v. Baker & McKenzie, 66
Wilson v. City of Chicago, 69
Wright v. Universal Maritime Service Corp., 152, 159

INDEX

Affidavits, 96–97
Age of harassment target, 25–26
Age variables in harassment cases, 22–24
Agency relationship, 76
Alternative dispute resolution, 160
arbitration, 152, 158–160
Civil Rights Act (1991) provisions, 151
employer involvement, 151–152
fact-finding investigation in, 153–155
mediation, 152, 155–158
settings for, 152
suitability of sexual harassment cases for, 152–153
Americans with Disabilities Act (1990), 4, 50
Amicus briefs, 4
Anxiety
as child sexual abuse outcome, 135–136
as harassment outcome, 127, 128
as job stress reaction, 139–140
preexisting, in targets of harassment, 136–137
Approach–rejection theory, 45
Arbitration, 152, 158–160. See also Alternative dispute resolution
Attorney's fees, 61

Back pay, 61
Biological model of sexual harassment, 39–40
Borderline personality disorder, 108–109, 136
Bush (G. H. W.) administration, 7–8

Causation of harm, 62–63, 86
expert testimony, 68
plaintiff's prior sexual abuse and, 104, 105–108
victim's unconscious incitement of sexual conduct, 105–106
Civil Rights Act (1871), 50
Civil Rights Act (1991), 48–49, 64, 151
Civil Rights Act (1964) (Title VII), 4, 6–7, 9, 48–49, 51, 52, 53, 57, 58
forms of legal relief, 60, 61
good faith compliance, 64
Clinical interviews, 91–92
Clinician Administered PTSD Interview, 90–91
Clinton administration, 8
Cognitive functioning
assessment instruments, 89–90
coping strategies of harassment targets, 123–124
court-ordered forensic assessment, 80–81, 103–104
harasser characteristics, 30–32
misogynists, 31–32
Collateral interviews, 92–93
Common law, 50–51
Compensatory damages, 9, 60, 61–62
Confidentiality and privacy issues
collateral interviews, 92–93
in forensic evaluation, 73–74
informed consent for forensic evaluation, 88–89
in neutral fact-finding investigation, 154, 155
in nontestifying forensic consultation, 81
psychologist–patient privilege, 74, 76–77
See also Privilege
Constructive discharge, 61, 146–167
Contingency fees, 78
Contract law, 50, 158–159
Contrapower sexual harassment, 28, 40
Coping with harassment, 123–125
Cost of litigation, 61
compensation for forensic psychologist, 77–78
Costs of sexual harassment
damage awards, 60–64
social costs, 3–4

Court-ordered forensic assessment, 80–81, 103–104
Court orders, 96
Credibility assessment, 10–11, 57
by juries, 65
Cultural differences, 117

Damages
compensatory, 9, 60, 61–62
cost of litigation, 61
expert testimony by forensic psychologists on, 67–69
goals of forensic assessment, 122
legal standards, 60
liability testimony and, 102
make-whole relief, 60, 61
nonmonetary, 61
punitive, 60, 63–64, 68–69
types of, 60–61
Defenses against harassment claims by employers, 59–60
Definition and conceptualization of sexual harassment, 6, 13–14, 18, 19–20, 114–115
Demand–control model of job stress, 141–142
Depositions, 85, 97
Depression
employment status and, 137
as harassment outcome, 127, 128
as job stress reaction, 139–140
preexisting, in targets of harassment, 136–137
Diagnostic Interview Schedule, 91
Disability law, 50
Dual-role relationship, 78–79, 82

Educational institutional, 49
Effects of sexual harassment, 44
contextual variables, 125
course over time, 149
damage awards, 60–64, 122
disability, 50
establishing causation of harm, 62–63
expert testimony by forensic psychologists on, 67–69
gender differences, 36
goals of forensic assessment, 121–122
involuntary discharge of complainant, 146–167
legal considerations, 121
phases of plaintiff's experience, 122
posttraumatic stress disorder, 130–131
preexisting fragility of plaintiff and, 122
presumption of emotional distress, 63
psychological impacts, 125–132
research limitations, 126–127
social costs, 3–4
tangible employment harm, 60
in theoretical models of sexual harassment, 45
tort claims, 50–51
victim response, 122–125
waiver of client privilege in determination of, 102
work-related problems as, 131–132
Employment contracts, 158–159
Equal Employment Opportunity Commission, 48, 51, 52, 62
Equal protection, 48, 50
Ethical practice, 11
conflict check, 82
financial arrangements, 77–78
guidelines, 81
informed consent for forensic evaluation, 88–89
neutral fact-finding investigation, 154, 160
privacy and confidentiality issues, 73–74
psychologist–client relationship, 74–77
testimony by plaintiff's psychotherapist, 78–79
Evidence. *See* Rules of evidence
Evolutionary biology, 39
Expert consultant, 81–82
Expert testimony, 71
compensatory damage awards for cost of, 61
conflict check, 82
in establishing liability, 66–67, 101, 102–119
knowledge base for, 69, 83

nontestifying forensic consultation and, 81–82
psychologist's preparation for, 97–98
by psychotherapist treating plaintiff prior to harassment experience, 78–79
record maintenance after, 99
role of mental health experts in sexual harassment cases, 4, 66–69, 75–76
scientific framework testimony, 76, 84
standards for admissibility, 5–6, 69–70, 79–81, 102
timelines and deadlines, 83–84

Fair Employment Practice Acts, 51
Federal Arbitration Act, 160
Federal courts, 48
evolution of sexual harassment law, 52–56
Federal Rules of Civil Procedure, 80–81
Federal Rules of Evidence
Rule *403*, 66
Rule *412*, 102–103
Rule *702*, 5–6, 79–80
Rule *404(a)*, 66
Feminist thought, 7
Filing of claims, 51
Forensic assessment
activities of, 10–11
appointment with plaintiff, 87–88
case reports, 10
clinical interviews, 91–92
compensation for, 77–78
consideration of harasser characteristics, 27–28, 32
court-ordered, 80–81, 103–104
for determination of reasonableness, 110–114
discussion with counsel before reporting, 94–95
ethical practice, 11
goals, 121
of harassment claims arising from former romantic relationship, 38
informed consent issues, 88–89
interpretation of data, 93–94
of job stress reactions, 138–144
knowledge base for, 5, 9–11, 13, 83
legal context, 47
for liability determination, 66–67, 101, 102–119
neutral fact-finding investigation, 153–155
phases of plaintiff's experience, 122, 147–148
of plaintiff's history of child abuse, 132–136, 148
of preexisting psychopathology in target of harassment, 136–138, 148
pretrial investigation, 10, 84–95
privacy and confidentiality issues, 73–74
psychologist–client relationship, 74–77
purpose, 4–5, 9–10, 75–76, 78
recording, 87, 91–92
report preparation, 80, 95
standardized interviews, 90–91
standards for, 84
of target's response to harassment, 122–125, 144, 145–149, 148–149
test selection for, 89–90
third-party interviews in, 92–93
See also Expert testimony
Forensic consultation, nontestifying, 81–82

Gender differences
age patterns in harassment cases and, 23–24
attributions of responsibility to targets of harassment, 22
in credibility assessment, 65
distribution in workplace, 33, 41–42
expert testimony on, 66
in filing of sexual harassment claims, 9
in nonharassment job stress, 142–143
perceived violation of gender role expectations, 22, 32, 41, 42, 54
in perception of sexual harassment claims, 6, 8, 58, 65
power relations in harassment experience, 28–29
racial patterns in harassment experiences and, 24–25
in reporting of sexual harassment, 36

Gender differences, *continued*
same-sex harassment, 34–35
in sexual harassment experience, 17, 18–20, 21, 22, 35
Governments, claims against, 48
punitive damage awards, 63
Grievance arbitration, 158–159

Harasser characteristics
community perceptions, 114–117
expert testimony by forensic psychologists, 66
forensic significance, 27–28, 32
misperception of social behavior, 30
personality characteristics, 29–32
physical attractiveness, 116–117
power relationship with target, 28–29, 40–41, 116
theoretical model of sexual harassment, 42, 43
Health Information Portability and Accountability Act, 76–77
Hill, Anita, 7–8
Histrionic personality disorder, 108, 109
Homoanathema, 36
Hostile workplace environment claims, 52–54, 58–59
expert testimony by forensic psychologists, 66
Hypermasculine perceptions and behaviors, 35–36
Hypersensitivity, plaintiff's, 112–113

Idiographic data, 94
Informed consent, 88–89
in neutral fact-finding investigation, 154, 160
Interrogatories, 85
Interviews
clinical, 91–92
collateral, 92–93
neutral fact-finding investigation, 154, 155, 160
standardized, 90–91

Judges and magistrates, 6
Jury trials, 64–65

Law
admissibility of expert testimony, 5–6, 69–70, 79–81, 102
disadvantages of mediation, 157
evolution of anti-harassment law, 6–9, 44, 47–48, 52–56, 70–71
judge *vs.* jury trials, 64–65
liability evaluation, 57–59
liability of employers for actions of employees, 55–56
pre-trial settlement, 64
protection from sexual harassment, 48–51
review of, in preparation for forensic evaluation, 87
same-sex harassment, 56–57
sexual orientation discrimination, 56
types of allowable damages, 60–61
types of courts, 48
See also Alternative dispute resolution
Lawyers, 5–6
attorney–client privilege, 74, 77
compensation for forensic assessment, 77–78
psychologist–lawyer relationship, 74–77
Letter of protection, 78
Liability
damage awards, 60–64, 102
employer defenses against, 59–60
of employers for actions of employees, 53, 55–56
forensic evaluation in determination of, 66–67, 101, 102–119
legal standards for evaluation of, 57–59
Likelihood to Sexually Harass, 29, 30–31
Los Angeles County survey, 15–16

Make-whole relief, 60, 61
Malingering, 90
Mandated arbitration, 158–159
Marital status, 117
Mediation, 152, 155–158. See also Alternative dispute resolution
Medical records review, 86
Men as targets of sexual harassment, 17, 18–19, 21
age patterns and, 24

gender role expectations and, 22
harassment effects, 36
racial patterns and, 24–25
same-sex harassment, 34–36
Military personnel
prevalence of sexual harassment among, 17–21
relationship between harasser and target, 28–29
Tailhook scandal, 7
See also U.S. Department of Defense studies of sexual harassment
Millon Clinical Multiaxial Inventory, 89–90
Minnesota Multiphasic Personality Inventory, 89
Misogynistic harassers, 31–32

Nomothetic data, 94
Notice of Right to Sue, 51

Organizational characteristics
comprehensive theories of sexual harassment, 43–44
determination of punitive damages, 63
gender distribution, 33, 41–42
hostile workplace environment, 52–54
liability of employers for actions of employees, 53, 55–56
reporting behaviors of harassment targets and, 124
responses to harassment claims, 33–34, 59–60, 66–67
retaliation against harassment complainants, 49, 61, 144–145
theoretical models of sexual harassment, 41–43
tolerance of sexual harassment, 44

Panic disorders, 137
Person X Situation model, 42–43
Personality Assessment Inventory, 89–90
Personality characteristics predisposing to sexual harassment
harasser characteristics, 29–32
victim characteristics, 108–110
Person–environment fit, 140–141
Pornography, 32, 58
Posttraumatic stress disorder, 90–91, 106–107, 112–113
child sexual abuse outcomes, 135–136
comorbid conditions, 138
employment patterns and, 138
as harassment outcome, 130–131
preexisting, in targets of harassment, 137–138
Power relations
biological theories of sexual harassment and, 39–40
community perception of harassment mediated by, 116
comprehensive theories of sexual harassment, 43–44
exploitative personalities, 30–31
in impact of harassment, 125, 132
organizational responses to harassment, 33–34, 59–60
patterns in harassment experiences, 28–29
theoretical model of sexual harassment, 40–41
in workplace, 3
in workplace romances, 37, 38
Pretrial investigation, 10
for forensic evaluation, 84–95
nontestifying forensic consultation, 81–82
Prevalence and incidence of sexual harassment, 8–9, 14–21, 25, 114
gender distribution in workplace and, 41–42
victim's age and, 22–23, 25–26
workplace characteristics, 32–34
Prevention of sexual harassment
damage awards and, 64
EEOC guidelines, 52
employer responsibility, 55
expert testimony on adequacy of, 66
military programs, 18
workplace interventions, 33
Privacy. *See* Confidentiality and privacy issues; Privilege
Privilege
lawyer–client, 74, 77
psychologist–patient, 74, 76–77, 102
waivers of, 102

Productivity, 3–4, 131–132
Proximate cause, 60
Psychosocial dysfunction, 91
child sexual abuse outcomes, 135–136
effects of job loss, 147, 149
evaluation of harassment effects, 125–132
natural history of harassment response, 149
nonharassment job stress and, 139–140
plaintiff's unconscious incitement of sexual advances, 105–110
preexisting, in targets of harassment, 136–138, 148
Public attitudes and beliefs
age variables in, 117–118
attributions of responsibility to targets of harassment, 22
community tolerance of harassment behaviors, 58, 65
definition of sexual harassment, 6, 13–14, 114–115
evolution of anti-harassment law, 6–9
jury trials and, 64
perception of harassers, 116–117
perception of targets of harassment, 117–118
perception of workplace romances, 37, 38
psychological research on sexual harassment perceptions, 114–118
racial stereotypes, 25
reasonable person evaluation, 57, 58–59, 65, 110–114
sex-role stereotypes, 41, 42, 65
Punitive damages, 60, 63–64
expert testimony on, 68–69

Quid pro quo harassment, 52, 53–54, 115

Race/ethnicity, 24–25
Reasonable person test, 57, 58–59, 65, 110–114
Recording forensic assessments, 87, 91–92
Records maintenance after expert testimony, 99
Redbook magazine survey, 14–15
Repetition compulsion, 105–108
Reporting of sexual harassment, 21, 123
expert testimony by forensic psychologists, 66
gender differences, 36
outcomes for target, 124
retaliation against complainant, 49, 61
retaliation against whistle-blowers, 144–145
victim's prior harassment experience and, 26
Research methodology, 13–14
conceptual models of sexual harassment, 38–39
consequences of sexual harassment, 126–127
Respondeat superior, 53
Responses to harassment claims by employers, 33–34, 59–60, 66–67
retaliation, 49, 61, 144–146
Retaliation against complainants, 49, 144–145
damage claims arising from, 61
paranoid reactions to, 145–146
Retention of psychologists, 74–77
Romantic relationships in workplace, 36–38
Rules of evidence
affidavits, 96–97
depositions, 85, 97
determination of compensatory damages, 62
determination of punitive damages, 63
discovery of consulting experts, 81–82, 96
plaintiff's sexual history, 102–103
psychologist–patient privilege, 74, 76–77
scope of discovery, 102
in tort law, 50–51
See also Expert testimony
Rules of procedure
compelled forensic evaluation, 80–81, 103–104
filing claims, 51
forensic report, 80

subpoena of testimony, 96
timelines and deadlines, 83–84

Same-sex harassment, 8, 34–36, 56–57
power-based theories of sexual harassment and, 40–41
Schedule of Affective Disorders, 91
Scientific framework testimony, 76, 84
Self-blame, 124
Settlement cases, 64
Sexism, 44–45
Sexual abuse, prior to harassment experience, 104, 105–108, 112–114, 130, 146
family characteristics, 134–135
forensic assessment, 132–136
incident characteristics, 134
Sexual Experiences Questionnaire, 19, 90
Sexual harassment
approach–rejection theory, 45
biological theories, 39–40
case reports, 10
classification of harassing behaviors, 19–20, 21, 25, 35, 43, 115, 128
community standards, 58, 65
comprehensive theories of, 43–44
conceptual models, 38–39, 45, 69–70
dynamic nature of, 121
evolution of legal environment, 6–9, 11, 44, 47–48, 52–56, 70–71
following romantic relationship, 37–38
as function of sexism, 44–45
generalizability of social science research on, 13–14
incidence and prevalence, 8–9, 14–21
individual-based models, 42–43
legal protections, 48–51
legal standards for establishing, 57–59
organizational models of, 41–42
plaintiff's unconscious incitement of, 105–110
power relations model, 40–41
public attitudes and beliefs, 6, 13–14, 58–59, 65, 114–119
role of forensic assessment and consultation in claims of, 4, 9, 75–76, 78–83
same-sex, 8, 34–36, 56–57
social costs, 3–4
trends, 16, 18–19, 21
Sexual orientation discrimination, 56
Social identity, 3
Social support, 124–125
effects of job loss, 147, 149
nonharassment job stress and, 143–144
Somatic manifestations of job stress, 139, 141–142
Standardized interviews, 90–91
State courts, 48
State laws, 51
Structured Clinical Interview for DSM–III–R Disorders, 91
Structured Interview for DSM–IV Personality Disorders, 91
Subpoena of testimony, 96
Substance abuse, 129, 138

Tailhook scandal, 7
Targets of sexual harassment
age characteristics, 22–24, 25–26
attributions of responsibility to, 22
benefits of informal resolution of claims, 152
coping strategies, 123–125
gender differences in harassment experiences, 17, 18–20, 21
hypersensitivity in, 112–113
investigation of sexual history, 102–103
involuntary discharge, 146–167
legal protections, 48–51
legal standard for evaluating perceptions of, 58–59, 104–105
multiple plaintiff trials, 75
nonharassment job stress in, 138
paranoid reactions in, 145–146
power relationship with harasser, 28–29, 40–41
preexisting fragility in, 122
preexisting psychopathology in, 136–138, 148
prior harassment experiences, 26

Targets of sexual harassment, *continued*
prior sexual abuse history, 104, 112–114, 130, 132–136, 146
psychotherapy prior to harassment, 78–79
reasonable person evaluation, 110–114
responses to harassment, 122–125, 144–149, 148–149
substance abuse by, 129, 138
theoretical model of sexual harassment, 42–43
unconscious incitement of harassment by, 105–110
victim characteristics mediating perception of harassment claim, 22, 117–118
See also Men as targets of sexual harassment
Test of Memory Malingering, 90
Test selection and interpretation, 89–90, 93–94
Therapeutic relationship
conflict check, 82
dual-role concerns, 78–79
Thomas, Clarence, 7–8
Title VII. *See* Civil Rights Act (1964)
Tort law, 50–51
Totality-of-circumstances test, 59

U.S. Department of Defense studies of sexual harassment, 17–21, 24–25, 28, 34, 35, 42
U.S. Merit Systems Protection Board survey, 16–17, 22–23, 24, 28, 34

Validity Indicator Profile, 90
Victims of harassment. *See* Targets of sexual harassment

Wechsler Adult Intelligence Scale, 90
Whistle-blowers, 144–145
Workplace
anti-harassment law, 48–51
disruptions caused by harassment complaints, 152–153
evolution of anti-discrimination law, 7
gender distribution in, 33, 41–42
harassment prevention, 33, 52
nonharassment job stress, 138–144
organizational responses to harassment, 33–34, 59–60
power relations in, 3, 28–29
prevalence of sexual harassment, 14–21, 114
romantic relationships in, 36–38
social relations in, 3
See also Organizational characteristics

ABOUT THE AUTHORS

William E. (Bill) Foote, PhD, has been in private practice as a forensic psychologist for 25 years in Albuquerque, New Mexico. Dr. Foote's practice has centered on the application of forensic psychology in criminal and civil cases. He is the clinical director for the Society of Northern Renewal, a not-for-profit organization that provides treatment to Inuit sex abuse victims in Arctic Canada. He has been a consultant to the New Mexico State Hospital, the Indian Health Service, and the New Mexico State Police. He has served on the adjunct faculties of the School of Law, the School of Medicine, and the Department of Psychology of the University of New Mexico. He received his diplomate (board certification) in forensic psychology in 1984, and was president of the board of directors of the American Board of Forensic Psychology in 2003–2004. He has been active in his state psychological association (president, ethics chair, legislative chair) and with the American Psychological Association (APA; council representative, chair of the Committee on Legal Issues, Committee on Professional Practice, Division 31 president). He is a fellow of the APA and received an APA Presidential Citation for his activities in psychology and law.

Jane Goodman-Delahunty, JD, PhD, directs the postgraduate program in forensic psychology at the School of Psychology, University of New South Wales in Sydney, Australia. She hails from Johannesburg, South Africa, where she began her career as a French and English teacher. She lived in the United States for 25 years, completing a Juris Doctor in 1983 at the University of Seattle School of Law and a PhD in 1986 at the University of Washington. For 10 years she divided her energy between psychology research on the cognitive faculty in the Department of Psychology of the University of Washington in Seattle and legal practice, litigating employment discrimination cases for the U.S. Equal Employment Opportunity Commission (EEOC) and in private practice with Frank Rosen Freed Roberts LLM. From 1992 to 2001, she served as an administrative judge at the Los Angeles District Office of the EEOC. During this time she developed a practice in mediation, arbitration, and neutral fact-finding techniques. She has taught employment discrimination on the adjunct faculties of the Seattle University School of Law and Whittier Law School. She was president of Division 41, the American Psychology–Law Society in 1995, and is a fellow of the American Psychological Association. Since 2000, she has served as editor-in-chief of the interdisciplinary journal and law review, *Psychology, Public Policy, and Law*. She has been a part-time commissioner on the New South Wales Law Reform Commission since 2002.